STEP DANCING IN IRELAND

*Dedicated to my family, John, Mark and Rachel,
and to the memory of my parents, Johanna and Patrick*

Step Dancing in Ireland
Culture and History

CATHERINE E. FOLEY
University of Limerick, Ireland

ASHGATE

Published by
Ashgate Publishing Limited
Wey Court East
Union Road
Farnham
Surrey, GU9 7PT
England

Ashgate Publishing Company
110 Cherry Street
Suite 3-1
Burlington, VT 05401-3818
USA

www.ashgate.com

British Library Cataloguing in Publication Data
Foley, Catherine E.
  Step dancing in Ireland: culture and history. – (Ashgate popular and folk music series)
  1. Step dancing – Ireland. 2. Step dancing – Ireland – History.
  I. Title II. Series
  793.3'19415–dc23

The Library of Congress has cataloged the printed edition as follows:
Foley, Catherine E.
  Step dancing in Ireland: culture and history / by Catherine E. Foley.
      pages cm. – (Ashgate popular and folk music series)
  Includes bibliographical references and index.
  ISBN 978-1-4094-4892-1 (hardcover : alk. paper) – ISBN 978-1-4094-4893-8 (ebook) – ISBN 978-1-4724-0130-4 (epub) 1. Step dancing—Ireland—History. 2. Dance—Social aspects—Ireland. 3. Folk dancing, Irish—History. 4. Ireland—Social life and customs. I. Title.
  GV1646.I8F65 2013
  793.3'19415—dc23

2012049942

ISBN 9781409448921 (hbk)
ISBN 9781409448938 (ebk – PDF)
ISBN 9781472401304 (ebk – ePUB)

Bach musicological font developed by © Yo Tomita

MIX
Paper from
responsible sources
FSC
www.fsc.org FSC® C013985

Printed in the United Kingdom by Henry Ling Limited, at the Dorset Press, Dorchester, DT1 1HD

Contents

List of Illustrations and Maps

List of Labanotation Examples

General Editor's Preface

The upheaval that occurred in musicology during the last two decades of the twentieth century has created a new urgency for the study of popular music alongside the development of new critical and theoretical models. A relativistic outlook has replaced the universal perspective of modernism (the international ambitions of the 12-note style); the grand narrative of the evolution and dissolution of tonality has been challenged, and emphasis has shifted to cultural context, reception and subject position. Together, these have conspired to eat away at the status of canonical composers and categories of high and low in music. A need has arisen, also, to recognize and address the emergence of crossovers, mixed and new genres, to engage in debates concerning the vexed problem of what constitutes authenticity in music and to offer a critique of musical practice as the product of free, individual expression.

Popular musicology is now a vital and exciting area of scholarship, and the *Ashgate Popular and Folk Music Series* presents some of the best research in the field. Authors are concerned with locating musical practices, values and meanings in cultural context, and may draw upon methodologies and theories developed in cultural studies, semiotics, poststructuralism, psychology and sociology. The series focuses on popular musics of the twentieth and twenty-first centuries. It is designed to embrace the world's popular musics from Acid Jazz to Zydeco, whether high tech or low tech, commercial or non-commercial, contemporary or traditional.

Professor Derek B. Scott,
Professor of Critical Musicology,
University of Leeds, UK

Preface and Acknowledgements

This book has been in gestation for many years. Dance and music have been important to my life ever since I was a young child, and my understanding of step dance has been shaped and coloured not only by my own step dancing and music experiences, but also by the step dancing experiences, comments and stories of others. Researching this dance form has therefore been for me an organic process of investigation.

The book would not have been written without the encouragement and support of numerous people. I therefore thank all those who kindly gave me their knowledge, time and friendship over the years. I particularly thank all the Molyneaux step dancers of North Kerry who trusted me with their dance material and taught it to me in the early 1980s. I thank them for their hospitality and kindness and for sharing their knowledge and passion for step dancing. The following step dancers, and their families, I particularly wish to thank: Phil Cahill, Seán Cahill, Michael Carroll, Jack Dineen, Sheila Lyons Bowler, Marie Finucane Kissane, Willie Goggin, Paudy Hanrahan, Jimmy Hartnett, John McCarthy, Eileen Moriarty MacNamara, Jerry Nolan, John Joe O'Donnell, Michael Walsh and Mossie Walsh.

I thank Fr Pat Ahern, Founding Artistic Director of Siamsa Tíre, the National Folk Theatre of Ireland, for introducing me to the Molyneaux style of step dancing and for sharing his knowledge and passion for this dance style with me. I also thank the board members and staff of Siamsa Tíre, in particular Honor Hurley, Oliver Hurley, Jonathan Kelliher, Tara Little, Michael Murphy, John Sheehan, Carl Wallace and Martin Whelan for their support of my work and for always making me feel welcome at Siamsa Tíre.

I thank Honor Flynn and Jimmy Smith, Founding Teachers of *Rinceoirí na Ríochta,* for their friendship and support over the years and for their willingness to make their school of dance available to me for my research. I also thank the following people for assisting me with my research: Lorraine Bailey, Tríona Breen, Kay Carmody, John Flavin, Geraldine Fitzgerald, John Fitzgerald, Irene Gould, Patricia Hanafin, Tim Hanrahan, Jimmy Hickey, John B. Keane, Brendan Kennelly, Eileen Lade, Patricia Lawlor, John Lynch, Michael Lynch, Dr Bryan MacMahon, Declan Malone, Aideen Morgan, Phil Mulally, Ríonach uí Ógáin, Seosamh Ó Bruadair, Wil O'Donnell, Liam Ó Duinín, Miriam O'Sullivan, John Pierse, Bridie Trant, Tom Paiti Walsh and Will Wixted.

A lot of the research material in this book is based on my original fieldwork from the early 1980s and the early 2000s but archival materials from personal and institutional archives together with published material have also been included. For permission to include these materials, I wish to thank the following: An Coimisiún le Rincí Gaelacha; Siamsa Tíre, the National Folk Theatre of Ireland; the Trustees of Muckross House (Killarney) Ltd; John Egan and FeisPix; *Rinceoiri na Riochta,* Tralee; the National Archives of Ireland (NAI), Dublin, and the Director of the National Archives of Ireland; the Archives of the National Folklore Collections at University College Dublin; Oxford University Press; Bloodaxe Books Ltd UK; the Institute for Musicology of the Hungarian Academy of Sciences, Budapest; Eighteenth Century Ireland Journal; The Journal of Dance Research, Edinburgh University Press; Cork University Press; *The Kerryman*, Tralee; Kevin Coleman; Bridie Trant; J. Anthony Gaughan; Gráinne McArdle; Jimmy Smith, John Fitzgerald; Mark Franko, University of California, Santa Cruz;, and Jimmy Deenihan, Minister for Arts, Heritage and the Gaeltacht and North Kerry Literary Trust, Listowel, for permission to use material from my book, *Irish Traditional Step Dancing in North Kerry: a Contextual and Structural Analysis* (2012 – Book and accompanying DVD).

In addition, I wish to acknowledge and to thank sincerely the following who at different stages of this research, and in their different ways, gave of their expertise and knowledge: Andy Adamson, Dr Peter Brinson, Professor Theresa Buckland, Paul Filmer, Hubert Kwisthout, Dr Alastair MacFadyen, Peggy McTeggart, Dr Valerie Preston-Dunlop, Pat and John Ryan, Dr Harold Silver and Dr Trevor Wittock.

At Ashgate Publishing, I would sincerely like to thank Derek Scott, Laura Macy, Heidi Bishop, Huw Jones, Barbara Pretty and Beatrice Beaup for their wonderful support and assistance throughout the publication process.

At the Irish World Academy of Music and Dance, University of Limerick, I wish to thank all my colleagues for their support but particularly Professor Micheál Ó Súilleabháin, Dr Orfhlaith Ni Bhriain, Dr Mats Melin, Dr Sandra Joyce, and Dr Niall Keegan. I thank Dr Colin Quigley, for reading an early draft of the manuscript and for his helpful comments. I would also like to thank the National Dance Archive of Ireland at the University of Limerick and Dance Research Forum Ireland for their support.

I would like to acknowledge the support of the two men who initiated the Muckross House Collection of Irish traditional music, song and dance. They and I were not to know then how this project would shape my life. They are the late Edmond Myers, Muckross House, Killarney, and the late Ian O'Leary, Killarney. I thank them both. I also wish to thank Pat Dawson and the Trustees of Muckross House, Killarney, for their support over the years, and the late Tom Munnelly, who provided me with my first class in fieldwork methods.

For awards and assistance with funding the initial stages of this research (1983–1985), I wish to thank the Trustees of Muckross House (Killarney) Ltd; the Arts Council of Ireland; the American Irish Foundation, and my parents and family. However, this book would not have been written without the love, support and trust of those closest to me. My parents, Johanna and Patrick, nurtured a deep love of music, dance, books and Irish culture in me. My father inspired me to dance and sing to his wonderful music on the melodeon. I owe my passion for music and dance to him. I thank my sisters, Pat Ryan and Breda Long, and my brothers, Gene Foley and Joe Foley, for their constant friendship and support throughout the years and for always being there for me. To my husband, John Dawson, I would like to express my heartfelt thanks for his love, support and encouragement. He has always been the first reader of everything I have written, and assisted in the preparation of this manuscript. I also thank our son and daughter, Mark and Rachel, for their constant love and for deeply enriching my life.

Chapter 1

An Ethnochoreologist in 'The Kingdom' of Kerry

Introduction

This book is concerned with the development of one dance form in Ireland from the eighteenth century to the twenty-first century. It examines the interrelationships between step dancing and the changing historical and cultural contexts of colonialism, nationalism, postcolonialism and globalization. This examination illustrates how step dancing is a powerful tool of embodiment and meaning that provokes important questions relating to culture and identity through the bodies of those who perform it. It also shows how step dancing through time has assisted to shape, and has been shaped by, changing notions of culture and identity.

Written from an ethnochoreological perspective, the book aims to provide an appreciation and an understanding of step dancing as both an expressive and an embodied vehicle of culture and identity. To this end, the book focuses on one rural region, North Kerry, in the south-west of Ireland, and selects three step dance practices to illustrate how different manifestations of step dance can embody, express and shape culture and history: (1) the rural Molyneaux step dance practice, representing the end of a relatively long-lived system of teaching by itinerant dancing masters in this region; (2) Rinceoirí na Ríochta, the urbanized staged competition-orientated practice, cultivated by the cultural nationalist movement the Gaelic League established at the end of the nineteenth century, and (3) the stylized folk-theatrical practice of Siamsa Tíre, the National Folk Theatre of Ireland, established in North Kerry in the 1970s. These three practices embody and represent three different cultural meaning systems, and reveal and comment upon transformations in Irish culture from the end of the eighteenth century to the beginning of the twenty-first century.

This period witnessed Ireland changing from a colonial country under British rule in the eighteenth century to a postcolonial, European, modern nation-state in the twenty-first century. Throughout this period, step dance was shaped by influences from both within and outside Ireland. The book examines these influences, utilizing both a historical perspective and an ethnographic perspective.[1]

---

[1] Since the closing decades of the twentieth century, the ethnographic perspective from the field of anthropology has been applied by a number of disciplines, including ethnochoreology and ethnomusicology. For the different uses of fieldwork and ethnography, see the articles by Kaeppler and Williams in Buckland (1999); see also Barz and Cooley (1997 and 2008).

While the historical perspective provides the story of step dancing in North Kerry as it has unfolded through time, the ethnographic perspective provides the immediate, richly detailed descriptions, and the voices of the dancers and others, in the field. Both perspectives contribute to illustrating how step dancing interacts with and responds to the different cultural processes in Ireland of colonialism, famine, nationalism and globalization. As Theresa Jill Buckland states:

> the study of dance as representative practice requires the skills and perspectives of history and ethnography, not only to explore legacies of colonialism and nationalism, but also to interrogate the continuing impact of globalization and the politics of identity articulation.[2]

Step dancing as a genre is some two hundred and fifty years old. To provide an understanding of its emergence in Ireland, I examine dance during the period of the European Renaissance to establish connections between the European dancing masters and dancing masters in Ireland. The European dancing masters' aesthetic and codified dance practices were disseminated by dancing masters across Europe – and indeed, across the Atlantic – to different sectors of society through instruction in dance and ballroom etiquette. Ireland was no exception. Here, a hierarchical system of dancing masters existed for different sectors of society. These dancing masters provided instruction in dance and ballroom etiquette as an integral part of the 'civilizing process'[3] prevalent throughout most of Europe during the eighteenth and nineteenth centuries.

The book investigates these dancing masters, especially the itinerant dancing masters of North Kerry. Itinerant dancing masters were positioned at the bottom of the social hierarchy of dancing masters, working predominantly with rural communities. It is these itinerant dancing masters who cultivated step dancing as a dance form in Ireland within the context of British colonialism. The book identifies and examines these dancing masters throughout this period to the middle of the twentieth century, when the last of them, Jeremiah Molyneaux (1882–1965), died. Based upon intensive periods of fieldwork during the 1980s and 2000s with step dance students of Jeremiah Molyneaux and others, this book hopes to provide a unique glimpse into the world of these dancing masters and their students. Through interviews with these students, younger step dancers and others, I trace the changing trajectory of step dancing over two hundred years as it has reflected, responded to and negotiated historical and cultural processes of colonialism, famine, nationalism and globalization. In addition, through my own training in step dancing and through learning step dances directly from Molyneaux's step dance students, I offer a subjective and embodied understanding to this discourse on step dancing. This has assisted me to appreciate and to interpret the worlds that are referenced by step dancing.

---

[2]   Buckland (2006), p. 17.
[3]   Elias (1994).

I have researched into the field of step dancing in North Kerry for thirty years, with some intensive periods of fieldwork during 1983–86 and in 2004. This book is based on this research and my 'native' experience as an Irish step dancer, teacher, musician and ethnochoreologist.

Cognisant of the fact that step dance has, for the most part, been taught, practised and performed within the context of social or communal dance practices, the book also refers to these dances in order to contextualize the practice of step dancing. The focus of the book, however, is on step dancing as a solo dance practice.

Step Dancing

Step dancing is a solo dance-music practice that exists today not only in Ireland, but also in countries and regions including Scotland, England, mainland Europe, Scandinavia, the United States, Canada, Australia, New Zealand, Africa, Japan and Russia. For many people, step dancing is associated with the Irish step dance stage show *Riverdance*, which from 1995 assisted in promoting and disseminating the dance form and in placing Ireland globally.[4] The situation for step dance is much more complicated and fluid, however.

Step dancing may be performed informally by friends and neighbours, or in formally structured classes; it may be performed by young and old, male and female dancers; it may be performed in either highly organized, formal, competitive staged contexts, or in informal social settings; it may be performed in spectacular stage shows such as *Riverdance* or *Lord of the Dance*, or in smaller theatrical venues; it may be performed with highly elaborate costumes, or ordinary everyday wear; it may be danced with specialized hard or soft dance shoes, or ordinary everyday shoes; it may be improvisatory, or it may be a set repertoire, and step dancers may be either professionals or amateurs. Step dancing is a multi-faceted practice that does not hold one meaning for all step dancers; it holds diverse meanings, generated by different historical, ideological and socio-cultural contexts. Step dancing as a dance form is dynamic and adaptable, and assists in reflecting, shaping and contributing to different socio-political circumstances and changes in culture and society.

Step dancing is meaningful practice; it is danced by people who ascribe meaning to it. To those who do it or actively watch it, step dancing is considered meaningful in and of itself. Step dancing refers to a particular way of dancing. Generally, it is regarded as a solo dancer's performance practice, and may be considered joyous, serious or virtuosic. As the name implies, step dancing is the art of rhythmical stepping with the feet in dialogue with traditional music genres; in Ireland, these music genres include Reels, Jigs[5] and Hornpipes (see the Appendix). The feet and legs have most significance in step dancing, while the torso remains erect with arms

---

[4]   Foley (2001).

[5]   I am including Slip Jigs or Hop Jigs in $\frac{9}{8}$ time within the category of Jigs.

held in place at the sides of the body. Particular kinaesthetic movements are common to all forms of step dancing, and step dancers aim to acquire cognitive, corporeal, aesthetic and cultural competence in these, relative to their contexts of practice.

Step dancers dance for numerous reasons: they love the dance form; they love the music; they love the rhythm; they love the way they feel when they are step dancing; they love the challenge of moving in a specific way to traditional dance music; they enjoy the social element associated with the form; they like to keep fit; they like to compete, and they feel pride when they express and embody their heritage and culture. Step dancing is all of these and more. Step dancing, as a structured, human movement system,[6] does not exist in a vacuum. It is located in time and place, and has been generated by people and institutions within specific social, cultural and historical circumstances. Step dancing is therefore a complex, multi-faceted expressive and embodied practice that evokes deeper meanings when viewed within the contexts of culture and history.

An Ethnochoreological Perspective

This book is written from an ethnochoreological perspective. Ethnochoreology is an interdisciplinary field of study drawing from concepts and research methods within multi-disciplinary areas including anthropology, sociology, cultural studies, folklore, philosophy, education, linguistics, dance studies and performance studies. Its focus is the academic study of dance (or any human movement system) as product and as social process and its relationship to the culture of which it is a part.

An ethnochoreological perspective embraces the study of all dance and human movement systems, including popular dance, urban dance, traditional dance, theatrical dance and other movement systems which are not classified under the Western term 'dance'.[7] It is the study of people *in situ* engaged in a cultural movement activity that is somatic, social, highly symbolic and meaningful. While an ethnochoreological perspective generally implies that one engages in fieldwork to obtain firsthand context-rich data for description, analysis and interpretation, other resources are also used, including archives, libraries and the Internet. Written histories of dance have existed since the early decades of the eighteenth century[8] and collections of dances in Europe, carried out by predominantly middle-class intellectuals, have been closely associated with the discipline of folklore and eighteenth and nineteenth century European romanticism and cultural politics.[9] Although dance was not the focus of anthropological studies in the early twentieth century, a number of anthropologists included their observations and analyses of dance in their studies. For example, Radcliffe-Brown (1922) looked

---

[6]   Kaeppler (1986), pp. 25–33.
[7]   Kaeppler (1978).
[8]   Royce (1977).
[9]   Giurchescu and Torp (1991); Foley (2012c).

at the importance of dance for the Andaman islanders for the transmission and maintenance of sentiments, Evans-Pritchard (1928) looked at the role of the *gbere buda* (beer dance) within religious ceremony in Azande, while Mead (1928) looked at the educational role of dance and the transmission of sentiments in Samoa. Boaz (1944) laid the foundation for examining dance within the context of cultural relativism while Mitchell (1956) examined the *Kalela Dance* in an attempt to analyse aspects of the system of social relationships among Africans in the towns of Northern Rhodesia.[10]

Academic investigation into the body commenced with the French sociologist Marcel Mauss in his seminal work, *Les Techniques de Corps* (1935). Research into dance and human movement as culturally-derived systems began around the 1960s, when anthropologists, ethnochoreologists and dance ethnologists in both the United States and Europe began to focus on their significance in understanding not just dances, but also the cultures out of which they had emerged.[11] These scholars argued for the importance of anthropological and ethnochoreological investigations of dance and human movement in order to gain insight into the deeper structures of human movement and culture. Studies were undertaken into the structural analysis of dance where the dance itself was documented and analysed to shed light on the structure of the dance as a culturally-derived and cognitive system.[12] From the 1970s, studies of dance were developed further to include embodiment, ethnicity, gender, globalization, identity, politics, ritual, social relations, social structure, somatics, and worldview.[13] In 2008, Hughes-Freeland states '[the] importance of dance both as embodied practice and as representational system is now recognized, socially, culturally and politically'[14] It is also now acknowledged that cultures express and differentiate themselves through symbolic activities which are important loci of people's most deeply held values, beliefs and meaning systems.[15]

The ethnochoreological perspective offers the opportunity to encounter, to examine and to draw attention to different dance or human movement practices, lifestyles, belief and value systems, modes of thought and experiential opportunities. It teaches us about different ways people conceptualize and experience their world through the lens of movement and dance.

---

[10]   Spencer (1985).

[11]   See, for example, Kurath (1960), Hall (1960), Martin and Pesovar (1961), Birdwhistell (1972); Kealiinohomoku (1972a), Kaeppler (1978; 1986; 1991), Hanna (1980), Royce (1977), Williams (1991) and Giurchescu and Torp (1991); see also Buckland (1999), Kaeppler (2000) and Reed (1998) for overviews of the field; and Foley (2012e) for an examination of ethnochoreology in Ireland.

[12]   Kaeppler and Dunin (2007).

[13]   Ibid.

[14]   Hughes-Freeland (2008), p. 11.

[15]   Royce (1977), Hanna (1980), Kaeppler (1972; 1986; 1991), Kealiinohomoku (1972a), Williams (1991).

Following the work of anthropologists such as Adrienne Kaeppler, Cynthia Bull Novack, Joann Wheeler Kealiinohomoku, Anya Peterson Royce, Yvonne Daniel, Sally Ann Ness and Deidre Sklar, the book interprets dance as an important part of culture. In this book, step dancing is interpreted as culture.[16] This perspective provides a particular way to view dance and dancing within the complex rituals and social processes in society, and it also enables us to view culture as expressive of particular worldviews which assist in telling us something about the culture and about the dance as an embodied practice.

This chapter looks at some of the theoretical concepts which frame the writing of the book – embodiment, culture, *habitus*[17] and identity – but first it will discuss my role as an ethnochoreologist researching step dancing in North Kerry.

Locating Myself in the Field

According to the ethnomusicologist Bruno Nettl: 'if the ethnomusicologist considers himself the student of music in all cultures, his "field" may also be his own environment, and he is part of it'.[18] As an ethnochoreologist, my interest is in all dance and other human movement systems, but my field of research is step dancing in North Kerry. I grew up in Ireland, and I have step danced and played music for most of my life. My father, Patrick Foley, played the melodeon, and his mother, Abbey Lane, played the concertina and fiddle. Both were also singers and dancers. I played the concertina, tin whistle and piano. I played these at home with my father, and outside of the home I learned classical piano and step dancing formally. My sister Pat and myself would often step dance at home to our father's music. I chose to study classical music for my undergraduate degree. Throughout my life, I have participated in diverse roles in different dance and music communities: I competed at traditional music and step dance competitions from the age of six; I performed traditional music and dance informally at home and formally at concerts and exhibitions in Ireland and abroad; I participated in informal pub sessions, and I formally taught traditional music, classical music and dance at primary, secondary, undergraduate and postgraduate levels within the education system. Also, I worked as a collector of Irish traditional music, song and dance; I presented dance workshops and lectures in different parts of the world, and I have been, and continue to be, a member of international, academic dance and music communities. These experiences have shaped my own sense of identity and my own interpretations and understandings of step dance practices in Ireland. However, the seed for this book was planted in 1980, when I commenced my work as a collector of Irish traditional music, song and dance for Muckross House, Killarney, Co. Kerry.

---

[16]   See also Snyder (1972) and Merriam (1974).

[17]   Bourdieu (1977).

[18]   Nettl (1964), p. 63.

Fieldwork in Kerry and the Muckross House Collection

Kerry is one of 32 counties on the island of Ireland, and is one of the 26 counties in the Republic of Ireland. These counties are sub-national land divisions for administrative, political and geographical purposes, and they also assist in demarcating conceptual boundaries between counties. Kerry is situated on the south-western coast of Ireland, and is commonly referred to as 'The Kingdom'.[19] It consists of villages and towns of various sizes surrounded by bogs, mountain ranges, rivers and lakes, and numerous scattered farms engaged in dairying and mixed tillage. The majority of the population are Catholic. Due to its landscape, considered to be one of the most beautiful in Ireland, Kerry attracts many tourists, and consequently a thriving tourist industry has emerged there which has contributed to the economy and the culture of the region.

In 1979, Muckross House[20] in Killarney, Co. Kerry, initiated a regional collection of Irish traditional music, song and dance. The collection was instigated by Edmond Myers, then Manager of Muckross House, and Ian O'Leary, a Trustee of Muckross House and a local journalist with *The Kerryman* newspaper. The objective of the collection was to document, record and preserve for posterity the traditional music, song and dance practices of the elderly population of the County of Kerry. The collection focused on elderly performers due to the rarity, value and worth of the repertoire of these performers, and also for historical, educational, research and heritage purposes. The collection would be housed in Muckross House, and would be available to the general public.[21]

I was employed as one of two collectors; the other collector was Geraldine Cotter.[22] Both of us were music graduates of Professor Aloys Fleischmann at

---

[19] In Irish: *An Ríocht.*

[20] Muckross House is a Victorian mansion situated in Killarney National Park, Co. Kerry. The house, together with its gardens and farms, is open to the public. Built in 1845, the house was owned by the Herbert family, then the Ardilaun family, and finally the Bourne Vincent family. In 1932, Muckross House was handed over by the Bourne Vincent family to the Irish State; it is now managed by a Board of Trustees. Integral to the house is the Muckross Research Library, and housed in this library is the Muckross House Collection of Irish Traditional Music, Song and Dance. In 2001, the library received the prestigious Museum of the Year Award for Best Collections Care.

[21] Foley (2012c).

[22] In 1983, another collector, Mary Mitchell, took over from Geraldine Cotter in North Kerry, and Patricia Connery, another collector, took over from me in South Kerry as I had been asked to transfer my attention to traditional step dance in North Kerry. At a later stage, Mary O'Flynn, another collector, participated in the collecting process for Muckross House. Between 1980 and 1990, in excess of 400 tapes, almost 3,000 items, of traditional music, song and dance were collected. The audio collection was recorded on reel-to-reel, full-track magnetic tape, size 5.25 inches; these recordings were later digitized. Step dance recordings were made on standard VHS video tapes; these were also digitized (I was the only step-dance collector). The Muckross House Collection received much support. Initial

University College, Cork. Geraldine focused on the north of the county, since it was closer to her home town, Ennis, Co. Clare, and I focused on the south of the county, since it was more accessible to my home city, Cork, and also to the West Cork Gaeltacht,[23] Baile Mhúirne, where I was a secondary school music teacher at that time.

The collection process took place annually, during ten weeks of the summer season; the first summer was 1980. With our Uher reel-to-reel tape recorders, we located individuals to record. We did this through the help of shopkeepers, publicans, postmasters and others who lived locally, and once a few sources were located, the rest was word of mouth. Most of the elderly population I recorded lived in rural areas, and the majority of them were retired. Most had been involved in farming, while others had been builders, home makers, and shopkeepers. Since it was summertime, I sometimes had to accommodate myself to the agricultural timetable to find a convenient time to record. Consequently, I might record at 10 a.m. or at 10 p.m. into the early hours of the morning, and if the repertoire was extensive, I would return on other occasions. I took relevant notes during these events, and on returning to my bedsit, I transcribed the music and song material. At the end of each summer, I ended up with some twenty reel-to-reel tapes of recorded traditional musicians and singers together with transcriptions of their repertoires. The collected material was deposited in Muckross House, where it is today. Some information about the performers, their material and the location and conditions of the recordings was also supplied, but it was the music, songs and dances, as artefacts or cultural 'texts', which carried most importance.

During the summers of 1980–81, I based myself in the town of Kenmare and collected from musicians and singers around the Kilgarvan and Kenmare areas; in 1982, I moved my base to the village of Sneem, where I continued to locate and collect from performers. Throughout this time, I sourced, located and encountered many traditional musicians and singers and made numerous recordings of their repertoires; however, there were very few elderly solo traditional step dancers. Most of the dancers in the area at the time were involved in either competitive step dancing, in which case they were young and outside the remit of the collection, or were engaged in social dancing, which included set dancing (similar to Quadrilles or square dancing), cabaret dancing or disco dancing.

---

funding for the collection came from the Trustees of Muckross House and the Kerry County Board of Comhaltas Ceoltóirí Éireann. Later, a grant for the collection was secured by Billy Vincent, President of the American Irish Foundation. Professional and technical assistance was received from Dr Micheál Ó Súilleabháin of the Music Department, University College, Cork; Tony Perrott of the Audio-visual Department, University College, Cork; Tom Munnelly, the full-time collector with the Department of Irish Folklore, University College, Dublin, and Fr Pat Ahern, Founding Artistic Director of Siamsa Tíre, the National Folk Theatre of Ireland, Tralee.

[23]   A *gaeltacht* is an Irish- or Gaelic-speaking area. In Baile Mhúirne, I therefore taught through the medium of Irish.

In 1983, Edmond Myers, the Manager of Muckross House, requested that I turn my attention to collecting solo traditional step dances in North Kerry. Fr Pat Ahern, the Founding Artistic Director of Siamsa Tíre (see Chapter 7), had requested that the Muckross House Collection might include some elderly step dancers in the region of North Kerry. I was informed that these step dancers performed a style of dance that was special to the area, but that it was no longer being transmitted live. They had been taught by an itinerant dancing master, Jeremiah Molyneaux, and their step dances and style of dancing were considered old, of cultural value, and in decline. My research field was thus determined.

In February 1983, I met these elderly step dancers for the first time (see 'The Jerry Molyneaux Commemorative Night' in Chapter 2), and in June 1983 I commenced my fieldwork in step dancing in the region of North Kerry. Most of the Molyneaux step dancers were retired; some of them lived with their families, while others lived on their own. As a collector of their dances, my method was to visit each of them in their homes and to physically learn their individual repertoires (see below); I did not have a personal video camera at my disposal at the time, therefore learning to embody the dances was a primary research tool.[24]

As I learned and embodied each dance step, I also documented it mnemonically.[25] I used the mnemonic system which I had learned from my step dance teacher, Peggy McTeggart of Cork. This system consisted of terms associated with particular step dance vocabulary which was embodied, and sometimes, when practising or teaching, these terms were vocalized in time with the dancing and the accompanying rhythmical metre of the music. This vocabulary included terms such as batters,[26] hops, tips, toes, heels, cuts and stamps. I decided to use this system for documenting the dances. It would act as an *aide-mémoire*, and it would accompany the video recordings of each individual dancer which were made at the end of each summer.[27]

However, the video recordings gave insight into one performance only, and the mnemonic system was accessible only to those trained in it; also, it was not an accurate documentation tool. Having used Western music notation for transcribing

---

[24]   See Chapter 6 in this volume, and Foley (2012c).

[25]   Catherine Foley Step Dancing Collection, Muckross House Archive (1983–85).

[26]   These terms were used by my step dance teacher, Peggy McTeggart of Cork, by her students, and also by step dancers in North Kerry and elsewhere; however, the terms are not universal. For example, the movement named the 'batter' here is also sometimes referred to as a 'shuffle, rally'.

[27]   Video recordings of the Molyneaux step dancers took place at the end of each summer during 1983–85 in the Teach Siamsa, Finuge, North Kerry. Generally, I co-ordinated these events. Since I had collected and learned the dances from these step dancers during the summers, it was thought best at the time for me to sit in with the dancers during the recordings, since they knew me and it might put them at their ease. Phil Mulally of Dublin worked the camera in 1983; Fr Pat Ahern, Artistic Director of Siamsa Tíre, worked the camera in 1984 and 1985.

the collected music and songs, I was aware of my lack of an equivalent movement notation system for the documentation of the step dances. Therefore, in 1984, with an award from the Arts Council of Ireland and additional funding awarded by the American Irish Foundation, I went to the Laban Centre for Movement and Dance in London to equip myself with the necessary dance research methods and skills,[28] and in particular Labanotation, the movement notation system. I registered for an MPhil., and I familiarized myself with relevant research methods and available literature in multi-disciplinary fields such as ethnochoreology, ethnomusicology, anthropology, sociology, cultural studies, folklore and linguistics. I upgraded to a PhD, and in 1988 I completed my doctorate in ethnochoreology, 'Irish Traditional Step Dancing in North Kerry: A Contextual and Structural Analysis'.[29]

During the years I was in London, I returned each summer to Ireland and to Kerry for further fieldwork and research. In 1985, I completed my work as a collector for Muckross House, but I continued until 2004 with my own research, conducting short, intensive periods of fieldwork in North Kerry. At this stage, I had broadened my academic and research interests to include other step dance practices in the region.

Therefore, together with the Molyneaux step dance practice, two other step dance practices are included in this book. These all co-existed in North Kerry during the 1980s, albeit at different stages of their development. The Molyneaux step dance practice as a rural, living tradition was considered to be in decline (see Chapters 2, 3 and 4); the cultural nationalist practice of An Coimisiún le Rincí Gaelacha[30] had been operating in North Kerry for thirty years (see Chapters 5 and 6), and Siamsa Tíre[31] had just employed its first professional dancers/actors (see Chapter 7).

Dance Ethnography in North Kerry

Due to a paucity of literature in the field of Irish dance in the 1980s, it was essential for my research to undertake ethnographic together with archival and bibliographic research methods.[32]

---

[28] This was made possible by an award I received from the Arts Council, Ireland, and by some funding from the Trustees of Muckross House and the American Irish Foundation.

[29] Foley (1988b).

[30] The Irish Dance Commission.

[31] *Siamsa Tíre* literally means 'lively entertainment of the country'. Siamsa Tíre, the National Folk Theatre of Ireland, theatrically presents Irish folklore, customs and myths through Irish traditional music, song in Irish, dance and mime. In recent years it has broadened its theatrical work to engage with wider cultural issues (see Chapter 7).

[32] Since the beginning of the twenty-first century, published scholarship on dancing in Ireland has increased; these texts include: Brennan (1999); Foley (2001; 2011); F. Hall (2008) and Wulff (2007).

Generally speaking, ethnography is the study of people *in situ* over an extensive period. It was established as a primary research method by the anthropologists Bronislaw Malinowski and Franz Boas in the 1920s, and has remained the hallmark of anthropology ever since. It is also an important research method in ethnochoreology.[33] Generally, ethnography involves doing fieldwork: observing people, participating in their culture in a role that is acceptable to them, taking field notes, gathering *collectanea*, selecting ethnographic informants, interviewing and recording them, and possibly transcribing recordings in the case of music and dance ethnography. Ethnography also requires familiarity with theoretical concepts in multi-disciplinary fields, particularly those found within the social sciences, and a final written product which describes, analyses and interprets the ethnographic process – academic proof that one was actually there. Ethnography is a practice of embodiment, and as such, it is well suited to dance research since it empowers the body as a locus of knowledge.

According to the anthropologist Bronislaw Malinowski: 'The goal of ethnography should be ... to grasp the native's point of view, his relation to life, to realize his vision of his world'.[34] Dance ethnography, as a method in ethnochoreology, facilitates an examination into how indigenous people think, construct, experience, understand and represent their world through dance. Although I am Irish, I am not a native from the Kerry perspective. The dance was therefore a significant place for me to start to grasp both the Kerry perspective and a better understanding of its inhabitants' reality and their worldview or ethos through dance.

To gain access to this information, I learned the dances, as mentioned above, and I carried out interviews with primary informants in the field.[35] These included dancers, teachers, actors, local historians and others knowledgeable about step dancing and step dancers in the region. I recorded the majority of these interviews to present the voices, expressions and stories of the informants, and also to acquire

---

[33]   Buckland (1999).

[34]   Malinowski (1922), p. 25.

[35]   I adopt the term 'informants' here as it is most commonly used within the field. Primary informants for this research included representatives of the different step dance practices in the region of North Kerry. Informants for the Molyneaux step dance practice included: Fr Pat Ahern, Phil Cahill, Seán Cahill, Michael Carroll, Jack Dineen, Máire Finucane Kissane, John Flavin, Willie Goggin, Paudie Hanrahan, Tim Hanrahan, Jimmy Hartnett, Jimmy Hickey, Michael Kavanagh, Sheila Lyons Bowler, Eileen Moriarty MacNamara, John McCarthy, Jerry Nolan, Seosamh Ó Bruadair, Liam Ó Duinín, John-Joe O'Donnell, Willie O'Donnell, Tom Joe O'Sullivan, Jack Stack, Michael Walsh, and Mossie Walsh (for biographies of some of the Molyneaux step dancers, see my PhD thesis, Foley 1988b; and 2012b). Informants for An Coimisiún in the region and Rinceoirí na Ríochta included Tríona Breen, John Fitzgerald, Honor Flynn, Irene Gould, Eileen Lade, Miriam O'Sullivan, and Jimmy Smith. Informants for Siamsa Tíre included Fr Pat Ahern, John Fitzgerald, Patricia Hanafin, Honor Hurley, Oliver Hurley, Jonathan Kelliher, Tara Little, Michael Murphy, Jimmy Smith, Ray Walsh and Martin Whelan.

their perspectives and feelings on their dance practice and history; direct quotations are included in this book. Video recordings were also made of the dancers at the end of each summer in order to provide audio-visual representations of the dancers *in* practice.

The step dancers I researched knew that I was a step dancer, and my dance competence was taken for granted. My role as an ethnochoreologist was that of dancer, musician, researcher and documenter of their cultural knowledge. However, many years prior to this, when I was recording traditional music and songs in South Kerry, some of the musicians there thought that I was something between a social worker and a television researcher. I can understand how they might have thought this. I spent much time talking to these elderly people about themselves, their lives, their health and their music and dance, and recording their music and songs was to them reminiscent of some radio and television programmes that they had heard or seen. My role as an ethnochoreologist and step dancer in the field was perceived as active, combining social interaction with ethnochoreological research methods. In this role, I attended and participated in social events, concerts and *feiseanna*[36] in the area and entered into dialogue with the local people to uncover their views, feelings and values on step dancing, and indeed their broader culture. I participated in dance events when and where culturally appropriate, and I gradually developed friendships with many of the dancers I encountered.

The anthropologist Sally Ann Ness suggests that there are three stages to ethnographic production: home office – field site – home office.[37] We could translate this to: fieldwork preparation (practically and theoretically) – fieldwork experience – writing up the fieldwork experience, the monograph. My experience did not work as neatly as this. When entering the field in 1983, I had been prepared practically by my experiences and embodiment of the traditional performing arts in Ireland – music, song and dance. I was also familiar with the literature in these fields and some literature in other related fields, including ethnomusicology, which I studied during my undergraduate music degree. However, a deeper theoretical engagement with the available literature in ethnochoreology, anthropology, sociology, cultural studies and linguistics came later, during my PhD studies in London during the 1980s. My PhD, together with this book, have become the writing up stage. However, the process is never complete.

Representing the Field

The notion and nature of representation is a matter of significance in the social sciences. How does one represent a culture, a people or a dance community within the domain of academia? How does one represent these communities within

---

[36]   The plural of *feis*, literally 'festival', referring here to competitive step dance festivals; see the Appendix and Chapter 4.

[37]   Ness (1992), p. 141.

one's own back yard? Conscious of the discourse of representation within the literature,[38] my objective is to attempt to represent a selected and 'partial' view of the three step dance practices and their communities in North Kerry. Throughout the ethnographic process, questions relating to representation influenced the methodologies I applied in the field, and will also influence the final outcome of the ethnographic process: the written and recorded material.

In writing this book, total objectivity cannot be attained, and neither is it wished for. My own biography, dancing background and experiences, together with my own prejudices and biases, were constantly present in the field, and influenced and shaped social interactions and ethnographic decisions made during and after field research. Therefore, I realize that the representations I will present will be partial, speaking from a particular place – geographically, culturally and historically.

Ethnographically, researching the three step dance practices in North Kerry presented me with a rare opportunity. It was not only a dance endeavour. The process was one of human interaction with dancing and dancers at the centre of the research. My ethnographic experiences with these dancers remain part of my cultural memory. On a personal level, the experiences were enriching and transformative; from a dance perspective, they extended my step dance knowledge and understanding of different step dance practices through my embodiment of these practices; and from an ethnochoreological perspective, they provided me with the opportunity to gain a deeper understanding of how cultural expressive practices assist people in shaping, and being shaped by, a sense of place, history and cultural identity.

Insider–Outsider Continuum

Born and brought up in the city of Cork, I may be viewed as an 'insider' to Irish culture. However, since I am not 'native' to the ethnographic region in question, Kerry, I may also be viewed as an 'outsider'. Insider–outsider relations play a significant role in the ethnographic process, both in terms of interactive dialogue between the researcher and the researched, and in matters of written representation, where power/knowledge relationships may exist.[39] I perceived the Molyneaux community of elderly step dancers as 'Other' in the sense that their dance practice was aesthetically different to the one in which I had been trained, and they were also 'Other' in that I was younger, female (the majority of the Molyneaux step dancers were male), and grew up in an urban location as opposed to their rural one. Consequently, my use of 'Other' here is within the context of describing cultural differences. Conversely, however, I was an insider, in that: (1) I was Irish, and shared a common cultural knowledge of Ireland with

---

[38]   Dumont (1978), Herzfeld (1983), Marcus and Fischer (1986), Clifford (1988), Said (1978).

[39]   Said (1991); McKenzie (1995); Clifford (1988).

the dance communities being researched; (2) I spoke English and Irish, and could communicate directly with informants; (3) I was an Irish step dancer and qualified Irish step dance teacher, and shared common knowledge and dance experiences with the step dance teachers of An Coimisiún; (4) I was an insider, in that we all shared a passion for step dancing and traditional Irish music, and (5) I had an intimate knowledge of the contexts associated with the traditional performing arts due to my parents' rural background and the rural house dances associated with it. I was therefore never wholly an insider or an outsider. I was positioned at different times somewhere along the continuum of insider–outsider, depending on differences in social, cultural and contextual circumstances.

Dance Performance as an Ethnochoreological Research Tool

With ethnographic role positions dialogically shifting between insider and outsider, I placed myself as a reflexive performer within the research arena. My dance competence became an ethnochoreological research tool.[40] This concurs with what the anthropologist Sally Ann Ness states: that for one to fully understand what performing a choreographed movement means, one must have 'some appreciation of how getting oneself physically through a choreographed movement can affect a human being, and how it can affect one's own cultural understanding'.[41] This is further reiterated by Anya Peterson Royce, who argues:

> We cannot get to the heart of the place without committing ourselves to embodied ways of knowing … through which access may be only through a body that holds its insights tight.[42]

This use of performance in my dance research and the notion of fieldworker as performer enabled active participation in the research. By integrating performance as a research and experiential method and by embodying the Molyneaux movement practice through direct one-to-one transmission with each individual dancer in their homes during fieldwork, I acquired a subjective and embodied kinaesthetic awareness of their dance steps. Also, as Solis states:

---

[40]   This physical and kinaesthetic way of knowing has also been advocated by scholars such as Novack (1990), Browning (1995), Daniel (1995), Royce (2002), Noland and Ness (2008), Sklar (2008) and Hahn (2007). Also, in the field of ethnomusicology, Blacking (1973a) and Koning (1980), for example, have emphasized the use of performance as a research tool.

[41]   Ness (1992), p. 2; see also Browning (1995), Daniel (1995), Royce (2002), Savigliano (1995), Hahn (2007); Blacking (1973b) and Koning (1980).

[42]   Royce (2007), p. 4

> In learning to dance and sing in new ways, one becomes vitally aware of issues
> of self and other, and of 'here' and 'there', challenging the distancing that takes
> place in much disembodied scholarship.[43]

My dancing body became both a tool for sensing, collecting and remembering their dances, and a repository that assisted my subsequent reflexivity, analysis and subjective understanding. Indeed, by embodying and documenting the dances (mnemonically and in Labanotation), I acquired a phenomenological understanding of the Molyneaux step dance practice. However, as Susilo suggests: 'Learning a culture … is not just learning how the natives physically do it, but also how they think about it.'[44] Therefore, in an attempt to understand the three step dance practices examined in the book I used phenomenological hermeneutics as a framework to assist me to interpret them.

Phenomenological Hermeneutics

Phenomenological hermeneutics has its roots in the thinking of philosophers such as Heideggar, Gadamer and Ricoeur. Phenomenology deals with the lived, emotional and immediate experience of Man; it deals with the philosophical notion of *being*.[45] According to Heiddegar "Being is understanding" and "being-in-the-world" is a mode of experience which grounds understanding"[46] Maxine Sheets-Johnstone suggests that, phenomenology deals with 'descriptions of man and the world as man lives in-the-midst-of-the-world, as he experiences himself and the world … before any kind of reflection whatsoever take place …'.[47]

As an ethnochoreologist, I was interested in how the Molyneaux step dancers and the other step dancers of North Kerry experienced and perceived their world through dance. Being a step dancer and a step dance teacher, I had also experienced step dancing over many years. I therefore had a pre-understanding of step dance practices. However, as the philosopher Paul Ricoeur (1981; influenced by Hans-Georg Gadamer) suggests, pre-understanding is only the first step in the self-conscious task of understanding 'text', and in this instance dance as 'text', and of translating this understanding into language.[48] Ricoeur states: 'Text is any discourse fixed by writing,'[49] and 'What is fixed by writing is [thus] a discourse which could be said.'[50] This notion of 'text' as forwarded by Ricoeur considers

---

[43]   Solis (2004), p. 17.

[44]   Susilo in ibid., p. 4.

[45]   Heidegger (1962); see also Foley (2005a), pp. 48–55.

[46]   Ibid: p. 70.

[47]   Sheets-Johnstone (1979), p. 10.

[48]   Foley (2005a).

[49]   Ricoeur (1981), p. 146.

[50]   Ibid., p. 145.

any meaningful action as 'text'. Dance can, therefore, be considered a 'text' which can be experienced as meaningful action and interpreted or read as 'text'. Ricoeur names this process the *hermeneutic arc*, which involves pre-understanding, followed by explanation, interpretation, and finally, a new understanding.

Hermeneutics is, generally, understood to mean the act of interpreting texts. Nineteenth-century scholars such as the theologian Schleiermacher and the philosopher Dilthey sought to interpret and understand the works of genius produced by so-called Others; they are generally regarded as the founders of Romantic hermeneutics.[51] This tradition, like that of the Enlightenment tradition, advocated objective research methods: *etic* research methods. Since, we now understand, however, that the 'outsider stance is not objective'[52] and since dancing is somatic and affective as well as social and cultural, I sought to mediate dichotomies inherited from the western Enlightenment tradition of objective/subjective, etic/emic, outsider/insider, and interpretation/experience. Therefore, following Ricoeur and the ethnomusicologist Timothy Rice,[53] I sought an understanding 'in hermeneutic terms as a dialectic of experience and interpretation'.[54] This process is what Rice calls *phenomenological hermeneutics*. He states:

> In phenomenological hermeneutics, the world, far from being doubted by the subjective ego, is restored to its ontological and temporal priority over the ego or subject. The world – or in our terms, the culture or the tradition – exists and the subject/ego is 'thrown' into it, According to Heidegger, 'being-in-the-world' is the ego's ontological condition before knowing, understanding, interpreting, and explaining. What the ego/subject comes to understand and manipulate are culturally and historically constructed symbolic forms such as language, dress, social behavior and music. In hermeneutic jargon, the unbridgeable gulf between subject and object is mediated as the subject becomes a self through temporal arcs of understanding and experience in the world. The self, whether as a member of a culture or a student of culture, understands the world by placing itself 'in front of 'cultural works[55]

Thus, in phenomenological hermeneutics, the community of Molyneaux step dancers existed in North Kerry prior to my entering the field or prior to my being 'thrown' into it. Through my encounters and experiences with the Molyneaux step dancers, through placing myself 'in front of' their dancing, I achieved 'temporal arcs of understanding' and became a 'self', This assisted me in mediating the gulf

---

[51]   Rice (2008).

[52]   Ibid, p. 55.

[53]   Rice's thinking here was particularly influenced by the work of Martin Heidegger, Hans-Georg Gadamer, Paul Ricoeur and Clifford Geertz.

[54]   Clifford in Rice (1994), p. 10.

[55]   Rice (1997), p. 114.

between subject and object, between me and the Molyneaux step dancers of North Kerry. Rice further states:

> When, as in ethnomusicological research, a new world of music is encountered, new understanding results when the horizons of the researcher's world are expanded to include at least part of the world that the new music symbolically references. From this perspective, the researcher seeks to understand not so much the inner experience of people from another culture, but rather the world suggested by music sounds, performances and contexts. Because ethnomusicologists often find themselves at some cultural or historical distance from the traditions they study, appropriation is the dialectical counterpart of that initial distanciation. Even so-called insider ethnomusicologists, those born into the traditions they study, undergo a productive distanciation necessary for the explanation and critical understanding of their own cultures.[56]

The new world of dance encountered by me was the Molyneaux step dance practice. The act of physically learning and embodying the Molyneaux step dances, together with researching the practice and familiarizing myself with relevant literature and social theories, expanded my horizons,[57] allowing me to become a 'self' and to gradually reach new understandings. Distanciation for me occurred when I went to London and engaged in the relevant literature and learned to 'other' myself in order to critically understand step dancing and my own culture.

Phenomenological hermeneutics thus provided me with a framework for looking at dance and dancing in North Kerry as both subjective experiential knowledge and as meaningful action to be read, analysed and interpreted for a new critical cultural understanding.

Key Themes and Concepts

Key themes and concepts in this book include cultural change, embodiment, *habitus*[58] and identity. The three step dance practices with their different aesthetic and value systems reveal different worlds or cultures of dance and different ways of being-in-the-world (Heidegger 1962) through dance. They reference particular histories, places and worldviews, and illustrate how step dancing expresses, shapes and embodies different meanings and notions of culture and identity – self, affinity group, regional, national, global or imagined.[59] They also show the different ways that step dancing is situated in people's lives.

---

[56]   Rice (1994), p. 6.
[57]   Gadamer (1986) explores the metaphor of a world with horizons.
[58]   Mauss (1973) and Bourdieu (1977).
[59]   Anderson (1983) and Foley (2011).

Step Dancing as Culture, *Habitus* and Identity

Ireland is an island with a population of over 6 million people in 2010 (around 4.5 million in the Republic of Ireland, comprising 26 counties, and 1.7 million in Northern Ireland, comprising six counties). With a history of migration to other countries and continents for employment, Ireland is considered 'home' to many more people in the diaspora. In her 'Cherishing the Irish Diaspora' address to the Joint Houses of the Oireachtas (1995), former President of Ireland Mary Robinson reached out to the '70 million people worldwide who can claim Irish descent'. Therefore, when referring to Irish people, we need to acknowledge the large diaspora that exists outside the physical island of Ireland. The island of Ireland does not exist in isolation; it is part of a broader international, economic, political and socio-cultural network.

Ireland also has a long history of invasions and colonizations, and these have all left their mark on its culture. These historical events, together with travel and migration between Ireland, the United States, Canada, Australia, England, Scotland, mainland Europe and elsewhere over the centuries, have ensured that Ireland has no single, homogenized or fixed cultural identity, despite the fact that the Catholic Church and cultural nationalist movements in Ireland have made efforts to promote a uniformity of culture in Ireland (see Chapter 5). The development of step dancing in Ireland is intertwined with these historical and cultural developments, and its practices owe much to a combination of indigenous and non-indigenous influences.

Step dancing is interpreted in this book as culture. Following Clifford Geertz's concept of culture, influenced by Max Weber, that 'man is an animal suspended in webs of significance he himself has spun',[60] I interpret each step dance practice as culture with its own complex 'webs of significance'. Geertz's concept of culture is a semiotic one in search of meaning, and suggests that culture is not something that is locked inside people's heads, but is embodied in public symbols to communicate a people's ethos or worldview[61] to themselves and others. According to Geertz:

> A people's ethos is the tone, character, and quality of their life, its moral and aesthetic style and mood; it is the underlying attitude toward themselves and their world that life reflects. Their world view is their picture of the way things in sheer actuality are, their concept of nature, of self, of society. It contains their most comprehensive ideas of order.[62]

The three step dance practices in this book are public symbols that carry meaning, and each expresses and communicates a particular worldview or ethos.[63] When

---

[60]   Geertz (1973), p. 5.

[61]   Ortner (1984).

[62]   Geertz (1973), p. 127.

[63]   Snyder (1972).

these practices are performed by step dancers in contexts appropriate to their performance, they generate meaning. However, for step dancers to perform and communicate their practices, they are required to possess cultural knowledge, which can be equated with cultural capital.[64] This knowledge is learned over many years, either formally in structured contexts of learning, or informally within families or the wider community. This knowledge relates both to the dance itself and the behaviour around the dance appropriate to specific contexts. Step dancers are enculturated into communities of step dancers, and acquire, embody and negotiate dance knowledge experientially and progressively as a semiotic system of kinaesthetic symbols and signs. These systems have specific dance vocabularies, grammars, syntax and aesthetic modes of performance, and step dancers learn, perform and negotiate these systems to the accompaniment of Irish traditional dance music within contexts appropriate to their practice. Over time, step dance movement systems become embodied, and they constitute what Pierre Bourdieu (1977), following Marcel Mauss (1973), calls taken-for-granted knowledge; in effect, they become what Bourdieu calls the dancer's *habitus*. Bourdieu defines *habitus* as:

> systems of durable, transposable dispositions, structured structures predisposed to function as structuring structures, that is, as principles of the generation and structuring of practices and representations which can be objectively 'regulated' and 'regular' without in any way being the product of obedience to rules.[65]

The *habitus* is a set of dispositions or a system of encoded, cultivated and inherited practices inscribed on the body over time. Disposition, according to Bourdieu, 'designates a way of being, a habitual state (especially of the body), and in particular, a predisposition, tendency, propensity or inclination'.[66] In the field of competitive Irish step dance, for example, discipline and training are synonymous with the form (see Chapter 5). With years of training, generally commencing at a very young age, step dancers who acquire mastery, bear the evidence of the practice as an "inscribed practice".[67] Sklar notes, however, that 'the hold of the *habitus* is not absolute, and we do sometimes transcend its automatic and efficient grip … inviting opening beyond routine'.[68] The *habitus* is therefore not static.

Each of the three embodied practices of step dance in this book has its own history, a system of encoded practice, moral and aesthetic values, particular stylistic uses of the body, and recognisable music soundscapes. Each dance community has its own knowledge base, stylistic characteristics and repertoires, and each has its own transmission structures and performance contexts. In short, each dance

---

[64]   Bourdieu (1984).

[65]   Bourdieu (1977), p. 72.

[66]   Ibid., p. 214, and Cowan (1990).

[67]   Ness in Noland and Ness (2008), p. 13.

[68]   Sklar (2008), p. 92.

community performs, expresses and embodies a particular *habitus* which assists in both shaping and being shaped by step dancers and their practices.

Step dancers in this book are understood to be active social agents who negotiate within relatively fluid, objectified cultural systems of structured movement. Therefore, although step dancers, teachers and others assist in reproducing the step dance systems they practise, they also assist in gradually developing, re-negotiating and extending them experientially and cognitively. Also, individuals within these dance communities construct and develop their own individual, multi-dimensional *habiti*. For example, in this book, I illustrate how some contemporary step dancers within a modern, globalized Ireland participate in disparate social and cultural institutions, thereby constructing and developing their own multi-dimensional sense of identity, and indeed their own individual *habitus*.

Step dancing as culture, and as a dancer's *habitus*, is also identity. Similarly, identity is both individual and social, and is interpreted here as fluid, inventive and mobile.[69] According to the sociologist Stewart Hall, identity is:

> a matter of 'becoming' as well as of 'being'. It belongs to the future as much as to the past. It is not something that already exists, transcending place, time, history and culture. Cultural identities come from somewhere, have histories. But, like everything that is historical, they undergo constant transformation. Far from being eternally fixed in some essentialised past, they are subject to the continuous 'play' of history, culture and power. Far from being grounded in a mere 'recovery' of the past, which is waiting to be found, and which, when found, will serve our sense of ourselves into eternity, identities are the names we give to the different ways we are positioned by, and position ourselves within, the narratives of the past.[70]

Dancing as identity is shaped by, and assists in shaping, a sense of place and history. This identification can be perceived and felt both locally and nationally;[71] but one can also feel oneself to be placed globally. Cultural expressive practices thus have the power to actively construct, reinforce, contest and shape a sense of place, history and identity, and the three step dance practices in this book express, embody and shape different senses of place and identity: self, local, regional, national and global. According to the social theorist Manuel Castells:

> construction of identities uses building materials from history, from geography, from biology, from productive and reproductive institutions, from collective memory and from personal fantasies, from power apparatuses and religious

---

[69]   Mendoza (2000).

[70]   Hall, S. (1990), p. 225; see also Hall, S. (1996).

[71]   This is in line with Benedict Anderson's definition of nationalism: 'an imagined, political community' (Anderson 1983, p. 6) where members will never meet or know most of their fellow members.

revelations … in general terms, who constructs collective identity, and for what, largely determines the symbolic content of this identity, and its meaning for those identifying with it or placing themselves outside of it.[72]

The three step dance practices examined in this book use different historical and cultural 'building materials', and consequently possess different 'symbolic content'. These assist in constructing different notions of individual and collective identities, and at the same time they provide the 'means by which people recognize identities and places, and the boundaries which separate them'.[73]

Step Dancing as Embodied Practice

My understanding of the term 'practice' includes the doing, embodying and experiencing of step dance, be it in private or public spaces; the conceptualization of step dance by those who do it and observe it; the process involved in the creation, transmission, rehearsal and performance of step dance, be they formal or informal contexts; and the notion of practice or praxis as research. This understanding has been influenced by the writings of Pierre Bourdieu (1977) on practice and the earlier writings of Marcel Mauss (1973) on the *techniques de corps*.

Step dancing is not fixed or fossilized. It is an embodied, dynamic, dance-music cultural activity that is constantly undergoing transformation according to transformations and interactions in, and between, step dancers, musicians, history, culture and society. My understanding of embodiment is in line with the anthropologist Thomas Csordas, whose paradigm of embodiment, influenced by Merleau-Ponty, sees the body as the subject of culture, or as 'the existential ground of culture and self'.[74] As Deidre Sklar notes:

> Csordas recognizes that the phenomenologists' 'lived experience' is never merely individual and subjective but develops as relational and cultural constructions in social space. On the other hand, he understands that the sociologists' practice is not only a collective sedimentation passed on through the generations but an opportunity for individuality, agency, and somatic awareness …. Csordas addresses embodiment as 'the starting point for analyzing human participation in a cultural world'.[75]

---

[72] Castells (2004), p. 7.
[73] Stokes (1994), p. 5.
[74] Csordas (1990), p. 6; see also Mauss (1973), pp. 70–87.
[75] Sklar (2008), p. 92.

The body is socially and culturally constructed, and it is through the body that we experience culture and reality.[76] The body is therefore a field of both perception and practice, and is tool, object and agent. It allows us to experience, sense, feel, perceive, communicate and express our notions of culture and reality, while simultaneously allowing us to shape culture and reality. Culture is grounded in the human body and is embodied in dance, and in this instance, step dance. According to the anthropologist Cynthia Novack:

> Culture is embodied. A primary means of understanding, knowing, making sense of the world comes through shared conceptions of our bodies and selves and through the movement experiences society offers us. Movement constitutes an ever-present reality in which we constantly participate. We perform movement, invent it, interpret it, and reinterpret it, on conscious and unconscious levels. In these actions, we participate in and reinforce culture, and we also create it … the history of the dancing serves as a vehicle for investigating the powerful interrelationships of body, movement, dance, and society.[77]

Step dancing is an expressive and embodied practice. The three step dance practices in this book provide an understanding of how different communities of step dancers come to know and make sense of the world around them – and indeed, their being-in-the-world – through shared, or not shared, conceptions of their bodies and selves. They also illuminate the interrelationships between these step dance practices and the societies and cultures out of which they have emerged and developed.

Chapter Outline

In Chapter 2, I offer an ethnography of 'The Jerry Molyneaux Commemorative Night' in North Kerry, a local event celebrating and remembering the last of the itinerant dancing masters of the region. I then examine the professional dancing masters in Continental Europe to shed light on their influences on itinerant dancing masters in Ireland, and in particular North Kerry. I look at their aristocratic and gentrified associations, and the development of a codified dance aesthetic and foot technique. I posit that these dancing masters and their Continental European dance fashions and codified practices, together with dancing masters in England, influenced dance and a hierarchical system of dancing masters in Ireland beginning in the seventeenth century. I examine how dancing masters in Ireland taught the fashionable dances of the day and ballroom etiquette to the gentry and upper classes to prepare them for balls and parties, and how they also worked in theatres,

---

[76]   The body is discussed here in its totality, not as in the so-called Cartesian mind–body split.

[77]   Novack (1990), p. 8.

private houses and academies for young ladies in Ireland. The primary function of these was one of socialization, where people from similar class systems could ultimately meet, socialize, and hopefully find a marriage partner. The chapter looks at newspaper advertisements pertaining to these dancing masters and finds that no such advertisements for itinerant dancing masters existed, suggesting that itinerant dancing masters taught dance and ballroom etiquette to the peasantry, and relied on word of mouth and their dancing skills to advertise their profession.

Chapter 3 identifies the itinerant dancing masters of North Kerry and examines how they emerged on the rural cultural landscape of North Kerry towards the end of the eighteenth century and within a context of colonialism. It was these dancing masters who cultivated step dance as a cultural movement practice. In this chapter, I provide a history of these dancing masters from the end of the eighteenth century to 1965 within a changing historical and cultural landscape. I also explore how these itinerant dancing masters during this colonial period mimicked practices of wealthier and more established dancing masters in Ireland, and assimilated and made their dances local. I examine their system of transmission, the dance schools and the dancing master's quarter, the benefit night system, and the repertoire taught. The function of these dancing masters was similar to that of those who taught fashionable dances of the day to the higher echelons of society: to assist their patrons in matters of socialization, deportment and education. The dance classes of the dancing masters, with their aesthetic of order, were important sites for the 'civilizing process'.[78] The chapter concludes with an examination of Jeremiah Molyneaux, the last of the itinerant dancing masters of North Kerry, and looks at his transmission of step dance and the contexts in which it was transmitted.

In Chapter 4, I look at my own *habitus* and my phenomenological hermeneutic approach to embodying, analysing and interpreting the Molyneaux step dance practice and aesthetic. I also examine the more formal aspects of the dance, together with the contexts of its practice: where, when and how the Molyneaux step dancers would, or would not, perform step dance. I further explore the importance of creativity for the Molyneaux step dancers and the rural people of North Kerry through an examination of the creative process involved in the practice of step dancing. In addition, I discuss the deep significance that 'steps', as cultural artefacts, 'texts' and embodied knowledge, had for these step dancers. I examine the notion and ethno-aesthetic of gendered steps: what was considered to be a 'masculine' step or a 'feminine' step within the context of this particular practice. Finally, I identify the different social contexts in which step dance was practised, and the role it played in these contexts and within the economic system of mutual aid in the region.

In Chapter 5, I examine the second step dance embodied practice, which emerged around the end of the nineteenth century within a discourse of cultural politics and nationalism. I examine the appropriation of step dance by the cultural nationalist movement, the Gaelic League, and how in the postcolonial period it was institutionalized, urbanized and popularized by An Coimisiún le Rincí

---

[78]   Elias (1994) and Hobsbawm (1977).

Gaelacha, the Irish step dance organization which functioned under the auspices of the Gaelic League. I discuss how step dance was adapted and 'Irish' dance was invented[79] to project and embody a unified and 'national' sense of place, community and identity.[80] In this chapter, I also focus on issues of control, power, hierarchy, transmission, discipline and training; I examine the latter within a Foucauldian perspective, illustrating how cultural values and sentiments believed to be appropriate for the new Irish nation-state were embodied in step dance training, discipline and practice. I illustrate how step dance as an embodied and expressive practice was a powerful vehicle of thought and sentiment in promoting a cultural nationalism in Ireland from the early decades of the twentieth century.

Chapter 6 concerns itself with processes of cultural change in the region of North Kerry. I look at the modernization of Ireland and North Kerry, and the decline in transmission and practice of the traditional style of step dancing as taught by the itinerant dancing masters. I examine the changing function, contexts and meaning in step dance practice in the region as the organization An Coimisiún, with its cultural-nationalist agenda, became assimilated into North Kerry. I select the local dance school, Rinceoirí na Ríochta,[81] as representative of this embodied practice in the region. Since competition is the primary context and motivation for dance schools within An Coimisiún, I investigate the most important competition within its hierarchical structures – Oireachtas Rince na Cruinne, the World Championships of Irish Dance. I examine the system of ranking, winning and losing at these competitions, and I explore students' motivations to participate in competition culture. Finally, I examine the relationship between the Gaelic League and An Coimisiún today.

In Chapter 7, I examine the third of the three embodied practices in North Kerry: Siamsa Tíre, the National Folk Theatre of Ireland. Influenced by the Moiseyev Dance Company of Russia and the Ballet Folklorico de Mexico, Siamsa Tíre was established in 1974 in the region of North Kerry as a regional response to developing cultural tourism and as a national response to processes of modernity and globalization. I examine how Siamsa Tíre developed, re-presented and commoditized Irish folk culture while developing artistically and professionally within a broader European theatrical context. I explore how concepts of community and identity were significant in the conceptualization, organizational structure and artistic work of the theatre. Further, I examine the Siamsa Tíre company, its repertoire and its ongoing negotiation as a folk theatre. While the commoditization of Irish culture, focusing on *Riverdance*, the Irish step dance stage show, has previously been documented and analysed,[82] in this chapter, I examine the commoditization of Irish culture within the context of Siamsa Tíre.

---

[79]   Foley (1988b); Hall, F. (2008); see also Hobsbawm (1977).

[80]   Foley (1988b); see also Anderson (1983).

[81]   'Dancers of the Kingdom'.

[82]   Hall, F. (1997); O'Connor (1998); Foley (2001); Ó Cinnéide (2002); Wulff (2007).

I also examine how the local Molyneaux style of step dancing became a kinaesthetic iconic marker for the artistic and folk-theatrical work of the theatre.

In the final chapter, I conclude that step dancing as culture is not static. Today, it continues to be a dynamic and transnational dance form that expresses and embodies different notions of culture and identity. In the twenty-first century, step dancing, a socio-cultural activity, continues to assist individuals to express their identity at a time when a multiplicity of identities is the norm and when many individuals choose and construct their own sense of identity.

Chapter 2
The Professional European Dancing Masters

'The Jerry Molyneaux Commemorative Night'

It is mid-evening on 23 February 1983, and as I drive along the dark, wet country roads from Baile Mhúirne in the West Cork Gaeltacht, where I am a teacher, to Listowel in North Kerry, I wonder about the dancers and the dancing I am about to encounter. I also wonder about the place, North Kerry. I was told that the dancers I am about to meet are the last performers of a particular and unique style of step dancing in North Kerry, that it is no longer being transmitted, and that I am to collect the dances for posterity for Muckross House in Killarney.[1] I wonder what it is about this style of step dancing that makes it so unique. How is it different, if indeed it is, from the Irish step dance form in which I have been trained? And why is it no longer being transmitted? These are some of the questions that are on my mind as I make my way to the village of Finuge, some three miles from the town of Listowel.

The North Kerry region has a scattered population which is primarily agricultural and for the most part Catholic. Listowel is a heritage town, and is the main town of the region. It is situated to the north of the county, nine miles from the coast of the Atlantic Ocean, and until recently was relatively remote. Listowel, with its attractive square, narrow streets and colourful shops, commercial premises, schools, churches, pubs, hotels and houses, is drawn upon by the people of North Kerry for employment and for educational, religious, commercial and social purposes. The River Feale flows through the town and is an attractive fishing location. Listowel had a population of 3,650 in 2004, and has all the modern amenities and facilities of other similarly sized towns in Ireland.

Listowel has a Racecourse and holds annually the Listowel Races. It also holds other annual events such as the Harvest Festival[2] and Writers Week. The All Ireland Fleadh Cheoil[3] has been hosted by the town on a number of occasions. Like other

---

[1] Muckross House Folk Museum in Killarney has since developed, and is no longer referred to as a 'folk museum'. It is now called Muckross House, Gardens and Traditional Farms. I will refer to it simply as Muckross House.

[2] Listowel is widely known for its Listowel Races, an annual summer horse race meeting. The Harvest Festival is an important part of race week, at which the All-Ireland Wren-boys' competition takes place.

[3] An annual traditional music festival organized by Comhaltas Ceoltóirí Éireann, an organization for traditional Irish musicians, but which also includes singers and dancers. It was founded in Dublin in 1951, and by 2002 it had 35,000 members in 400 branches.

towns and villages in Ireland, Listowel and its surrounding areas have branches of Comhaltas Ceoltóirí Éireann,[4] Macra na Feirme,[5] the Gaelic Athletic Association (GAA) and the Irish Countrywomen's Association (ICA). These organizations also provide important venues for socializing for the people of the region. Dancing and music are important leisure-time activities, and during the summer season the town caters for the tourist trade with traditional music and dancing often featured in pubs or hotels. Also, *Seisiún*,[6] a concert of Irish traditional music, song and dancing, is organized by Comhaltas Ceoltóirí Éireann on a weekly basis during the summer season.

Historically, the town of Listowel grew around Listowel Castle, a twelfth-century fortress built by the Anglo-Norman earls of Kerry. Listowel became an English garrison town, and as a result of the sixteenth- and seventeenth-century plantations, many English Protestant colonists were settled in both the town and the surrounding areas. This sector of society represented the gentry and land-owning classes, and they came to dominate both the commercial and professional life of the district of Listowel until the early decades of the twentieth century.

On this particular evening, I do not go into Listowel town; my destination is the Teach Siamsa[7] in Finuge, North Kerry, where I have been invited by Fr Pat Ahern to witness 'The Jerry Molyneaux Commemorative Night'. The Teach Siamsa, a whitewashed thatched cottage, was built in 1974 for the purpose of teaching local children the traditional music, song and dance repertoire of the region; it also functions as a local traditional arts community venue. The Teach Siamsa project was instigated by Fr Pat Ahern, a parish priest and founding artistic director of Siamsa Tíre, the National Folk Theatre of Ireland, based in Tralee, the largest town in the county of Kerry and some 16 miles from Listowel. The Teach Siamsa in Finuge was one of two such venues (the other was built in Carraig, near Dingle in the West Kerry Gaeltacht), built principally for pedagogical, training and cultural purposes (see also Chapter 7).

On arriving at the Teach Siamsa, the door is closed, but I can hear the chant of prayers coming from inside. I am joined outside the door by Bryan MacMahon, the

---

Although these branches are predominantly in Ireland, there are also branches in the UK, the USA, Canada, Australia, Japan, Hungary, Sweden, Sardinia and Italy. Listowel has its own branch of Comhaltas Ceoltóirí Éireann, where *céilís* (Irish social dance events; see Chapter 7) are sometimes held, and where the All-Ireland Fleadh Cheoil na hÉireann (the most significant competition within the competitive structures of Comhaltas Ceoltóirí Éireann) have been hosted there some 14 times. According to J. Anthony Gaughan (2004), 4,000 musicians took part in the All-Ireland Fleadh Cheoil na hÉireann competitions and concerts in 2002; 6,000 more musicians arrived to play at spontaneous sessions, and it was estimated that approximately 220,000 people visited Listowel throughout the event. See also Henry (1989).

[4]   'The Organization of Musicians of Ireland'.
[5]   'The Farmers' Organization'.
[6]   'Session', a gathering of traditional musicians, singers and dancers.
[7]   'House of Entertainment'.

well-known author and schoolmaster from Listowel. We stand for a few minutes under Bryan's black umbrella in the rain, chatting generally about our respective functions at this occasion. We wait for an opportune moment to enter the Teach Siamsa, a moment that will not disturb too much the prayerful chant inside. We eventually hear the familiar cadential refrain: 'In ainm an Athar, agus an Mhic, agus an Spriod Naomh, Amen.'[8] Both of us know instinctively that this is our cue to enter.

Inside, Mass had been celebrated. The celebrant was Fr Pat Ahern. With Mass over, people leave their positions of prayer and start to mill around, talking to those gathered; musicians tune up, and creaking chairs are dragged across the grey flagstone floor in preparation for the concert that is to follow. The space was designed mindful of recent times past in rural Ireland; indeed, the space jolts my own memory: the open hearth, the flagstone floor bring me back some twenty years to my own childhood in the 1960s when we visited my father's rural home in Inchinaugh, Glenville, Co. Cork. My father's home had been a rambling house, a place where neighbours and relatives, including local musicians, dancers and singers, came to socialize. I remember the oil lamps, the open hearth, the bellows and settle to its right, the milk churns, the concrete floor and the dancers' feet. I remember the music, my father's music on the melodeon, which called the dancers to dance 'The Stack of Barley', 'The Step of Cipín', the Polka set and the Waltz. Singers sang and stories were told in between the dances. I remember my sister Pat and I would do a step dance, reminding all that although we now lived in Cork city, we were still connected through the dance to our parents' rural roots. Our dance was trained dancing, disciplined, competitive-style step dancing, but after our demonstrations, we joined in with our mother, our siblings and the rest of our relations and danced the set or any of the couple dances, mentioned above. We all gave our 'two-pence worth' in contributing to the success of these occasions in whatever capacity we could: singing, dancing, playing music, making tea and sandwiches or making conversation. Teach Siamsa was a recent, purpose-built, modern replica of this scene: the open hearth, the flagstone floor, the butter churns, the wooden half door and a fiddle hanging from the whitewashed wall. This purpose-built space sets the scene for 'The Jerry Molyneaux Commemorative Night', an evening consisting of a concert of traditional dancing, with music and singing items in between. This is the event to which I have been invited in order to see the elderly Molyneaux step dancers perform. There is no formal stage or platform. The room is an informal space that facilitates the bringing together of a community to celebrate their shared social, cultural and economic existence. Jeremiah Molyneaux, the region's itinerant dancing master, is the reason for their coming together.

'The Jerry Molyneaux Commemorative Night' was held for the first time in the late 1970s. Afterwards, it became an annual event, always falling on the same date, 23 February. The date is significant for those assembled as it marks the death of the itinerant dancing master Jeremiah Molyneaux in 1965, aged 84. Jeremiah Molyneaux is also known locally as Jerry Molyneaux, Jerry Munnix or Gerrín

---

[8] 'In the name of the Father, and of the Son, and of the Holy Spirit, Amen.'

Illustration 2.1   Liam Tarrant dancing in Carraig, Dingle, Co. Kerry, 1974. Used
with permission of Siamsa Tíre

(pronounced 'Gereen'), and he is important to the community as he represents the
last of the rural itinerant dancing masters and their system of teaching in Kerry –
and indeed, to the best of my knowledge, in Ireland. The event was instigated by
Fr Pat Ahern to celebrate Jeremiah Molyneaux and the Molyneaux step dancers,
living and deceased.

The inspiration for the event came from Liam Tarrant's family. Liam Tarrant
was a pupil of Jeremiah Molyneaux, and had won a trophy for step dancing some
years earlier. When he died suddenly, while dancing in Carraig, Dingle, in 1974,
his family approached Fr Pat Ahern with the hope of establishing an occasion to
commemorate Liam and the other dancers (see Illustration 2.1). The outcome of
the meeting was the annual 'Jerry Molyneaux Commemorative Night' at which
Liam's trophy would be awarded to one of the surviving Molyneaux step dancers.
The criteria for this award were not in any sense competitive, but were based
on entertainment value or seniority. The final 'Jerry Molyneaux Commemorative
Night' was held in 1989. This step dance context is therefore a recently created and
a relatively short-lived one.

On this occasion, I am greeted by Fr Pat Ahern, who introduces me to some
members of the gathered community. He formally announces that I will be visiting

the dancers that summer to collect their step dances for Muckross House. Fr Ahern gives a short speech explaining the context of the evening and its history. After this, the musicians take their places at the side of the hearth and tune up. The instruments include fiddle and button accordion, but could have included any combination of the following instruments: melodeon, button accordion, concertina, fiddle, flute, tin whistle, uilleann[9] pipes, *bodhrán*[10] and spoons. The number of musical instruments, together with the particular combination of instruments, depended on which musicians had been invited, which musicians were able to attend, together with those who subsequently arrived.

The members of the community gathered at this 'Jerry Molyneaux Commemorative Night' include relatives, friends and neighbours of the step dancers, together with other interested individuals. Men, women and children are represented at this relatively small and intimate local gathering. All age groups are represented, from young children to the senior fraternity. On this particular evening, members of the community warmly chat as they position themselves facing the hearth; some sit, while the more agile of the community stand, but enough space is left in front of the hearth for the step dance performances to follow. The space in front of the hearth is the customary space for a step dance performance, since traditionally the flagstone located there offered the best acoustics for percussive dancing. This was due to the fact that traditionally there was a hole underneath this particular flagstone where a pot or a horse's head was placed.[11] During the course of the evening, each of the invited Molyneaux step dancers in turn will perform solo in front of the hearth, facing the audience. Each dancer wears a badge with the words 'Iardhalta de chuid Jerry Molyneaux',[12] given to them by Fr Pat Ahern. At the end of the evening, the Liam Tarrant Cup will be presented to the step dancer of the community's choice.[13]

---

[9] 'Elbow'.

[10] A single-membrane frame drum.

[11] The flagstone in front of the hearth is associated with step dance performances. Different theories concerning these flagstones exist in oral history. Some assert that they exist purely for their acoustic properties for step dancers; others assert that these flagstones are associated with bygone sacrificial burials, and still others assert that they are associated with fertility and good fortune. Whatever their history, they are associated today with their beneficial acoustic properties for step dance performances.

[12] A past pupil of Jerry Molyneaux.

[13] I would like to thank Mossie (Maurice) Walsh for supplying me with one of the Molyneaux badges and for the letter of invitation he received to partake in 'The Jerry Molyneaux Commemorative Night' in 1980. The letter I received from Mossie is interesting, since in 1980 not only did the event include the commemoration of Jeremiah Molyneaux and his dance, but it also illustrated the desire for the event to include other traditions of North Kerry. In 1980, story-telling on the theme of ghost stories was included. The event that year commenced with the pupils of the Teach Siamsa, Finuge (see also Chapter 7), presenting a short dramatized piece based on one such ghost story.

Having spent some time chatting with friends, relatives and neighbours, the step dancers are requested to perform by Fr Pat Ahern, who is the *fear 'n tí*.[14] There is no particular order in which these dancers will perform; it is left to the individual to either volunteer or to be volunteered. I look around, and it is not obvious who is or who is not a dancer. Eventually, the first dancer is coaxed up by those sitting near him. He is about 65 years of age and wears no particular dance costume, but his 'Sunday best'; the shoes he wears are ordinary leather shoes. It is announced that the first dancer will be Jerry Nolan from Moyvane, Listowel. Jerry makes his way slowly to the flagstone in front of the hearth at the top of the room amidst gentle, encouraging words from friends and family. He speaks to the musicians seated to the left side of the hearth and informs them what dance type he will perform; it is the Reel.

All those gathered are at this stage intent on seeing the performance. The musicians commence to play a Reel, and as is customary with an Irish step dance performance, an eight-bar musical introduction precedes the commencement of the actual dancing. During this time, Jerry keeps still in his natural posture, his hands hanging simply by his sides. Jerry directs his gaze towards the floor, at times as if in deep concentration, and towards the audience at other times, as if in preparation for the performance. Individual members of the community are shuffling closer to find the best position to see the performance. There is no formal sense of ritual here; it is an occasion of commemoration, fun and *craic*[15] mixed with feelings of admiration and respect for the skill of these elderly dancers as holders of a local dance tradition. Throughout these eight bars, Jerry waits for that moment when he will join the music, and that moment comes. On bar six, Jerry, unexpectedly, sets sail with a little meander, and traps the notes of the tune under his feet.

The music finds visual, rhythmical, auditory and kinaesthetic expression in Jerry Nolan's dancing. This expression, combined with energetic and rhythmically uplifting music, brings a cheer and a 'huup' from the gathering. The music and movement become one. It is not, however, just any kind of movement; neither is it the style of step dancing in which I have been trained. It is a local way of moving to, embodying and knowing the music. It is a localized system of movement that speaks from a particular place and about that place. The place is North Kerry.

Jerry performs the dance close to the floor in order to sound out the detailed movements and rhythms of the step dance. Each note of the music is visually, audibly and kinaesthetically represented by Jerry's feet, the majority of the movements taking place underneath his centre of weight. Even at 65, and as I find out afterwards, suffering from arthritis, Jerry moves with a gentle, rhythmical grace and a musicality of the body. Most of the movements are spatially confined to the flagstone in front of the hearth, but Jerry also does some small travelling, linear, movements to his right and to his left. However, the emphasis is on perfecting

---

[14] 'Man of the house' or 'master of ceremonies'.
[15] 'Sport' or 'fun'.

the visual, audibly rhythmical and kinaesthetic quality of the dance in order to illuminate and enhance the dance–music dialogue.

All eyes of the community continue to focus on the dancer on the flagstone. A few little comments and smiles from observers make manifest that they are enjoying Jerry's performance. This is not the first time they have witnessed Jerry perform. He is known in the locality, and those gathered have a good idea what to expect from him as a holder of a dance practice that is special to them. After a Lead[16] and two steps,[17] consisting of movements such as batters, cuts, stamps and drums and lasting about two minutes, the performance eventually comes to an end. Jerry, the musicians and all those gathered come together on that final chord: the community give out shouts and claps of applause; Jerry triumphantly traps with his feet the last note of the tune, and the musicians give the final note a strong and long-held punch. Feelings of pride and elevation abound, and in the midst of long applause, Jerry slowly returns to his seat in the middle of his community.

The rest of the evening continues with each of the remaining elderly Molyneaux step dancers performing the dance of their choice: either a Treble Reel, Jig or Hornpipe. 'The Blackbird', a Hornpipe solo set dance, is also performed, as this was a favourite dance of Jeremiah Molyneaux. Each dancer performs in a similar close-to-the-floor style, but each has their own individual style and favourite repertoire. But whatever dance is performed, it celebrates the choreographic skills of Jeremiah Molyneaux and the performance skills of the step dancers. Similarly to Jerry Nolan, each dancer is welcomed onto the flagstone and each dancer is complimented and applauded. There are fewer women than men performing, and when the women dance, they wear black, laced, heavy step dance shoes as opposed to the men's ordinary leather shoes. Some of the step dancers improvise during the performance; however, it is primarily the male step dancers who do so. All the dancers are familiar figures in the community, and in the act of performing, these dancers re-establish themselves as dancers before the eyes of the community and re-establish the community's link with their past through dance. Throughout the evening, there are also musical interludes by the local musicians, who play selections of Reels and Jigs and sing a few songs. There are also refreshments and sandwiches halfway through the evening, with much talk concerning the agility and technical ability of these elderly step dancers, other older dancers who are now dead, the weather, and current local and national affairs.

Before the community are asked for their final decision concerning who should be awarded the Liam Tarrant Cup, I am asked if I will dance. People start to coax me to dance, so I oblige and make my way onto the same flagstone in front of

---

[16]   The Lead or the Lead Around is the opening or introductory step in specific solo step dance genres. Therefore, there are Reel Leads, Jig Leads, Hornpipe Leads and Slip Jig Leads. As well as commencing a step dance performance, sometimes Leads also conclude a performance.

[17]   The step is generally eight bars long, and it is customary to repeat it to the opposite side or symmetrically for another eight bars.

the hearth. I inform the musicians that I will dance a Reel. The musicians start up, and I decide to dance a Treble Reel which I had learned some years earlier from Aidan O'Carroll, a fellow musician and dancer at the Music Department, University College, Cork. We had both been invited by our Professor of Music, Aloys Fleischmann, to perform together at the International Choral Festival in Cork. Since we did not share the same repertoire, I learned Aidan's, which he had learned and performed with Siamsa Tíre, the National Folk Theatre in Tralee. I knew that this repertoire would be familiar to some of those present. My decision to dance these Treble Reels was precisely because I was in North Kerry.

Although I had performed this material before, it was especially poignant performing it here in North Kerry. I wait for the customary eight-bar introduction from the musicians and prepare myself psychologically and physically for the performance. I think of my training: upright torso, arms by my sides, my gaze directed straight ahead, and I also think of my father and Inchinaugh, his foot tapping to the music as he played, and the intimacy and support of those warm and informal occasions. I dance a Lead of the Treble Reel, and I follow that with two steps. The music soars and takes me with it. It feels good to dance to this lively, energetic music in the intimacy of this warm space. I feel one with the music and this space. I also feel I am contributing in some small way to this celebratory occasion for Jeremiah Molyneaux, even though I never met him. At the end of the performance, I too am applauded. I feel good, and I also feel that I have been tested and that I have passed. Afterwards, other step dancers present, particularly those from Siamsa Tíre, also perform. It is an evening of sharing and celebration.

Finally, the community are asked to whom the Liam Tarrant Trophy should be awarded; the criteria for the award being based upon entertainment value, seniority or fairness. After some discussion, a consensus is reached and the Molyneaux dancer to be awarded the trophy is named; everybody is pleased with the outcome.

To complete the evening, all the Molyneaux step dancers take to the space in front of the hearth, and facing the audience in a line, they hold hands and perform together in unison the side-step of the Treble Reel. Watching these elderly dancers hold hands and dance together, I sense the reinforcement of unity, strength and harmony within the room. This concord is felt by all gathered, the line of step dancers metaphorically representing the community itself. Once the side-step is completed, each step dancer in succession performs one step dance solo. The music is picked up by each step dancer, allowing no break between the individual performances. After the last step dancer has performed solo, all the step dancers hold hands again and repeat the side-step in a line facing the spectators. The rest of the community join in with remarks such as, 'You're doing great,' 'That's the man,' 'Great stuff,' and 'Lovely.'

At the end of the performance, there is a warm and uplifting applause. Some people leave their seats and join the dancers around the flagstone by the hearth and congratulate them and talk; others remain seated in close conversation with friends and neighbours; there is much laughter and feelings of goodwill. On this note, the evening gradually ends and people, in their different groups, start to slowly make their way home. It has been a successful evening, by all accounts!

I watched the dancers perform this particular evening with bodies that were shadows of their former selves, but which were still willing and able. I watched as they performed with pride in their skill, and it seemed that their dance was itself a prayer that mediated between the living and the deceased in the community. During this Molyneaux Night, the voices and step dances of the dead, particularly Jerry Molyneaux, made themselves felt through the elderly bodies of the living Molyneaux step dancers. Both the living and the deceased were being honoured, remembered, celebrated and commemorated. The dancers, through their dancing bodies, made reference to and re-enacted an image of their past, and the community's past. This past included their common values, sentiments, beliefs, social behaviours and experiences. As Connerton states:

> Our bodies, which in commemorations stylistically re-enact an image of the past, keep the past also in an entirely effective form in their continuing ability to perform certain skilled actions.[18]

The Molyneaux step dancers embodied and performed 'skilled actions' at this event according to a local and communal lexicon, and in performing these actions, not only was the lexicon remembered, shared and celebrated, but so too was the whole cultural system and world which it referenced. 'The Jerry Molyneaux Commemorative Night' provided a space and a platform that generated a cultural memory and a sense of nostalgia for the past. As Edward Said states: 'space acquires emotional and even rational sense by a kind of poetic process, whereby the vacant or anonymous reaches of distance are converted into meaning for us here'.[19]

I wondered about these 'reaches of distance' – the past. I wondered about the dance practice and the evening I had just witnessed. I wondered about Jeremiah Molyneaux, the itinerant dancing master, and the history and culture out of which he had choreographed these step dances. What was his role within this rural community? Where did his dance training come from? I knew that step dance had been taught by dancing masters, but what was its history here, in North Kerry? And what was its connection, if any, with the European dancing masters?

Jeremiah Molyneaux, or Jerry Munnix as he was referred to locally, was part of a broad cultural historical narrative. He was the last of the rural itinerant dancing masters of North Kerry, and worked within a system of teaching that survived into the mid-twentieth century in North Kerry. This system was cultivated by rural itinerant dancing masters from the eighteenth century to the twentieth century, and was influenced by a European dance aesthetic and system of teaching. It is therefore appropriate that I provide a brief historical overview of the European professional dancing masters in order to contextualize and to historicize the itinerant dancing

---

[18]   Connerton (1989), p. 72.
[19]   Said (1991), p. 55.

masters of North Kerry and their dance aesthetic,[20] and to provide an appreciation of how step dancing as a genre developed in Ireland, and in particular North Kerry.

The Continental European Aesthetic

The dance aesthetic, vocabulary and the dances as practised and developed in Continental Europe influenced dances taught, practised and developed in Ireland. These influences are noted from medieval times with the introduction of the *Carole* into Ireland through to the twentieth century. Here, however, I will focus on the dancing masters of Continental Europe and England, and I will examine their role, practice and dance aesthetic and how their dances and dance aesthetic were disseminated to the western fringes of Europe.

The Continental European dancing masters were authorities on the art of dance, and they also had other responsibilities that extended to their students' intellectual and artistic education. They were teachers and composers of music as well as competent instrumentalists. They had knowledge of poetry, mathematics, geometry, philosophy, aesthetics, sculpture and painting. Their duties included the teaching of dancing, music, fencing and riding, and they also instilled social behaviours and graces in their students.[21] These professional dancing masters taught in princes' palaces, courts and schools of dance. Some of them also performed in theatres. To understand these dancing masters, their role in society and the culture out of which they emerged, a brief historical introduction is required.

Italy, throughout the High Renaissance, consisted of states ruled by princes whose courts rivalled each other. Dance, together with music, painting and poetry, was utilized to create lavish spectacles in honour of specific princes. Philosophers, scientists and artists found patronage with these princes, who provided the conditions for the achievements of the High Renaissance. It was within these courts that the professional dancing masters emerged, and it was they who developed dance from a pastime to an art, by developing it technically, aesthetically and theoretically. Within this process, dance was codified and a dance aesthetic was developed.

The earliest known dancing master was Domenico of Piacenza (also referred to as 'Domenico of Ferrara' or 'Knight of the Golden Spur'). Domenico was in the employment of the Este court in Ferrara, one of the many courts in Renaissance Italy. Others included Medici, Gonzaga, Sforza, Bentivoglio and Arigon. Domenico named many of his early dances after people and places connected with the Este court, and according to the dance historian Barbara Sparti, Domenico

---

[20]   To the best of my knowledge, professional dancing masters on the European circuit were predominantly male. However, according to the Census of Ireland in 1861, there were 88 male dancing masters and 11 female dancing masters operating in Ireland at the time; see Friel (2004). In North Kerry, there were no references to female dancing masters, although women did learn and informally transmit step dances.

[21]   See Brainard (1998a).

was a 'great innovator, meticulous choreographer and brilliant theorist'.[22] It is not known exactly when Domenico was born, but it is believed that he died *c.* 1476.

Many of the dancing masters also wrote treatises on dance. The earliest known were produced in fifteenth-century Italy, and nine of these have survived. The first is an anonymous treatise with 23 dances and their accompanying music, together with the dance aesthetic teachings of Domenico (*c.* 1455). This is believed to be the first dance instruction book ever written. The second is by a pupil of Domenico, Antonio Cornazano; the remaining seven are attributed directly or indirectly to Guglielmo Ebreo ('William the Jew', also known as 'Giovanni Ambrosio' when he later converted to Catholicism), also trained by Domenico. It is known that Cornazano was a well-known poet, humanist and courtier, but whether he was a dancing master or simply 'an enthusiastic amateur of the art of dancing'[23] is not certain. Guglielmo Ebreo was an esteemed dancing master throughout the latter part of the fifteenth century. These Italian dance treatises have left valuable information on the dances (*Bassedanza* and *Balli*), the music, the aesthetic and the theory espoused by these dancing masters at that time.[24]

Guglielmo Emreo, in his *De Practica* (1463), argued for a similar status for dance as for music. In an almost humanistic apology, Guglielmo argued for dance to be accepted as both art and science. Guglielmo wrote on the moral and ethical worth of dance, and included a section on the 'fundamental principles' upon which the dance was composed. Indeed, this was the format for most fifteenth-century treatises on architecture, music, painting, philosophy, education or rhetoric.[25] The fundamental principles listed below gave weight to Guglielmo's claim that dance was both an art and a science. They included concepts of measure – keeping in time to the music, memory of the sequence of the steps, spatial awareness, manner of movement and ornamentation. Indeed, manner, measure and style were also important to the painter, while measure was a fundamental principle in architecture and music. These concepts or 'fundamental principles' were basic to the Renaissance dance aesthetic – an aesthetic which influenced later dancing masters and found its way to the other courts of Europe, and from there was disseminated further by dancing masters in their travels throughout Europe and by contacts through courts, armies, universities and trade. It would also make its way to Ireland, and would influence dancing masters there in constructing and developing step dance as a dance-music cultural practice.

Although Domenico and Cornazano appear to have concerned themselves with dances of the court, Guglielmo also arranged festivities for commoners. The distinction between theatrical and social dancing that exists today did not exist in the fifteenth century. According to Sparti:

---

[22] Sparti (1993), p. 3.

[23] Cornazano (1455 [1981]), p. 12.

[24] Sparti (1993).

[25] Ibid., pp. 10–12.

> Courtiers were the performers whether they danced the traditional, improvisatory saltarello and piva or donned costumes and danced, before an audience, the choreographed, spectacular moresce. If one of Guglielmo's bassedanze or one of Domenico's balli was danced by princesses during a great festivity, its purpose – in that context – would have been to impress the onlookers; if it was danced by the same ladies in their rooms at night, its intention would have been to delight the performers themselves; if it was danced during a moresca, it will have taken on another – possibly allegorical – significance.[26]

Consequently, context, function and the intentionality of the performer influenced the performance, but there was no distinction made in the fifteenth century between dances that were considered to be theatrical and dances that were considered to be social.

With the increased wealth of the urban middle classes, dance as an art or a skill spread from the courts to urban ballrooms and assembly halls, and dancing masters found themselves much in demand. Instruction manuals soon followed. The first of these was the anonymous *L'art et instruction de bien danser*, printed in Paris *c.* 1488. Other dance manuals followed in France, England, Scotland, Germany and Italy, and included codes of accepted behaviour on and off the dance floor.[27] Of these, *Orchesography* by the Frenchman Thoinot Arbeau (1589) is the best-known.

Two renowned sixteenth-century Italian dancing masters were Fabritto Caroso and Cesare Negri; both also wrote dance treatises. Caroso (born *c.* 1526 in Sermoneta, Italy, died after 1605) published two significant manuals of court dance, *Il ballerina* (1581) and *Nobiltà di dame* (1600; 1605). These manuals included steps, figures, rules for dance style, etiquette for both sexes, and choreographies for more than one hundred dances with music. *Il ballerina* included 80 dances and 54 rules for step patterns, while *Nobiltà di dame* included 49 dances and 68 rules.[28] Caroso's first treatise, *Il ballerina*, included sonnets and madrigals along with all the dances, and many of these sonnets were written by Caroso himself. All of Caroso's dances were social dances for aristocrats, and most of the dances were couple dances. According to Sutton, these were:

> dances for young gentlemen who recognized dance as a manly art demonstrating as much skill as fencing or riding; of young ladies who saw dance as an opportunity to display their charms with grace and energy; and of young aristocrats who sought always to enjoy themselves while ornamenting their surroundings and pleasing their observers. All the dances [were] flirtatious, but few [were] programmatic .... The paths of the dancers [were] always related both to their partners and the dancing space.[29]

---

[26]   Ibid., p. 61.
[27]   Brainard (1998a).
[28]   Sutton (1998a).
[29]   Sutton (1998b).

Negri (born in Milan *c.* 1535, died in Milan *c.* 1605) was also known as *Il Trombone*. He founded a dance academy in Milan in 1554 and was an active court choreographer for the nobility there. Throughout most of his life, he served the Spanish/Hapsburg overlords of Milan and catalogued state events in both Spain and the various Italian courts at which he performed and directed musical festivities. He wrote the important dance manual *Le gratie d'amore* in 1602. Reissued in 1604 as *Nuove Inventioni di balli*, it included not only descriptions of steps and Galliard variations, 43 choreographies and their music, but also details about his professional life and that of 44 of his colleagues (teachers and professional pupils). The details mentioned the specializations of the different dancing masters, including: gymnastics, horsemanship, swordsmanship, music and dance technique. According to Sutton, Negri demonstrated that 'dance was recognised in his time as one of the standard manly arts to be mastered by young gentlemen'.[30] Also, Negri's detailed accounts indicated his awareness that he was part of a strong Italian dance tradition: a tradition that was disseminated through publications, dancing masters and their pupils to the major courts in Europe. From here, they were undoubtedly further disseminated. Although Caroso and Negri dedicate their treatises to the nobility, some of their choreographies were, according to Brainard, 'addressed to the lesser nobility and gentry, and their lists of subscribers and patrons include[d] wealthy commoners along with high-ranking personages'.[31]

Dancing masters at court were highly respected and well rewarded for their work. These rewards included houses, grounds, clothing, wine and other payments in kind in addition to their financial remuneration. Some pupils of these dancing masters, on the completion of their training, opened schools in their own countries, teaching dance, music or the military arts. Members of the gentry also employed dancing masters in their own homes. We can infer from the ease with which these dancing masters travelled how their dances, influence and aesthetic eventually crossed wide geographical, social and cultural boundaries.

Foot Technique

Italy led in the field of professional dancing masters, and although France would dominate the development of ballet, Italy led in matters of technique (as the writings of Caruso and Negri show), where virtuosity was the preserve of male dancers. During the early Renaissance in Italy, much attention was paid to footwork that was facilitated by the marbled floors of the palace courts. According to Quirey, by the end of the sixteenth century:

> the beauty and simplicity of Italian Quattrocento dancing had disappeared on its
> home ground. It was hidden under a mass of fussy footwork and rather trumpery

---

[30] Ibid., p. 580.
[31] Brainard (1998a), p. 337.

music .... The old flowing spaciousness seemed to be out of favour with the late sixteenth-century dancing masters, of whom two, called Caroso and Negri, have left us substantial volumes of their compositions.[32]

During the sixteenth century, corsets (for both males and females), ruffs or stiff collars, swinging cloaks and a novelty of the 1570s – heels on the shoes – assisted in shaping the dance aesthetic of the High Renaissance.[33] Corsets precluded torso movements, and ruffs forced the head to remain in an upright position; consequently, the dance aesthetic and technique of the sixteenth century focused on footwork, performed with precision, dexterity and sometimes great speed. The introduction of heels on shoes allowed for these foot movements to be audible.

Negri's manuscript *Le gratie d'amore* (1602) is considered to contain the most complicated technical steps of the High Renaissance. The repertory consists of dances of both duple and triple time, with the frequent use of movements such as, cuts, foot crossings, leg raises and vigorous stamps. According to Brainard:

> The last were the chief ingredient of the canario, on record from the time of Caroso's *Il ballarino* [1581] and coincident with the advent of shoes with heels.[34]

These stylized foot movements would eventually also become characteristic movements of step dancing in Ireland.

Further information on dance, and in particular foot technique, on the Continent throughout this period is illustrated in another contemporary publication. Thoinot Arbeau,[35] Canon of Langres, left an important dance and music resource of the sixteenth century in his book *Orchesography* (1589). Written in the form of a dialogue, Arbeau, as dancing master, instructs his pupil, Capriol, in the art of dancing. He describes many sixteenth-century dances for all who wished to learn refined manners and dancing skills. From close examination of the illustrations supplied, some of these dances, particularly the Tordion and the Galliard as taught by the Continental dancing masters, have foot and leg positions and gestures in common with basic Irish step dance positions and gestures.[36] These gestures include:

- *pied croisé droit* (right cut);
- *pied croisé gauche* (left cut);
- *grève droite* (high right throw forward) or *pied en l'air droit* (low right throw forward);
- *grève gauche* (high left throw forward) or *pied en l'air gauche* (low left throw forward);

---

[32]   Quirey (1987), p. 33.
[33]   Brainard (1998b), pp. 336–40.
[34]   Brainard (1998b), p. 338.
[35]   An anagram: his real name was Jehan Tabourot.
[36]   See Labanotated inventories of elements in Foley (1988b).

- *raude droite* (right leg raised behind), raude gauche (left leg raised behind);
- jumps;
- hops;
- leaps.[37]

Although this implies that particular positions and gestures were common to some dance practices as taught by dancing masters on the Continent during the sixteenth century and step dance as later developed by rural, itinerant dancing masters in Ireland from the eighteenth century, it is worth remembering that they would have been developed differently to suit different social and cultural contexts. It is interesting to note, however, that some common gestures and positions were part of dancing masters' stock of foot and leg movement vocabulary which they adapted and developed to suit their respective patrons, the intended dance contexts and their functions within specific cultures, and the dance-music aesthetic systems of their patrons. How these movements may have contributed to the dance-music aesthetic and to the experiences of those who danced them is also interesting.

Certain principles were common. According to Arbeau, for the Galliard and the Tordion, there was one movement, or one basic step, to a note. This is similar to the method applied by the North Kerry dancing master Jeremiah Molyneaux in choreographing a basic step dance: one foot sound per note. In addition, Arbeau mentions how symmetry was important in both the Galliard and the Tordion – whatever series of movements was done on the left leg was required for proper performance execution to be repeated to the opposite side, commencing with the right leg. Again, symmetry is important in step dancing in Ireland. However, in step dancing, generally full dance steps of eight-bar structures are performed commencing with the right leg, and are symmetrically repeated for a further eight bars commencing with the left leg.[38]

A focus on male energetic athleticism and virtuosity was characteristic of the Galliard. According to Brainard (1998b), Negri used one particular Galliard, 'The Kick to the Tassle', as a competitive dance for men (in *Le gratie d'amore*, 1602). All the attention was on the man, with his jumps, hops, beats and cuts. The notion of foot and leg patterns for one body would be later developed further by itinerant dancing masters in Ireland in the form of solo step dancing.

---

[37] Arbeau (1589), pp. 84–90.

[38] This does not apply to *sean nós* ('old-style') step dancing as performed in Connemara, Co. Galway; see Brennan (1999) and Foley (1988b; 2001; 2007c and 2008). Following on from my earlier work, Chapter 4 also illustrates that exact identical repeats were not always the norm in the traditional step dance practice in North Kerry. Dancers in this region also improvised or varied steps on the 'repeat' of the 'left leg' section of the step.

To master the footwork technique, particularly the more difficult movements such as the *capriole*,[39] the Continental dancing masters during the High Renaissance suggested practising by supporting oneself 'with the strength of the arms' on the backs of two chairs or by holding on to a tightly stretched rope.[40] This was the origin of the ballet barre, and interestingly, in Ireland, step dancers were and are still advised by teachers to practise particular movements with the aid of the backs of one or two chairs.

Therefore, from the above we can see how dancing masters of the High Renaissance throughout Continental Europe taught and practised similar dance types, and how the dance system and aesthetic as espoused by these dancing masters were disseminated through their teaching, performances, publications and travel.

Dancing masters were also popular figures in England. During the reign of Elizabeth I, a French family of dancing masters, the Cardels, was established at court. However, Moryson writes:

> 1600: Her Majestie [Elizabeth I] is in verie good health, and comes much abroade these holidays; for almost every night she is in the presence, to see the ladies dance the old and new Country dances.[41]

Also:

> 1602: We are frolic here at court; much dancing in the privy chamber of Country dances before the queen's Majesty, who is exceedingly pleased therewith. Irish tunes are at this time much liked.[42]

Elizabeth I was fond of dance, and enjoyed what dances were in vogue at the time; country dances were the fashionable ones of the day, and John Playford's publication of *The English Dancing Master* in 1651 assisted in the dissemination of these fashionable country dances. Following the restoration of Charles II to the throne in 1660, French dances were also fashionable at court, in fashionable society and in entertainments.

---

[39] Although not performed in traditional step dancing in Ireland, a more recent movement (late 1990s) within competitive Irish step dancing is the *entrechat quatre*, borrowed from ballet. The earliest form of this particular movement dates back to the *capriole*. Both Caroso (1581) and Arbeau (1589) give a description of a *capriole* where the legs change positions at the height of the leap in the air. The more fashionable version during the High Renaissance included versions where the feet crossed three, four or even five times. Today, many Irish step dancers demonstrate their virtuosity by including *entrechat quatres* in their steps.

[40] Brainard (1998b).

[41] Moryson in Breathnach (1983), p. 15.

[42] Ibid.

Académie Royale de Danse

With the increase in the number of dancing masters on the European circuit, academies were established to develop and maintain standards of dancing and to facilitate greater control over dance, dancing and dancing masters. Dancing masters had belonged to the musicians' guild, the Corporation des Ménêtriers, since the fifteenth century; however, due to tensions that had arisen within the corporation around the middle of the seventeenth century, the dancing masters sought an organization of their own.[43] Also, around this time there was a perceived decline in standards of dancing, and with the objective of maintaining dance standards, a new academy, the Académie Royale de Danse, was established in 1661 under Louis XIV of France.[44] Louis was a staunch supporter of dance, and was himself a great dancer at court. The new Académie consisted of 13 dancing masters, or *anciens*, who were entrusted with 're-establishing the art in its perfection'.[45]

Particular statutes and rules called the 'twelve principle articles' were devised for the selected *anciens* of the Academy. They are translated and supplied by Mark Franko as follows:

1. Firstly, the said Academy will be composed of the oldest and most experienced of dancing masters, the most expert in Dance, in the number of thirteen

2. The said thirteen will meet once a month at a place or house chosen by them and taken at common cost, to confer amongst themselves on the state of Dance, to take council and deliberate on the means for perfecting it, and to correct the abuses that can have been introduced or that could be introduced.

3. Two of the said Ancients will be chosen in turn to meet on every Saturday with other Dancing Masters, or with others who may want to teach Dance, in order to instruct them on the manner to Dance, and to show them the old and the new Dances, that will have been or will be invented by the thirteen Ancients.

4. All sorts of persons of whatever quality or high condition they may be, Masters, sons of Masters, and others, will come to said place and will be received there to receive instruction in these things, and learn them from the mouth of the Ancients and by their instruction given to the other Masters of the said Art.

---

[43] Hilton (1981).

[44] Louis gathered around his court the best of musicians and noble dancers. The Italian Jean-Baptiste Lully was the composer of instrumental music, while Pierre Beauchamps was the main choreographer. Louis took classes once a day for twenty-two years with his dancing master, Pierre Beauchamp, who is credited with having defined the five positions of the feet as a basis of ballet technique; see ibid.

[45] Guest (1960 [1977]), p. 10.

5.   The other Ancients of the named thirteen can also be present in said place or hall, with the said Deputies, on the said day, to give their opinion on what will be presented there.

6.   The other Masters teaching Dance in the said village and environs of Paris can aspire to be among the number of Ancients and Academicians and to be received in the said Academy, if they are judged by the Ancients in a majority vote to be worthy and capable. The candidates will have to demonstrate the exercise of all sorts of Dances, old and new, as well as steps from ballets, on a day set aside for such auditions. They will pay the sum of 150 livres if they are sons of Masters, and 300 livres if they are other.

7.   All those who call themselves Dancers in the said city and environs will have to register their names and addresses on a register that will be held by the Academicians. If they do not, they will forgo any privilege in the said Academy, never to join the ranks of the said Ancients and Academicians.

8.   Those of the said Ancients, and others who Dance, who will have or want to invent and compose a new Dance will not be able to show it unless it has been previously viewed and examined by the said Ancients and approved by them in a majority vote when they are assembled on days set aside for such deliberation.

9.   The deliberations undertaken concerning the affairs of Dance by the said Ancients convened as specified above, will be carried out according to the form and tenor indicated by the said Ancients and by others who make Dance their profession and aspire to join the Academy, with the disciplinary actions mentioned and 50 livres of fine for any breach of these rules.

10. The said Ancient Academicians and their children will be able to show and teach all kinds of dances in the city and its environs and elsewhere throughout the realm, without being constrained or obliged under any pretext to acquire Letters of Mastery nor any other authority beyond what is conferred upon them by the said Academy, in the manner and the forms indicated here.

11. Since the King needs persons capable of participating and Dancing in his Ballets and similar divertissements, when his majesty honors the said Academy with notice, the Ancients will be expected to furnish incessantly from amongst themselves or others the number of dancers needed by his Majesty.

12. The common affairs of the said Academy will be pursued, maintained, and defended by the said Academicians, at their common expense whose fund will be earned between themselves, and they will decide on all necessary measures in a majority vote when they are assembled to that purpose as described.[46]

---

[46]   Franko (1993), pp. 178–80.

The establishment of the Académie Royale de Danse and the 'twelve principle articles' assisted in regulating and controlling dances and dancing masters. They also influenced further developments in dance, particularly theatrical dance and ballet, and more indirectly what became known as step dancing in Ireland through the influence of its dancing masters, their students, their choreographies, teachings, performances and publications.

Throughout this time, Ireland was a colony of England, and consequently, English and Anglo-Irish gentry who lived in Ireland, and in particular Dublin, the capital of Ireland, were interested in what was considered to be fashionable in Paris and London.[47] As professional dancing masters taught and performed in Paris and London, so too they taught and performed in Ireland, particularly Dublin. This accommodated the dissemination and adaptation of fashionable European dances and a European dance aesthetic in Ireland. This was further assisted by Irish family members who were employed or connected with European courts, armies, schools and universities. For example, as a result of the Treaty of Limerick in 1691, some 14,000 Irish soldiers left Ireland to fight in the army of Louis XIV; these soldiers were known as the Wild Geese. Irish connections with Continental European countries such as France, Spain, Austria and England were strong. In addition, dance publications also assisted in disseminating fashionable dances and theoretical treatises on dance across a wide geographic area, and as we will see below, across different sectors of society.

Dancing Masters in England

Although French dancing masters were employed in England, there were also English dancing masters of high repute, for example John Playford, Josias Priest and John Weaver.[48]

Young ladies' boarding and day schools were a common feature in England from the eighteenth century onward. In *The Life and Works of John Weaver* (Ralph 1985), the dance historian Richard Ralph suggests that although Weaver (1673–1760) practised as a social dancing master, he moved freely and comfortably between the theatre and the dancing school, as did most dancing masters of the day. Weaver taught in provincial boarding houses and schools in Shrewsbury, where he was born, and also spent much time in London performing and learning the art of theatrical performance and production. Indeed, Weaver appeared in Ann Oldfield's Benefit Night at Drury Lane in 1700. While in London, Weaver had access to the dancing masters of the gentry and worked with London's two leading dancing masters: Mr Isaac, Court Dancing Master, whose patronage of Weaver began in 1702, and Thomas Caverley. Also, while in London Weaver had access to French

---

[47] It is worth remembering that Dublin at this time was the second largest city in the United Kingdom.

[48] Hilton (1981), p. 53.

and Italian artists who influenced much of his early theatrical productions.[49] From 1721, however, Weaver devoted himself to his boarding school in Shrewsbury, where, according to Ralph, there was an abundance of ladies' academies.

Throughout the seventeenth and eighteenth centuries, dance and dance instruction were necessary prerequisites for persons of quality. It was through such instruction and practice that grace of movement and etiquette of polite society were attained. However, towards the latter part of the seventeenth century, 'the petty mercantile class sought to buy the refinements of society',[50] and Weaver, being aware of this, advocated dancing to serve social ambition. This class provided a huge source of income for the dancing master profession. Dancing was perceived as a social art that enabled those who could dance to move with confidence in society. Dance was valued. Weaver and the other dancing masters of the day were of the opinion that dancing, drawing and music were important recreations for ladies, but for Weaver, women's dancing was less important than men's dancing.

Weaver also undertook a series of lectures in the 1720s on 'the application of anatomical and mechanical theory to the understanding of dancing'.[51] These lectures were given at the Academy in Chancery to an audience of 31 dancing masters who subscribed to a printed version of the lectures, published in 1721. In his lectures, Weaver made reference to a 'military pedigree of dance'.[52] In court, men competed in agility and virility with each other, and often dancing and soldiery were linked. Indeed, fencing and dancing were often linked together in dance schools, 'the *one* to grace and beautifie ... the *other* to shield and defend'.[53] It is of interest that this connection was also made in Kerry, as itinerant dancing masters were reputed to have taught both dancing and fencing in the one school building. Thus, in attempting to elevate the status of the dancing master and the art of dance, Weaver and his contemporaries maintained that dance was artistic and useful, and in their arguments made reference to the golden classical era of dance in Greece and Rome. They also argued that dancing was a social and healthy exercise, and that it was a necessary social accomplishment.

Together with his lectures, theatrical performances and dance instruction, John Weaver also published. Isaac commissioned John Weaver to translate into English Raoul Auger Feuillet's book *Choreographie ou l'art de décrire la dance, par caracteres, figures et signes démonstratifs, avec lesquels on apprend facilement de soy-meme toutes sortes de dances* (Paris, 1700). Feuillet's book was a theoretical one, devoted to illustrating the Feuillet system of dance notation.[54] Weaver's

---

[49]   Ralph (1985).

[50]   Ibid. p. 122.

[51]   Ibid. p. 26.

[52]   Ibid. p. 126.

[53]   Brathwait in ibid. p. 126.

[54]   Although Feuillet published this system of notation, known as the Feuillet system, in 1700, Beauchamp, dancing master to Louis XIV, is generally regarded as the person to have created it some thirty years earlier. In 1704, Beauchamp filed a petition against

translation, entitled *Orchesography or the Art of Dancing, by Characters and Demonstrative Figures ... Being an Exact and Just Translation from the French of Monsieur Feuillet*, was published in London in 1706, and many later editions followed. Weaver devoted much time to promoting the use of the Feuillet system of notation in England, and according to Ralph, during the writing of *Orchesography* Weaver might have spent time as a peripatetic teacher of the Feuillet system of dance notation, since there was a demand for it at that time. Indeed, Weaver documented and notated the dances that Mr Isaac composed for the Queen's Court Balls. These dances were published annually from 1703, but none have survived.

Other published works of significance from this time included P. Siris's *The Art of Dancing, Demonstrated by Characters and Figures* (London, 1706). On the cover of this publication, it stated: 'one may learn easily, and of one's self, all sorts of dances, being a work very useful to all such as practice dancing, especially masters'. Again, this publication was based on the work of Feuillet, but with alterations in some characters and with two additional dances: 'The English Rigaudon' and 'The French Bretagne'. Another publication, Pierre Rameau's *Le Maitre à danser* (1725), discussed stance, social behaviour, the execution of steps, and finally, dances. Rameau's book was translated into English as *The Dancing Master* in 1728, by John Essex. In addition, Kellom Tomlinson wrote *The Art of Dancing*, which although completed in 1724, was not published until 1735 in London, when enough subscriptions had been collected. A later publication, but one which was popular, was Carlo Blasis's *Traité élémentaire, théorique, et pratique de l'art de la danse* (1820); translations of this book appeared in Italian, Danish, Spanish and English within a few months of its publication. The above publications were significant in that they contributed to standardizing dancing masters' repertoires and techniques across a wide geographical area and across different sectors of society. In Blasis's treatise, the first practical treatise on the technique of ballet, we find many instructions on technique. For instance:

> While practising take equal pains with both legs, and let neither yield to the other in performance ... which proves they have both attained mastery.

Concerning the body, Blasis gives the following advice:

> The body should be held erect .... Throw out your chest and hold your waist in .... Keep our shoulders down, your head raised .... A fine carriage is one of the principal merits in a dancer.[55]

Concerning the feet, Blasis states:

Feuillet, but lost the case (see Hilton 1981, pp. 45–6). Consequently, the system is today sometimes called the Beauchamp-Feuillet notation system.

[55] Blasis (1820), p. 23.

> Devote yourself to accuracy and precision in your dancing, making certain that your temps conform to the best principles you have been taught and your steps are executed with grace and elegance.[56]

These instructions, although intended for ballet dancers of the day, would resonate with many Irish trained step dancers today.

Dance as a Social Art

The Académie Royale de Danse survived only until the French Revolution in 1789, when the aristocracy was overturned. Post-revolutionary France was, in structure and values, *bourgeois*, but aristocratic influence was still prevalent. As Hobsbawm states:

> Rising classes naturally tend to see the symbols of their wealth and power in terms of what their former superior groups have established as the standards of comfort, luxury, or pomp. The wives of enriched Cheshire drapers would become 'ladies', instructed by the numerous books of etiquette and gracious living.[57]

When noble dancing in the courts declined after the French Revolution, the art of dancing in a noble manner continued to be taught not only in France and the Continent, but also in the western fringes of Europe. In Norbert Elias's words:

> as in the moulding of speech, so too in the moulding of other aspects of behaviour in society, social motivations, adaptations of behaviour to the models of influential circles, were by far the most important.[58]

Following the French Revolution and the Napoleonic wars, the increased wealth of the upper middle classes demanded that dance and dancing masters also be made available in city ballrooms and assembly halls. Dancing masters found themselves in demand, and under their tutelage and direction, dance came to play a significant role in the 'civilizing process' where notions of civility and respectability were important.

Also, the availability of published fashionable dances in the Feuillet notation system and other figurative systems allowed for the dissemination of new social dances, not only in the metropolis, but also in the provinces. Notation encouraged the standardization of figures, stepping movements and patterns. This standardization was seen as imperative to both canonizing repertoires and keeping abreast of all fashionable dances. Indeed, the publications of dances allowed dancing masters to

---

[56]   Ibid., p. 41.
[57]   Hobsbawm (1977), p. 224.
[58]   Elias (1994), p. 97.

receive them in the post in a reliable format: a format that would aid their teaching, preservation and dissemination.[59]

In Scotland, resident dancing masters were also to be found in every sizeable town from 1750 to 1850, and itinerant dancing teachers visited the smaller towns and villages. According to the dance historians Joan and Thomas Flett (1996), the more prominent dancing masters studied in London and France. One such Edinburgh dancing master was David Strange, who advertised in 1764 that he:

> last season studied Dancing, under the celebrated Signor GALLINI at London: he is now returned from Paris, where, for some time past, he has been improving himself in the MINUET; and learned, at the same time, several NEW DANCES under the first TWO MASTERS in France, Monsieur MALTERE, Teacher to the Royal Family of France, and Monsieur VESTRES first Dancer in the Royal Academy of Dancing at Paris.[60]

It seemed important to these dancing masters to validate their art by naming their teachers and their training, and French and Italian dancing masters were the order of the day.

Dancing Masters in Ireland

As outlined above, dancing masters from Italy and France travelled throughout Europe during the seventeenth and eighteenth centuries, and appeared on stages in European capitals including Paris, London, Edinburgh and Dublin. Also, some aspiring dancing masters from different regions of Europe travelled to the European capitals for training in fashionable dances and their aesthetic. This gave them the social and cultural capital to validate themselves as dancing masters. However, as mentioned above, England also had its dancing masters: dancing masters who also contributed to the history of dance in Ireland.

From the seventeenth to the nineteenth century, dancing masters were popular characters in Ireland. These dancing masters frequented houses of the gentry and boarding houses, where they taught the fashionable dances of Paris. In many cases, these dancing masters performed in the theatres of Dublin and supplemented their income with dance instruction in schools and houses of the gentry, both within and outside the capital.

With the establishment of the first theatre in Werburg Street, Dublin, in 1635 by the Earl of Strafford, Thomas Wentworth – then Lord Lieutenant of Ireland – John Ogilby, an English dancing master, was given charge of the running of the theatre.[61] According to the dance historian Gráinne McArdle, Ogilby had initially

---

[59] Hilton (1981), p. 53.
[60] Flett and Flett (1996), p. 5.
[61] McArdle (2003).

come to Ireland in 1633 as dancing master to the Earl of Strafford's children, and also as one of the Gentlemen riding in the Earl's troupe of guards. Prior to this, Ogilby had enjoyed a career as a dancer in London and had also taught dancing there; among his pupils were Mr Isaac, the famous court dancing master, and John Lacey.[62] Ogilby brought actors and musicians to Dublin for the theatrical productions, and although little is known of the early plays performed in Dublin at this time, there is some evidence concerning the dancing. On St Patrick's Day 1640, the play *Landgartha* (the first Irish play by an Irish playwright) included a masque with 'A short nimble Anticke Dance; a country dance called *The Whip of Dunboyne*; and a *Grand Dance in Foure Couple*'.[63] Although the theatre closed shortly afterwards due to political circumstances, Ogilby acquired the position of Master of the Revels in Ireland in 1660, which gave him the right to: 'build theatres and stage "all Comedies tragedies Operas and other enterludes of what kind soever decent and becoming and not prophane and obnoxious"'.[64]

Ogilby was responsible for building the Theatre Royal, Smock Alley, Dublin, which opened in 1662, and for many decades it had the monopoly on all theatrical productions.

However, 1729–43 'was a period of intense competition in the Dublin theatre world', due to the rivalry of two theatres for theatre audiences.[65] According to McArdle, it was a dance troupe, Signora Violante and her rope dancers, which specialized in 'dance and dramatic entertainments after the Italian manner', that initiated this rivalry by establishing a separate theatre. The establishment of this theatre motivated another group of dancers and actors to develop another new theatre. The rivalry that followed inspired much dance activity throughout this period, with an increase in visiting foreign dancers, visiting harlequins, and dramatic/pantomime entertainments.

Many visiting theatre dancing masters supplemented their income by teaching. For example, included in Signora Violante's company was a French dancing master, Charles Lalauze, from the Opera House in London. An advertisement in *Dickson's Dublin Intelligence* (8 March 1731) reads as follows:

> Mr Lalauze, Dancing Master, who has perform'd in the Opera Houses and Theatres in Paris (where he was bred) and in the City of London for several years past, intending to make his Residence for some time in this City, will teach Ladies and Gentlemen, Young Misses and Masters to Dance, after the newest and best Manner Practis'd at Court, Assemblies, Operas or Schools, and will either wait on them at their home or will teach them from his home at the New Booth in Dames Street, where the curious may be convinced of his performance, also his ability of Instruction; a Young Boy and Girl his scholars, being to be

---

[62]   Brainard (1998a).

[63]   McArdle (2003).

[64]   Ibid.

[65]   Ibid.

seen there, who are admir'd by all persons, and reckon'd to surpass any of their Age, in most kind of Dancing, Serious and Comick.

N.B. He teaches abroad Tuesday, Thursday and Saturday, and at his House Monday, Wednesday and Fridays, and will also Attend any persons of Quality, who have seats within three or Four Miles of the City twice a week. He may be spoke with any day from Nine o'clock in the morning 'till four in the afternoon.[66]

Dancing masters were commonly found within educated society in Ireland, and all educated persons, or those aspiring to present themselves as educated, required knowledge in both the social dances of the day and in the presentation of oneself. The role of the dancing master consisted not just of teaching fashionable social dances, but imparting knowledge of ballroom etiquette, such as instruction on how to enter a room, how to bow, how to salute or kiss a lady, how to stand straight, and generally how to behave appropriately in public.

Throughout the eighteenth century in Ireland, literate and polite society was educated in fashionable dances, including the Minuet and the country dances of Playford. The publication of John Playford's *The English Dancing Master* (1651) and the later publication of Weaver's translation of Feuillet's notation system in *Orchesography* (1706)[67] provided dancing masters with a common canon of dance theory and dance repertoire. It is known that Mr Delemain and Mr Smith, dancing masters in Dublin, subscribed to Weaver's *Orchesography*.[68]

Children of wealthy families were also taught by dancing masters in their homes. The following extract is an example of a 'dancing master's agreement' drawn up on 21 October 1718 between William Bayly, Gentleman, Cork, and Charles Stanton, dancing master:

It is agreed that the said Charles Stanton shall teach the said William's children to the number of four to dance until they perfectly understand Minutes, Hornpipe and Country Dances, and such dances to dance very well to one of understanding in that respect shall Adjudge. In consideration whereof the said Bayly shall pay unto the said Charles the sum of two Gynnies, or six and twenty shillings, when taught perfectly Not before. In witness whereof the parties above named have interchange theire hands and seales the day and the years above written. Memorand that it is further agreed that since the youngest may not perform to

---

[66] McArdle (2005), p. 71.

[67] See Ralph (1985).

[68] Dancing masters in Dublin at the beginning of the eighteenth century included Mr Delemain and Mr Smith, and also Mr Sloane, who with his wife, Mrs Sloane, kept a boarding school for 'young ladies' in St Mary's Abbey, Dublin, in 1706. Sloane's Boarding School admitted both boarders and day Schollars (*sic*) (see *The Dublin Mercury*, 25 March 1706). The advertisement also informs us that they had lately kept a boarding school in England. See also McArdle (2005).

be ready as soon as the rest that then Mr Bayly will consider that part, the said
Stanton doing his best endeavour to forward the said Child.[69]

This agreement is evidence of the fact that dancing masters, in order to supplement
their income, also taught the fashionable dances of the day to children of educated
and wealthy families. This tuition took place in private houses, both within the
confines of the capital, Dublin, and outside it. Another reference to dancing
masters teaching children outside Dublin is found in *Memoires of Arthur O'Neill*,
the eighteenth-century Irish harper. O' Neill states:

> Always on my return from Granard Balls I stopped at Counsellor Edgeworth's of
> Edgeworthstown, where I was always well entertained. I taught two young ladies,
> Miss Farrell and Miss Plunkett, the harp, who lived in that neighbourhood ....
> I next came to a Cormack O'Neill's, of Fardrumman in the County Longford. He
> was an eccentric genius and kept a house not unlike an academy, such as dancing
> masters, music masters, classical masters, [masters] of modern languages, he
> having four sons and three daughters on whom he spared no expense.[70]

The Granard Balls that O'Neill refers to above occurred in 1781, 1782 and 1783.
These were harp festivals for the promotion of the Irish harp and harp music, at
which O'Neill participated. His mention of dancing masters in Longford is further
indicative of the fact that the gentry outside Dublin also had their dancing masters.

Dancing masters also supplemented their income by teaching in schools and
academies, both within and outside Dublin. For example, on 13 October 1817, the
following advertisement appeared in *The Freeman's Journal* for a dancing school
in Dublin:

Mr Duval

Has the honour of announcing to the Nobility and Gentry, that for the purpose of
complying with their repeated solicitations, and of accommodating several Families, to
whom he found it Impracticable last winter to extend his exertions, he will, on Friday,
7th of November next, in the Ballroom at the Rotunda, open a Morning Academy,
where ladies who may please to favour him with their attendance, will be instructed in
the present Fashionable Quadrille Dancing.

Mr Duval will devote two Evenings in the Week to the Instruction of Gentlemen.
Letters addressed to No. 2, Cavendish Row.

This advertisement draws attention to the fact that the country dances were by
now being superseded by the Quadrilles as the fashionable dances. Mr Duval's

---

[69]   See 'Miscellanea', *Journal of the Royal Society of Antiquaries of Ireland*, vol. xviii
(1887), pp. 212–13.

[70]   O'Sullivan (1958 [1991]), p. 165.

Academy was again directed towards the gentry, and interestingly, not only was dance instruction separated by gender, but two evenings were devoted to gentlemen, as opposed to one morning class for ladies.

On 22 December 1818, the following advertisement for dance lessons in Dublin appeared in *The Freeman's Journal*:

> MESSRS. Simon. SEN. AND JUN. PROFESSEURS DE DANSE ET DE WALTZ, most respectfully inform the Nobility and Gentry, that they have commenced giving Lessons in Quadrilles, Waltzes, &c. &c. &c.
>
> Balls and Quadrille Parties attended as usual, for which purpose they have selected the Newest and most Fashionable Music.
>
> Terms known on application at their residence, 22 Suffolk Street.

Quadrilles and Waltzes were the dances of the day. The appearance of 'Professeurs de Dance et de Waltz' in this advertisement illustrated that these dancing masters marketed themselves as French Professeurs de Dance with a wide-ranging knowledge of dance for polite society.[71] Balls and Quadrille parties were significant social events within polite society, and dancing masters, particularly French dancing masters with knowledge of fashionable dances, were in demand. Indeed, we can infer that the combination of visiting dancing masters (English, French and Italian) and the publication of dances – including dance notation and dance technique – facilitated the assimilation of dance into polite society across a relatively wide geographical area.

The Continental European aesthetic was based on noble dancing for polite and 'civilized' society; ballroom etiquette was therefore also taught as part of dance instruction in Ireland. The following advertisement for a dance academy in Dublin in *The Freeman's Journal* (1 December 1855) is an illustration of this:

> DANCING, DEPORTMENT, AND CALISTHENIC EXERCISES, – MR. CHAMBERLAIN has the honour to announce that his Academy, No. 57. JERVIS STREET, is now open for instruction in all Fashionable Dances on the newest Parisien system, including La Polka, La Polka Mazurka, La Mazurka Quadrilles, La Polka Quadrilles, La Parisien Lancers, Caledonians and Hibernian Quadrilles, Coulon's Double Quadrilles, La Valse Cellarius, La Valse a Deux Temps, La Galop, La Schottische Simple, La Nouvelle Schottish, German and Sauteure Waltzing, Spanish Dances, Country Dance, &c.

continued

---

[71] It is interesting to note that following the French fashion, some dancing masters teaching 'Irish' dance in Ireland, England and the United States also gave themselves the title 'Professor' – for example, Professor P.D. Reidy of the London Branch of the Gaelic League around the beginning of the twentieth century (see Chapters 3 and 4).

Mr Chamberlain receives but a limited number of Pupils into his Academy, so that due attention may be paid to every individual Pupil, the system pursued being the same as in the Continental Schools, where elegant deportment and strict attention to the etiquette of society elicit undivided care.

Private Tuition at various hours every day, as per arrangement. Evening Class on Mondays and Fridays from Seven until Ten o' Clock. Schools and Families attended as usual. Terms may be learned on application at the Academy, 57 Jervis Street. A Morning Class for Ladies at Twelve o' Clock.

As discussed above, dancing masters established academies and taught in schools, academies and houses in Dublin, the environs of Dublin, and elsewhere in Ireland. In the region of North Kerry, there is also documented evidence of these dancing masters; for example, *Chute's Western Herald* printed the following advertisements on 16 February 1828:

SELECT ACADEMY FOR

YOUNG LADIES,

Under the Superintendence of

MRS GREGORY,

*Assisted by her Daughters, and a Lady of
considerable Experience*

———

Mrs Gregory begs leave to announce her intention of arriving at TRALEE in a few days, where she will, immediately after her arrival, open a Seminary for the Education of Young Ladies.

Her system will embrace English, French, and Italian; Geography, the Use of the Globes, Astronomy, and such other Branches of Science as are considered fashionable for Young Ladies to know. Useful and Ornamental Works – Music, Drawing, and Dancing by experienced Masters – French and Italian, by Monsieur ADAMO.

She will pay the strictest attention to the Religious Instruction, Address, and Manners of her Pupils; and will be assisted in the Writing and Science Departments by Mr. GREGORY, late Professor of General Science at the Clonmel Endowed School, and Head Master of the Dublin Academical Institution, which she hopes, will establish an additional claim to Public Support.

Terms, and other particulars may be known by applying to Mr Gregory, who is at present in Tralee.

February 13th 1828

YOUNG LADIES

Boarding and Day School
DENNY STREET

———

MISS O'SULLIVAN,

ANXIOUS to meet the wishes of many kind Supporters of her School, has engaged a Lady from Dublin, of the Established Church, of Competent abilities, as

RESIDENT GOVERNESS

She feels very grateful for the liberal patronage she has hitherto received; and she trusts that her impartial manner of conducting her Establishment will meet with general approbation.

Masters in the several branches of French and Italian, Writing, Dancing, Drawing, and Music, regularly attend the School

Tralee, 13th February, 1828

On 5 March 1828, another advertisement relating to dance at an academy in Tralee appeared in *Chute's Western Herald*:

DANCING

———

Mr Cronin, begs to inform his Pupils, and his Friends, that he has got a new Set of *Quadrils*, danced by 16, as also, a new Set of *Spanish Dances*, together with some *Fancy Dances*, &c. &c. Commands left for him at Mr Cassidy's Academy, will be duly attended to.

Terms in the town, 12s for every 24 lessons, and 5s Entrance. Mr Cronin engages to fit his Pupils for a Public Ball in one Months' teaching.

Throughout this period, dance advertisements in newspapers related to teaching dance and preparation for dance balls were common. So too were newsworthy articles relating to the Royal Family, the British Houses of Parliament, and issues relating to Ireland and agriculture. In *Chute's Western Herald* (24 May 1828) a report is published concerning 'The King's Juvenile Ball'. Much information is given in minute detail relating to the whole event. For instance, we are informed that:

'After half-past eight o'clock, his Majesty entered the Ballroom …. The party were formed into sets for quadrilles. The floor was chalked in the most tasteful manner with representations of foliage, executed in the boldest style ….' And later in the evening, 'Owing to the superior accommodation afforded by the addition of the second Ballroom, four sets were enabled to be danced. Quadrilles, with waltzing at intervals, were danced during the night.'[72]

These Quadrilles were danced to a 30-piece Quadrille band.

These advertisements and reports are interesting for a number of reasons. First, the 'young ladies' referred to in these advertisements were all Church of Ireland and were all connected to the gentry of the county, the majority of whom were Anglo-Irish. Although Catholicism was the religion of the majority of the population of Ireland, under British rule the gentrified Anglo-Irish minority supported His Majesty and the Church of England, and dominated both the commercial and professional life of the region. Indeed, Chute, the owner of *Chute's Western Herald*, was also of Church of Ireland denomination, and his newspaper, the first of its kind available in the district, was written with the Anglo-Irish nobility and gentry in mind. Second, the gentry in Ireland, although living in Ireland, kept abreast of all social, cultural and political happenings in England and Europe.

Thus, instruction in fashionable dances and ballroom etiquette for 'polite' society was generally available to the gentry and nobility in Ireland. But what dances were practised by the labouring classes? And where and from whom did the labouring classes learn these dances? The labouring classes learned from dancing masters, and according to Limerick historian and journalist Maurice Lenihan (1867), there were three classes of dancing masters in Ireland during the late eighteenth and early nineteenth century. These he categorized as follows:

1. 'the fashionable terpsichorean professor': the slightly pretentious dancing master at the top of the social ladder who generally gallicized his name, claimed he had been trained in France and aped the manners and dress of his clients. These dancing masters included *Garbois*;[73] his original name is said to have been Garvey, and his teaching circuit was the south of Ireland, particularly, Waterford, Wexford and Carlow. *Coreille* or *Von Coreille* was another dancing master whose circuit was around Connaught and whose original name was Curly;

2. the dancing master in the middle who was respectable enough to teach children of the Big Houses or 'gentlemen's houses' and children of the ordinary tenants; and

3. the dancing master at the lowest rung of the social ladder, the village 'hop merchant' who prepared young boys and girls for Sunday dances or dances at fairs. These dancing masters used 'gads' and hay-ropes to instruct their pupils and 'practised the heel and toe step' and the 'cut and the shuffle'.[74]

---

[72]   *Chute's Western Herald*, 24 May 1828.
[73]   Kennedy (1875); Friel (2004).
[74]   Lenihan (1867).

Lenihan does not mention the dancing masters who visited Ireland from abroad and who had been taught by French, Italian or English dancing masters. The dancing masters mentioned above by Lenihan are Irish dancing masters who all, to varying degree, attempted to make a living in dance by imitating the teachings and mannerisms of Continental European dancing masters. Of the three types of dancing masters listed by Lenihan, it is the second category that is most respected by him. In meeting one of this class of dancing master named Hennessy, Lenihan asks him for his 'experience of men and manners in his walk' (Lenihan 1867). Hennessy gives an account of the dancers and dancing masters he has met:

> The first dancer I ever met – he was the first in Munster, Leinster or Ulster, an inventor, sir, of dancing himself – his name was Edward Ellard; he was a Kerryman, sir. He danced Irish dancing with any man that ever laid foot to flure [floor]. He was unequalled at the Moneen Jig. Oh! to see him dance it, you would go any distance or spend any time; it was delightful, sir – aye, I say delightful! The Moneen Jig, you know, or ought to know, is the best dance that ever was known – a true, real, undoubted Irish dance; it would dazzle your eyes to see it danced, sir. Well, Ellard was transported for life! He got at the head of a great number of rebels, and he attacked the home of a gentleman where he was teaching, and was informed against by one of his own party, and sent over the seas for life! Oh, he was a great teacher – he taught myself …. He was a native of Listowel, in the county of Kerry – a great man entirely. Well the next dancer I met in my time was John Gunaine – yes, his name was John – John Gunaine, I say, a native of Templemore, in the County Tipperary. Gunaine had but one eye, but he had the execution of any man; he was tip-top – an inventor of hornpipes and reels and all sorts of dances. He was a celebrated man, sir – a stout, able, portly man, not very tall. Mr George O'Kelly was the next I met in my time. He was a general teacher, sir; he taught at gentlemens' houses; was a good fiddler; and was one of the very first elegant teachers of his day. O'Kelly knew the French style as well as the Irish. He learned the French style in Paris at one time, where he went with the family of a gentleman he taught. He was an inventor also. The next man was Mr Nicholas Lysaght; he was a general teacher; he was a Kerryman – there was no bounds to these Kerrymen for dancing and all sorts of fun; they'd beat the world hollow, sir, so they would these Kerrymen; their heels were as light as bits of cork. Why, sir, there was no equalling them in the dancing line.[75]

In North Kerry, the labouring classes learned dance instruction from dancing masters 'of their own rank' who, when given the opportunity, also taught in private houses. Influenced by the dancing masters of Continental Europe and England, these dancing masters imitated, assimilated and adapted their dances and aesthetic to suit their 'labouring class' and small farmer patrons. Within this

---

[75]   Ibid.

context, step dancing, as a particular dance-music practice, was constructed and developed by these itinerant dancing masters using the 'fundamental principles' as outlined earlier by the Continental European dancing masters, together with enough foot and leg patterns for the one body. However, step dancing in Ireland was also influenced by the accompanying traditional dance music in Ireland and a native aesthetic and conceptualization of dance. In the next chapter, I trace the rural itinerant dancing masters of North Kerry and discuss them within the social and historical contexts of their time to inform our understanding of the meanings generated by, and embodied in, the Molyneaux step dance practice of the region.

Chapter 3

Colonialism and the Itinerant Dancing Masters of North Kerry

The itinerant dancing masters of North Kerry emerged on the scene towards the end of the eighteenth century within the context of colonialism. Throughout the eighteenth century, Ireland remained a colony of England, despite having its own parliament in Dublin. The Irish Parliament was, in effect, a colonial parliament whose members were Protestant and who had passed a series of anti-Catholic laws, known as the 'penal laws'.[1] The enforcement of these penal laws placed the Catholic majority in a position of subjection; however, as the century progressed, these laws gradually became less strict. Towards the latter half of the eighteenth century, the country progressed in industry and trade, but the resulting wealth was of little benefit to the majority of the Irish population, the Catholic peasantry. The Declamatory Act passed in the 1780s allowed Ireland to legislate for itself, but sharing a common monarchy with England.

The American War of Independence and the French Revolution had a strong influence on those in Ireland who were seeking parliamentary reform. Irish newspapers covered the events in France, and the ideas of Liberty and Equality were welcomed by these reformers.[2] In 1793, a Relief Act to Catholics was passed, which gave them the right to vote, but still excluded them from parliament and the higher offices of state. At the same time, a Convention Act was passed which forbade meetings of groups which claimed to represent a large portion of Irish

---

[1]   The penal laws were passed with the intent of securing Protestant supremacy in Ireland. These laws debarred Catholics from parliament, from holding any government office, from entering the legal profession, and from holding a commission in either the army or navy. These offices were maintained largely by Protestants, since a qualifying oath – an anti-Catholic oath – was prescribed for all of them. Further Acts forbade Catholics to buy land, to take a lease for longer than 30 years, or to own a horse worth more than £5. In addition, the Bishop Banishment Act of 1697 forced Catholic clergy to leave the country, thus forbidding Catholics from practising their religion. The Act to Prevent the Further Growth of Popery (1704) forbade Catholics from buying or inheriting land from a Protestant.

[2]   For example, in 1791, the society of the United Irishmen was founded in Belfast and Dublin by Wolfe Tone, a Dublin barrister who was very much influenced by the political and religious events of France. These were middle-class debating societies that wished to mould public opinion, and although Protestant in origin, the societies supported Catholic emancipation as part of parliamentary reform.

opinion.[3] In the Listowel region of North Kerry, the colonists had Protestant militia to maintain the status quo in the area.

The Act of Union was passed in 1800, which made Ireland part of the United Kingdom. Consequently, during the first half of the nineteenth century, political activity focused on attempts to repeal this union and also to acquire full Catholic emancipation.[4] Emancipation was finally granted in 1829, but parliamentary reform was to be delayed. The Great Famine of 1845–48 interrupted political endeavours, as the attention of the masses was on food and survival and not on a national Ireland.

The political events leading up to the Great Famine, though important for the country as a whole, had little direct impact on the bulk of the rural population of North Kerry. The daily lives of these people were more influenced by local than national institutions. It was the local landlords (Protestant and absent in Dublin, for the most part), their agents and the local clergy who influenced these people's everyday lives. Their main concerns were domestic and local, while their calendar was marked by payments in tithes and rents.

Prior to the Great Famine in Kerry and in most of Ireland, society was divided into three distinct social groups: (1) the local Protestant landlords and their agents; (2) the professional class, made up of government officials, shopkeepers and the rural tenant farmers, and (3) on the lowest step of the social scale, the Catholic, landless peasants, the majority of whom lived in rural areas. This third class could be further subdivided into the cottier class, labourers who took conacre,[5] and the simple labourer class. It is estimated that 50–90 per cent of the people in North Kerry were landless and propertyless.[6]

These rural peasants lived in poor conditions, mostly due to the tithe payments to the established Church and exorbitant rents to the landlords. Services rendered by the blacksmith, tailor, weaver and priest, together with the loan of a horse to bring turf to their homes, were paid for in the form of labour; money was rarely handled.

As a result of poverty and discontent with their lot, evictions and common land enclosures, agrarian crime was widespread throughout the countryside. The Whiteboy movement, 'an organised campaign of terror', emerged to address the grievances of the peasantry.[7] At the beginning of the nineteenth century, the area from Tarbert to Listowel in North Kerry was considered to be populated almost entirely by Whiteboys, who resisted the tithe payment collection of the established Church and opposed the high rents demanded by the local landlords. Evictions,

---

[3]   McDowell (1984).

[4]   Daniel O Connell, a Kerry barrister, led the field in this movement, which was well supported by the people of North Kerry.

[5]   Conacre was a system of letting land, usually small portions of a farm, for the growth of a single crop such as potatoes.

[6]   Gaughan (1973), p. 117.

[7]   Beckett (1966), p. 109.

resulting from non-payments of rents to the landlords, were common among the peasants of North Kerry. Opposition to these Whiteboys arose from the middle of the eighteenth century to the middle of the nineteenth century; this was made manifest in the passing of Acts against them, the first of which was enacted in 1776. However, the Whiteboy movement continued to operate in North Kerry, despite further opposition from some of the Catholic clergy.

The period up to the Great Famine in 1845 saw an increase in population which led to competition for farms and higher rents. As the century progressed and throughout the early decades of the nineteenth century until the Great Famine of 1845–48, matters worsened for this sector of society in North Kerry, who for the most part were exploited by landlords and their agents.

The Great Famine left Ireland exhausted, politically and economically, and changed the whole rural structure of society. As a direct consequence of this famine, between 1845 and 1851, the population of Ireland fell from 8.5 million to 6.5 million. It was estimated that approximately one million succeeded in emigrating, while another million died.[8] The cottier class almost disappeared, with an estimate of 70 per cent decline in one-roomed cabins, while holdings of over 15 acres doubled.[9] One consequence of the Great Famine was an end to the subdivision of farms, which delayed marriages in some cases, while in others it meant emigration. Thus, in the mid-nineteenth century, the pattern of modern Irish agriculture emerged: a family farm engaged in livestock and mixed tillage. The two main political issues of the latter half of the nineteenth century would be land and national independence.

The relationship between local landlords and their tenants worsened after the Great Famine. By taking advantage of the Corn Laws of 1845, some local landlords evicted their tenants in order to change from tillage to pasture. The power of landlords over their tenants continued for another few decades, but had almost ceased with the founding of the Land League by Michael Davitt in 1879. In North Kerry, this movement was strongly supported, as the people were concerned with the policy of land tenure in the National movement. Boycotting and 'no rent' were tools used by the Land League during the Land War of 1879–82, and its greatest success came in 1881 with the granting to tenants of the three Fs: fair rent, fixity of tenure and freedom of sale. Consequently, the interest of landlords in the land diminished. Many landlords preferred to sell out to their tenants than to share the land with them.[10] A series of Land Acts followed, and finally, in 1903, the old system of Landlordism was abolished in Ireland.

Throughout the latter part of the nineteenth century, transport improved, as did the social life of the people. In North Kerry, the historian J. Anthony Gaughan states:

---

[8]   See Green (1984), p. 274.
[9]   See Beckett (1966), p. 146.
[10]   See Moody (1984).

Although some adults were to be seen bare-legged and bare-footed, fewer of them went about in this way. People's clothing was of a better quality than it had been previously. Comfortable and substantial houses were replacing the old-style mud cabins. And, on the inside, houses were decorated neatly, albeit simply – the interior decoration generally involving pictures of the Sacred Heart, the Blessed Virgin Mary, St. Patrick, the reigning pope and the popular Irish political leader of the day. At this time also there were few people who had not, in addition to their former staple diet of potatoes and milk, bread (griddle bread) and tea, and occasionally meat (generally fat bacon) of some kind.[11]

Improvements were also evident in the growth of literacy and education. The national school system, established in 1831, quickly expanded throughout the century, but was criticized for being modelled on the English system. No Irish history, poetry, music nor dance were taught, and the Irish language itself was excluded from the curriculum. English was the official language of use; spoken Irish was discouraged under threat of punishment. A 'tally stick' or a *'bata scoir'*, attached to a piece of string was worn by children around their necks and teachers in schools and parents at home put a notch on these sticks should a child speak Irish. On seeing the notch on the 'tally stick' children would be punished by teachers at school. Pádraig Pearse, the Irish patriot, referred to the system as a 'murder machine', as it lacked 'freedom and inspiration'.[12] Consequently, as in many European countries during the nineteenth century, there was a desire to resurrect a sense of national identity (see Chapters 5 and 6).

Throughout these historical developments in Ireland, dance played an important social, cultural, educational and ideological role. Step dancing as a solo dance-music genre was developed within these cultural and historical circumstances.

The Itinerant Dancing Masters

Dancing is very general among the poor people, almost universal in every cabin. Dancing masters of their own rank travel through the country from cabin to cabin, with a piper or blind fiddler, and the pay is 6d. a quarter. It is an absolute system of education. Weddings are always celebrated with much dancing; and a Sunday rarely passes without a dance; there are very few among them who will not, after a hard day's work, gladly walk seven miles to have a dance ....[13]

Arthur Young, the English agriculturalist, is the first to mention itinerant dancing masters of the peasantry, in *A Tour of Ireland* (1776–79). Interestingly, the dancing masters referred to are 'dancing masters of their own rank', and not French or

---

[11]   Gaughan (1973), p. 163.
[12]   See Lyons (1973), p. 89.
[13]   Young in Maxwell (1983), p. 153.

Italian dancing masters. Young also mentions the dances taught by these dancing masters:

> Besides the Irish Jig, which they can dance with a most luxuriant expression, minuets and country dances are taught; and I have even heard talk of cotillions coming in.[14]

It would therefore appear that the dances as taught by dancing masters to the peasantry and small farmer class were similar to the dance types taught by dancing masters in 'polite' society (see Chapter 2). Indeed, at the beginning of the nineteenth century, the Knight of Glin, of the Fitzgerald House of Desmond, Co. Limerick (near the border of North Kerry), ordered all the dancing masters within his territory to teach the Quadrille as it was performed in France and Portugal.[15] Therefore, as the King of England was performing Quadrilles in his majestic ballroom (see Chapter 2), and as the reigning dancing masters of the day were teaching Quadrilles and fashionable dances of the day to the gentry and upper classes in England, Scotland and Ireland, 'dancing masters of their own rank' in Kerry were also teaching Quadrilles and fashionable dances of the day to the labouring and small farmer class. However, although Quadrilles were being taught and danced by different sectors of Irish society, they would not have been taught or danced in the same way. They would have been adjusted and adapted by the different dancing masters to suit their respective patrons, the social contexts of their practice, the music accompaniment, the aesthetic requirements, and the dancing abilities of their patrons. In effect, different meanings were generated by the different contexts in which the dances were performed and by the diverse social groups who danced them.

Since most transactions in rural society in North Kerry were carried out in labour or in kind (see above), it is noteworthy that the peasantry paid the amount of 6d. a quarter (a significant fee at the time) for dance tuition for themselves and their families. They were not in a position to improve their lot financially, but through dance they endeavoured to improve their lot experientially and educationally in society. This is consistent with Norbert Elias's comment:

> as in the moulding of speech, so too in the moulding of other aspects of behaviour in society, social motivations, adaptations of behaviour to the models of influential circles, were by far the most important.[16]

Young remarked on dance being 'an absolute system of education' for the Irish peasantry; the system of education referred to related to the 'civilizing process'.

---

[14]   Ibid. p. 202.
[15]   Breathnach (1983), p. 28.
[16]   Elias (1994), p. 97.

This was an opinion that was not confined to Ireland. Concerning the Scottish peasantry of the same period, Dr Currie, Robert Burns's biographer, states:

> That dancing should also be very generally a part of the education of the Scottish peasantry, will surprise those … who reflect on the rigid spirit of Calvinism with which the nation is so deeply affected …. The winter is … the season when they acquire dancing …. They are taught to dance by persons generally of their own number, many of whom work at daily labour during the summer months. The school is usually a barn, and the arena for the performers is generally a clay floor.[17]

Young's reference to 'dancing masters of their own rank' is consistent with Burns's reference to 'persons generally of their own number'. Both authors distinguish between the French and Italian dancing masters familiar to the cities and larger towns of both countries, and the travelling or itinerant dancing masters of the rural townlands.

The educational value placed on dance at this time is further supported by the fact that dance was also taught in many of the hedge schools in Kerry.[18] Breathnach states that in some places in the county of Kerry, the teacher worked at one end of the school, which was generally a barn, while the dancing master taught his dances at the other end.[19] This is further illustrated by the painting *The Country Schoolmaster* by Nathaniel Grogan (died 1807), in which, written on a blackboard of a classroom, is the following inscription:

> Principia
> Legendi, Scribendi et Sallandi
> In hac Schola
> feliciter inculata
> They who to lustre will advance
> Must read and write and also dance.
> Descendens a veritice ad imum
> If your scull resist my pains
> Thro your breech I'll reach your brains.
> Proper pressure on the Middle
> Fits head for books and heels for Fiddle.[20]

---

[17]   Dr Currie in Flett and Flett (1985), p. 28.

[18]   Hedge schools: schools for the children of the peasantry that were often constructed by the side of a road – hence the name 'hedge school'. These schools were maintained by the peasantry themselves. See also Maxwell (1983), pp. 202 and 235. Also, for hedge schools in Kerry, see Gaughan (1973), pp. 223, 225–8 and 242–4.

[19]   Breathnach (1983), p. 23.

[20]   Gaughan (1973), p. 255.

Throughout this whole period, dance among the gentry and the rural labourers was observed as both a 'system of education' within the 'civilizing process' and a primary means of socializing within their respective classes. Also, as Ralph (1985) remarked, dance also assisted one to move with confidence within society, and indeed to buy the refinements of society (see Chapter 2). The emphasis placed on dance within the 'civilizing process' illustrated the value placed on control, order and regulation. This control and regulation of what were previously regarded as 'disorderly practices' would reconfigure dances and dancing in Ireland and, indeed, in Europe.[21] In Ireland, the Catholic Church would also play a part in the civilizing process based on issues of morality (see below and Chapters 5 and 6).

During the early decades of the nineteenth century, it would, therefore, appear that there were four categories of dancing masters to be found in Ireland. These categories were divided by class. One category of dancing master was the English, French or Italian dancing master (or those dancing masters who had trained with them), who taught the gentry and upper classes in the cities and larger towns of Ireland or in gentlemen's houses in rural areas (see Chapter 2); the patrons for these dancing masters were, for the most part, Protestant. A second category included the dancing master who Lenihan refers to as 'the fashionable terpsichorean professor' – the slightly pretentious dancing master who Gallicized his name and aped the manners and dress of his clients. A third category was the dancing master who was respectable enough to teach the young people of both the big houses and the ordinary tenants. A fourth category of dancing master was the one that Lenihan named 'the village hop merchant', who was on the lowest rung of the social ladder; he prepared young people for Sunday dances and dances at fairs.

All classes of dancing masters in Ireland prior to the Great Famine taught etiquette of the ballroom together with the fashionable dances of the day. Joan and Thomas Flett (1985) mention how teaching etiquette of the ballroom was common practice for all Scottish dancing teachers, whether the classes were held in a barn or an assembly room. And although the peasantry in both Scotland and Ireland might never enter a ballroom of the gentry, it did not stop them from imitating their behaviour, and indeed, their dance practices in their own manner to the accompaniment of their own indigenous dance music.

In his romantic, nostalgic and comic *Tales and Stories of the Irish Peasantry*, William Carleton (1845) provides an account of a number of characters peculiar and familiar to the Irish countryside prior to the 1845 famine. Carleton, an antiquarian and author, travelled much of Ireland, and based characters he wrote about on firsthand experience. In this book, Carleton states that each character sketch represents not one person, but a class. One of these sketches is based on a country dancing master named Dogherty.[22] Carleton knew this dancing master,

---

[21]   Reed (1998).

[22]   The sketch of William Carleton's Buckram-Back appeared first as 'The Country Dancing Master', *Irish Penny Journal*, vol. i, no. 9 (29 August 1840), pp. 69–72; later, it was published in Carleton (1845).

and named him Buckram-Back (a nickname) in his sketch. Carleton's sketch of Buckram-Back is the earliest written sketch of the character of the rural dancing master, providing comical and exaggerated details relating to his role, dress and tuition. According to Carleton, Buckram-Back had been a drummer in the army, where he learned to play the fiddle. However, not being cut out for the army, he abandoned it and became a dancing master. Buckram-Back apparently spoke with a rich Tipperary brogue, crossed with lofty, illegitimate English which he had picked up while away in the army.

In the sketch, Carleton emphasizes the social importance of dancing for the peasantry of rural Ireland throughout the eighteenth and nineteenth centuries. Of interest is Carleton's description of the dancing master. Carleton is emphatic that it is the dancing master 'of the old school' (prior to the Great Famine) he is concerned with, and not 'the poor degenerate creature of the present day, who, unless in some remote parts of the country, is scarcely worth description, and has little of the national character about him'.[23] According to Carleton, the dancing master of the old school was generally a bachelor. Robert Shelton Mackenzie (1855), however, mentions that dancing masters of the early decades of the nineteenth century around Fermoy, Co. Cork, were generally married, and some travelled with their wives.[24] Mackenzie further states:

> Such a being as a youthful dancing master, I never saw, I never heard of. They were invariably middle-aged men, at the youngest; but professors of 'the poetry of motion' who were about seventy, appeared the greatest favourites. It was dreaded, perhaps, that the attraction of youth and good dancing combined would be too much for the village beauties to resist. On the same system, in all probability, it was *a sine qua non* that the dancing master should be married.[25]

Generally, however, the itinerant dancing masters were bachelors and according to Carleton, they considered themselves to be superior in status to the itinerant musicians. This was shown by the way the dancing master dressed. He wore a castor, or Caroline hat, and an ornamental staff made of ebony, hickory, mahogany or some form of cane, to which was attached a silver head and a silk tassel. However, it was the dancing master's pumps and stockings that distinguished him from the fiddler. The dancing master seldom wore shoes. A characteristic feature of the dancing master of the old school was his general neatness. According to Carleton, the fiddler was more loved, the dancing master more respected. When travelling with a fiddle, the dancing master did his utmost not to be seen with it, for fear of being mistaken for a fiddler. However, he adds that these professions were changing, and 'neither the fiddler nor the dancing master possesses the fine

---

[23]   Ibid., p. 18.
[24]   Mackenzie (1855), p. 293.
[25]   Ibid.

mellow tints, nor that depth of colouring, which formerly brought them and their rich household associations home at once to the heart'.[26]

The dancing master described by Carleton, Buckram-Back, is of the 'shabby-genteel class' – a black second-hand coat, little pumps, little stockings, drab breaches, hat and gloves. His school of dance was open after the hours of labour, and was held in an uninhabited house. Together with tuition in the popular dances of the day, Buckram-Back also taught his pupils etiquette of the ballroom. He taught them how to enter a drawing room, how a gentleman should salute a lady, how a gentleman and lady should bow, the art of courtship as practised in Paris during the previous season, and how to write love letters and valentines. He taught them the five positions of the feet and the 15 attitudes,[27] and for those who were unable to identify their right foot from their left foot, Buckram-Back attached a *súgán*[28] and withe,[29] called a *gad*, to the dancers' feet. The *súgán* was attached to the right foot, while the *gad* was attached to the left.

In the eighteenth century, it was common to find a dancing master teaching fencing or cudgel-playing. According to Carleton: 'Fencing-schools … were nearly as common in these times as dancing schools, and it was not at all unusual for one man to teach both.'[30] As was discussed in Chapter 2, the association of dance with fencing was not uncommon among dancing masters within the European tradition. Together with teaching dance, fencing and etiquette of the ballroom, these itinerant rural dancing masters fulfilled other roles in society. Match-making was common among them, and often they negotiated between families as well as individuals.

Rivalry existed between dancing masters. Carleton refers to some solo step dances by name, such as 'The Jig Polthogue' and 'The College Hornpipe', and states how challenges between dancing masters often occurred at a distance, since they rarely met; each dancing master kept for the most part to his own circuit. These challenges took the form of the following: 'if he could not dance Jig Polthogue on the drum-head, he had better hould [*sic*] his tongue for ever,' or asking, 'if he [the rival dancing master] was the man to dance the Connaught Jockey upon the saddle of a blood-horse, and the animal at a three-quarter gallop'.[31]

Dancing masters had their own circuits. These circuits were known to the different dancing masters and the rural communities which they serviced. When a particular townland bordered two dancing masters' circuits, they would compete for the townland by step dancing against each other. The competition was assessed in terms of the quantity of step dances and the agility and fitness of the dancing master; the people assessed the competition. The dancing master who danced the longest won the competition and the right to teach in the townland.

---

[26] Carleton (1845), p. 20.

[27] Carleton does not supply information on the 15 attitudes.

[28] Straw rope.

[29] Flexible twig.

[30] Carleton (1845), p. 20.

[31] Ibid. pp. 27–8.

The Itinerant Dancing Masters of North Kerry

Múirín: Dancing Master

> Liam heard about Múirín. He was a dancing master after and a fiddler. He hadn't either dance or music first. He was travelling one day along the road from a neighbour's house and he fell asleep on the roadside near a fort. He had his crutches by his side. He was asleep when the voice called him and told him play a tune. He said he couldn't. The tune was 'ceol-sidhe' whatever kind of tune that is.
>
> 'Well', says the voice, 'try it.'
>
> He played it as if he was playing it all his life. I couldn't tell you where he got the fiddle. I suppose they gave it to him. After a bit he got up on his bottom and he was looking for his crutches to get up.
>
> The voice said, 'stand up.'
>
> 'I couldn't', says he, ''til I get my crutches.'
>
> 'Try it', says the voice.
>
> He did and he stood up.
>
> 'Well now', says the voice, 'play a tune and dance it.'
>
> He did and he was a great dancer after and a good fiddler too. His name was Tom Moore. He used go by Múirín. When they used speak of any good dancer they'd say, 'he was as good as Múirín'. Múirín lived at Fenit. He was an outlaw dancer you know.[32]

This myth was collected by Seosamh Ó Dálaigh from Muiris Seoighe in Killorglin, Co. Kerry, for the Irish Folklore Manuscript Collection in 1950. The myth is an example of a common folkloric belief that existed in Ireland prior to modernity: if an individual possessed great talents, particularly in music and dance, he or she had been given these gifts by *na sióga*[33] or *na daoine maithe*.[34] In the myth above, Múirín (pronounced 'Mooreen') was considered to have been given the gift of music and dance in this manner; this is indicative of his dancing and music skills.

---

[32]   The National Folklore Collection, University College Dublin, Manuscript no. 1169: 45. Muiris Seoighe, Killorglin, Co. Kerry. Collector Seosamh Ó Dálaigh (1950).

[33]   'The fairies'.

[34]   'The good people'.

In constructing a history of step dancing in North Kerry during the summers of 1983–86, this particular myth was not mentioned, but many dancers in the area orally traced back the dancing masters of North Kerry to Thomas Moore, or Múirín as he was referred to locally. Múirín is therefore the earliest known dancing master in the genealogical step dancing history of North Kerry, and is regarded as the 'father' of their dance.

According to the myth above, Múirín learned dance from the fairies, or *na sióga*. According to my informants in North Kerry, it is possible that Múirín learned step dancing from a dancing master named O'Kearin, an itinerant dancing master from Castlemaine in South Kerry.[35] According to the findings of O'Keeffe and O'Brien (1902 [1944]):

> In Kerry alone there were professors of Irish dance, whose fame was as wide, at least, as Ireland. The great O'Kearin, who flourished in the end of the eighteenth and beginning of the nineteenth century, was a man who, in a country like France of the seventeenth century, would have found his way into the history of the period as a man of genius. To O'Kearin was largely due the crystallization, if we may say so, of Irish dances; he it was who helped largely to reduce them to the order and uniformity they have attained, a uniformity which was very remarkable, and which was common to the four principal step dances.[36]

Breandán Breathnach (1977) concurs with this, and states:

> the great O'Kearin, a Kerry dancing master who flourished at the end of the eighteenth century … is reputed to have imparted to the basic step dances the order and style which obtained throughout the whole country.[37]

Other itinerant dancing masters, such as Tadhg Ruadh O'Scanlon from Glin, Co. Limerick, who came after O'Kearin, also contributed in shaping the step dance form into a system of precise stepping. Indeed, Tadhg Ruadh O'Scanlon was given a house and garden in Glin free of rent by the Knight of Glin. However, it is the itinerant dancing master Múirín who remains within the oral memory of the people of North Kerry. He was, by all accounts, a great dancer. This is illustrated in the following local anecdote:

---

[35]   Another itinerant dancing master from Castleisland, Co. Kerry, and who was also taught by O'Kearin was Reidy. Reidy taught dance to his son, Patrick Reidy, who later emigrated to London, where he taught for the London branch of the Gaelic League around the turn of the twentieth century; he was known as Professor Patrick D. Reidy, or Professor P.D. Reidy (see Chapter 5).

[36]   O'Keeffe and O'Brien (1902; 1944), p. 26. The four principal dances referred to are: Jig, Reel, Hornpipe and Hop Jig (also commonly known as the Slip Jig).

[37]   Breathnach (1977), p. 56.

> It was Moore brought it [the dancing]. I'd call it the Kerry style as I don't see it
> in any other county, that style …. Moore travelled a lot of the south of Ireland
> …. He came back here to North Kerry, and they used to say that he was gifted
> because one night at a circus, my father was there, and a fellow did tap-dancing,
> and the Ring Master, the MC, said that he would give a pound to any man that
> could dance the same dance, and Moore went out and did the tap-dancing. So he
> was gifted – no doubt in the world about it; and he got the pound.[38]

Thomas Moore, locally known as Múirín, was born in 1823. According to Paddy
White, one of the Molyneaux step dancers:

> When the land was divided by Cromwell, he gave an awful lot of property to
> a man by the name of Crosby … around Ballyheigue. Crosby came from Leix,
> Offaly, and Crosby brought three families from Leix, Offaly, with him by the
> names of Moore, Dowlings and Lawlors. They came from Leix, Offaly.[39]

According to this anecdote, Múirín (Thomas Moore) was a member of the Moore
family from Co. Offaly, who moved with the Crosby family to Kerry, where he
was taught step dancing. Although we cannot be certain where Múirín was born,
all sources agree that Múirín lived and worked as an itinerant dancing master in
the south of Ireland and also North Kerry. He died in Listowel on 27 March 1878.
On his death certificate, it states that he died while in a coma from exposure, in
Listowel Workhouse in North Kerry. He was aged 55. Under rank, profession,
occupation is written 'Dancing Master'. Múirín was buried in Cruaitín Bán, or
Teampaillín Bán as it is known today, a few miles from Listowel. This was a
common burial ground for all those who died in the local workhouse during and
immediately after the Great Famine. The fact that Múirín's profession and rank on
his death certificate was listed as 'Dancing Master' is significant. It implies that he
worked professionally as a dancing master.

Dance Contexts

From about the 1840s, Múirín travelled around the province of Munster, including
North Kerry, teaching the dances of the day: country dances, Quadrilles and step
dances. Buckley Shanahan, a fiddler, travelled with Múirín to play for his dance
schools; Múirín is also believed to have been a fiddler. Like many dancing masters
prior to the famine, Múirín was a bachelor. He taught in private houses and at
dance schools which he established at various rural locations for the duration of
six weeks, the dancing master's quarter. Those who learned to step dance were
called 'scholars', and of interest is that this same term was also used by Mr Lalauze

---

[38]   Paddy White, recorded interview. I thank Fr Pat Ahern for providing me with a
copy of this recording.
[39]   Ibid.

with reference to his dance pupils in his dance advertisement in *Dickson's Dublin Intelligence* on 8 March 1731 (see Chapter 2).[40] The dance schools were hosted either in barns or farmers' houses. These were places for tuition in dance and ballroom etiquette; venues for socializing for the youth and elderly of an area; and contexts where on occasions the dancing master fulfilled the role of match-maker. No fee was charged to attend the dance school, but the system of payment was that of a benefit night concert.

Mid-way through the six-week term, a benefit night concert was held for the dancing master. Similarly to the dance school, this took place in somebody's home, a barn, or any place that was suitable. Múirín's dance scholars aged 14 and upwards paid a contribution, usually a shilling or two, to Múirín at this event. There was no set fee; scholars paid what they could afford. This was also a social occasion, and amidst light refreshments, social dances such as Quadrilles and some country dances were danced. The scholars also exhibited some step dances which they had learned from Múirín, and Múirín also performed. The week after this event, if musicians were available to play for the dance school, another benefit night concert was held for the musicians. On this occasion, all contributions were given to the musicians. The format for this occasion was similar to the previous benefit night, and the same dances would be repeated.

Richard Ralph (1985) also mentions how the English dancing master John Weaver appeared at Ann Oldfield's Benefit Night on 6 July 1700, at Drury Lane, London. He danced an entry with Cottin and Miss Campion.[41] Also, Topham in the 1770s states:

> it is a custom in London for some of the principal dancing masters to have balls for their benefit, but here [Edinburgh, Scotland] it is a general thing from the one most in vogue to the humble teacher of a reel to the drone of the bag-pipe. Each has his ball and his public, or his two balls ... and endeavours to show his own excellence and skill as a master by the execution and performance of his scholars.[42]

Therefore, the benefit night system of payment or 'finishing balls'[43] of the dancing masters were characteristic methods of payment to dancing masters of different levels, not only in England and Scotland, but also in North Kerry.

Together with the dance school and the benefit night concerts, step dancing was performed at social events throughout the eighteenth and nineteenth centuries. These included weddings, Patterns, fairs, holy days, Sundays, St Stephen's Day, St Brighid's Eve, St John's Eve and the end of harvest. The dances performed

---

[40]   Since 'scholar' was the word used for those who learned to step dance with the itinerant dancing masters, I will use the word in this text in relation only to the itinerant dancing masters. Afterwards, 'pupil' or 'student' was the word used by teachers of step dance.

[41]   Ralph (1985), p. 8.

[42]   Emmerson (1972).

[43]   Ibid.

at these events would have been social dances such as Quadrilles and country dances, but step dancers would also have performed at them.

Throughout this period, the Catholic Church was perceived to be the natural leader of the peasantry in Ireland, and had since the seventeenth century condemned dance as immoral, and night-time dancing as sinful. The Catholic hierarchy abhorred the apparent unruly and obscene behaviour, together with excess drinking, which accompanied dancing at Patterns and pilgrimages. Consequently, parish priests were ordered to endeavour to oversee and control the behaviour of their flocks, and were empowered to excommunicate those who danced, or indeed played music. In the myth collected about Múirín above (p. 68), it stated that "He was an outlaw dancer". This may indicate that he was excommunicated by the Catholic Church or forbidden by the Catholic Church to teach dance in a particular area.

Being aware of the power of music and dance to assemble people together, some parish priests, in carrying out these orders, tried to stop music and dancing in their parishes. Some were fanatical on the subject, and it is reported that one parish priest, Fr John Casey (1769–1861), from Ballyheigue in North Kerry, went as far as banning dancing, together with music and card-playing, in his parish in Feriter. Consequently, a blind harper, Tom Kennedy, converted to Protestantism and joined the souper colony[44] at Ventry.[45]

In spite of these objections to dancing, Múirín continued to teach at his dance schools and performed on occasions. For instance, fairs were important contexts for step dancers and dancing masters. Fairs attracted people, and these events provided dancing masters with the opportunity to both display their dancing skills and to advertise and promote their profession. In North Kerry, fairs were held on particular days of the year in various places. In the oral history of the community of dancers of North Kerry, it is recalled that Múirín performed at Ballyduff Lamb Fair, which was held annually on 1 June.[46] He performed 'The Blackbird' set dance on a half-door placed on the street at Ballyduff Lamb Fair, and was accompanied by an uilleann piper named Thomas McCarthy, from Ballybunion (see Illustration 3.1).[47] McCarthy's life spanned three centuries, 1799–1904.[48] How Múirín performed 'The Blackbird' set dance and what exact movements he employed, we do not know. Today, there are different settings of 'The Blackbird' set dance which have been developed by different dancing masters, dancers and teachers over the years. It would be safe to say, however, that whatever Múirín

---

[44]   'Souper colony' referred to those who, having converted to Protestantism, were entitled to soup.

[45]   Breathnach (1983), p. 40.

[46]   John McCarthy (1985), ethnographic interview with the author.

[47]   Ibid.

[48]   See *Ros* (1978), p. 1. It is also of interest that McCarthy accompanied Patrick D. Reidy in 1868 when he gave a step dancing exhibition at the home of Dr Wren in North Kerry; see O'Neill (1973b).

Tom Carthy,   1904
Who lived to the wonderful age of 105. *d. c. 1910*
Irish Piper, Ballybunion, Co. Kerry.

Illustration 3.1   Thomas McCarthy, uilleann piper, Ballybunion, Co. Kerry *c.* 1875.
Postcard kindly given to me by Helen Leahy, Listowel, Co. Kerry

and other step dancers performed at fairs, it would have been observed by other dancing masters or step dancers who were present to witness these performances. Múirín's primary occupation was that of dancing master. He taught step dance, Quadrilles and country dances in his dance schools and private houses, and performed at social events of the agricultural communities he frequented. However, the advent of the Great Famine changed the whole social, cultural and economic fabric of Irish society.

The Great Famine and Step Dancing in North Kerry

According to William Wilde

> The failure of the potato crop, pestilence, famine, and a most unparalleled extent of emigration, together with bankrupt landlords, pauperized poor-laws, grinding officials, and decimating workhouses, have broken up the very foundations of social intercourse.[49]

> The old forms and customs, too, are becoming obliterated; the festivals are unobserved, and the rustic festivities neglected or forgotten; the bowlings, the

---

[49]   Ibid., pp. 9–10.

cakes and the prinkums (the peasants' balls and routs) do not often take place
when starvation and pestilence stalk over a country.[50]

The Great Famine of 1845–49 left Ireland exhausted. During 1845–51, the
population of Ireland fell from 8.5 million to 6.5 million. Itinerant dancing masters
who survived the Great Famine lost many of their patrons, thus depriving them of
both their livelihood and their status. Múirín was one of these dancing masters.
Many young people emigrated from rural communities, and consequently, the
demand for dance schools declined, as did a lot of other customary festivities;
private tuition also decreased. Thus, many dances, including step dances, were
lost, and the turmoil of the famine saw a time when there was a decline in the
composition, transmission and performance of step dance and other dances.

The Great Famine also affected the psyche of the Irish people. Numbed,
paralysed and starved, those who survived it and remained in Ireland were socially,
economically, psychologically and emotionally altered. Brendan Kennelly, a North
Kerry poet, conjures up these emotions, including shame, guilt and loss, in his poem
My Dark Fathers. He speaks of the famine, and how the 'green plant' – the potato
– was 'withered by an evil chance'. He reflects upon this historical Irish experience
and celebrates 'the darkness and the shame'. Kennelly speaks of the woman who
had once danced with such pride 'upon the sandy Kerry shore' because 'she loved
flute music', and who, as a consequence of the famine, 'heard the music dwindle
and forgot the dance'.[51] According to Declan Kiberd, the Great Famine produced in
Irish people 'a distrust of nature itself … since nature had failed them'.[52]

Survivors of the Great Famine suffered a temporary paralysis of mind and
body mixed with feelings of guilt and shame. As people tried to survive the
aftermath of the famine, dancing masters and their classes in ballroom etiquette
and dancing were no longer in demand. This left dancing masters without their
patrons and without their prior status. Although Múirín lived until 1878, his whole
livelihood had been threatened.. He died in Listowel Workhouse, and was buried
in a pauper's grave at Teampaillín Bán cemetery outside Listowel. As mentioned
in the myth above, 'When they used speak of any good dancer they'd say: "He
was as good as Múirín."' Under rank and profession, 'Dancing Master' – with its
Continental European associations – was the once honourable profession listed on
Múirín's death certificate.

Although people ceased to dance for a time, Múirín had succeeded in teaching
dance to others, including his successor in the genealogical history of step dancing
in North Kerry, Nedín Batt Walsh (see Illustration 3.2). Ballroom etiquette was no
longer taught but step dancing continued to be taught and performed.

Múirín was esteemed as a dancing master by the people of North Kerry and as
a contributor to the general education or 'civilizing process' of rural communities.

---

[50]   Wilde (1979), pp. 14–15.
[51]   Kennelly (2011).
[52]   Kiberd (2006), p. xiv.

Illustration 3.2   Nedín Batt Walsh and his wife, *c.* 1875. Used with permission of Siamsa Tíre

Step dancing was seen as a skill to be mastered: a skill that showed that individuals had control and mastery over their minds and bodies. This was contrary to the negative reputation that English colonizers generally spread about the Irish as 'uncivilized'. Thus in controlling their movements through step dancing, dancers were endeavouring to illustrate that they, like their colonizers, could also be controlled and 'civilized', but in an Irish way.

According to Doncha O Flartharta, 'Mooreen was the daddy of all the dancing masters. I heard he wouldn't break an egg under his feet.'[53] This lightness of foot and control of the feet and body when dancing was respected and valued in step dancers by the people of North Kerry. The controlled upper torso placed emphasis on this notion of control and uprightness, while the light stepping and soundings of the feet to traditional music accompaniment emphasized a visual and auditory domain. I suggest that the step dancing body with its soundings of the feet gave 'voice' to the colonized history and culture of the people. As the Irish language was 'silenced' throughout the nineteenth century by colonizers, the national school system, emigration, and by upper middle class Irish who wished to imitate

---

[53]   The National Folklore Collection, University College Dublin, Manuscript no. 1169: 314. Doncha Ó Flartharta. Collector: Seosamh Ó Dálaigh (1950).

the manners, worldview and language of the colonizers, step dancing continued to be developed further by dancers and itinerant dancing masters to provide a culturally expressive 'voice' for the peasantry (see also Chapter 4).

Nedín Batt Walsh: Dancing Master

Nedín Batt Walsh, Múirín's successor, was born *c.* 1835, in the townland of Tullamore (mid-way between Listowel and Ballylongford), in the parish of Ballydonohoe. His family, who were Catholic, possessed a small farm of 30 acres with a bog attached, which supplied them with turf for winter fuel. There were six children in the family. On marrying *c.* 1870, Nedín Batt Walsh inherited the farm and had a family of two sons and three daughters. Most of the small farmers in the area were self-sufficient, having a garden of potatoes and vegetables and fattening their own pigs. They also farmed some fowl – turkeys, hens, geese and ducks. However, for extra money during the winter, some small farmers drained land for the bigger landowners, together with quarrying stone and flags. Nedín Batt Walsh also taught dance to the rural communities to supplement his income, but he never taught in a full-time professional capacity, as had his predecessor, Múirín. Neither was Nedín Batt Walsh a bachelor, as many of the itinerant dancing masters before him had been. It is not known exactly when Nedín Batt Walsh commenced teaching dance, but he was doing so during the closing decades of the nineteenth century. It is not certain when Nedín Batt Walsh died, but local people estimate that he died *c.* 1901.[54]

Dance Schools

Nedín Batt Walsh held dance schools according to the dancing master's quarter and the benefit night system (see Map 3.1). These were held predominantly during the winter season when work on the farm was slack. He taught in houses in rural townlands which he had acquired for the purpose. For example, he taught in Lyons' cottage, Blanemore, in Tullamore. During the period of the dance school, Walsh taught beginners the basics of step dance from 5 p.m. to 6 p.m. and later in the evenings, sets (sets of Quadrilles) and Reels (Eight-Hand Reels) were danced by those in the wider community who attended. No fee was charged to attend the dance school, but like Múirín, the system of payment was that of a benefit night concert.

---

[54]   I would like to thank Tom Pattí Walsh, a relative of Nedín Batt Walsh, for supplying me with information on Nedín Batt Walsh.

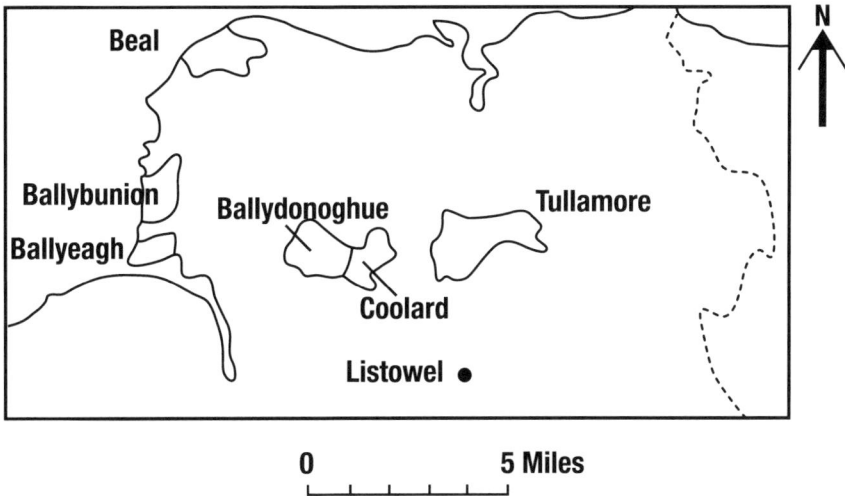

Map 3.1   Townlands in which Nedín Batt Walsh taught step dance

Nedín Batt Walsh often taught his step dance scholars without a musician, and would diddle or lilt the music himself. In these instances, one benefit night concert for Nedín Batt Walsh sufficed. Nedín Batt did not play an instrument as many of the earlier dancing masters had. Hence, Lyons' house is reputed to have been the first country house in the townland to have bought a gramophone for the dance school. Nedín Batt Walsh held dance schools in other rural areas too, such as Ballybunion, Coolard, Ballyeagh and Lisselton, at which the same system applied. Nedín Batt also taught in some national school buildings, but only with the permission of the local parish priests.

Nedín Batt Walsh's son, Edward Walsh, also taught at dance schools, but the most noted step dance scholar of Nedín Bat Walsh was Jeremiah Molyneaux, who learned at Walsh's school in Coolard, outside Listowel, and who in turn continued the tradition of the itinerant dancing masters in North Kerry. Jeremiah Molyneaux, the last itinerant dancing master of his type in the county, continued to teach step dancing according to the dancing master's quarter and the benefit night system in the rural areas of North Kerry and West Limerick. The elderly step dancers I encountered during the 1980s were some of Molyneaux's scholars. Their dances represent a step dance practice and knowledge that was developed over a 200-year period by both step dancing scholars and itinerant dancing masters of the area, including Múirín (Thomas Moore), Nedín Batt Walsh and Jeremiah Molyneaux.

Jeremiah Molyneaux: Dancing Master

> A small accurate hammer of a little man, who once held great sway in the North
> Kerry countryside.[55]

Jeremiah Molyneaux, or Jerry Munnix as he was locally known, was born at
Gunsborough Cross, about five miles from Listowel, *c.* 1881. He was the youngest
of a family of seven – four boys and three girls. Four of the family later emigrated
to America, where they died, but Jeremiah, his brother William and his sister Bridge
remained in Gunsborough. His father, William Molyneaux, was a blacksmith, and
owned a forge at Gunsborough Cross; his mother, Ellen Scanlon, was a dressmaker.[56]
Jeremiah Molyneaux attended the local national school at Coolard until he was 14
years of age, after which he apprenticed himself to his father in the forge.

Around the beginning of the twentieth century, Nedín Batt Walsh, the
itinerant dancing master, held dance schools in the area of Coolard, and Jeremiah
Molyneaux attended one (see above). It is not known for how long Molyneaux
was tutored, but he reputedly competed in a number of step dance competitions at
races and sports meetings and won several step dance championships as a teenager
(see also Chapter 6). In 1903, at the age of 20, Molyneaux held his first dance
school according to the dancing master's quarter and the benefit night system
(see above). After this first school, Molyneaux extended his teaching to include
other rural areas of North Kerry and West Limerick, where he set up other dance
schools, provided private tuition to children in their homes, and also taught in
national schools. Molyneaux practised his profession as an itinerant dancing
master during the early decades of the twentieth century, and in 1953, at the age
of 70, he terminated his dance schools. Afterwards, and until his death in 1965, he
taught the odd step to those who were interested. Molyneaux's patrons were for
the most part the agricultural community.

Molyneaux had a number of accomplishments. He was a dancing master, first
and foremost, and he was also a cobbler, a carpenter, and worked in the forge
with his father. He also bred canaries as a hobby. However, it was as a dancing
master that he is best known. He spent most of his life creating and teaching step
dance, and it is remembered within local memory how he made up step dances
using his fingers in lieu of feet, and how, when seated by the fire, he would create
choreographic patterns with a stick on the ashes in the fire. Jeremiah Molyneaux
held dance schools around the region of North Kerry, but during the summer
season, Lent, Advent or whenever he was unable to receive permission from the
Catholic priests to establish a dance school, he generally fell back on his other
trades, which he practised locally.

---

[55] Bryan MacMahon, the Listowel author and schoolmaster, speaking about
Molyneaux, personal communication.

[56] John Flavin (1983; cousin of Jeremiah Molyneaux), ethnographic interview with
the author.

Molyneaux was no more than five feet tall. He was a lean man with small, neat feet. It is said that he dressed better than the gentry at the time and had his clothes specially made by a tailor in Listowel named Jackie O' Connell, who had learned his trade in America. According to my informants, Molyneaux enjoyed the perceived exoticism associated with his Gallic surname. He married a woman from Lixnaw, North Kerry, when he was in his forties; her maiden name was Fuller. They had two children. The first child was born in Saint Catherine's Hospital, Tralee, but died there at birth. The second child died in early childhood. With the eventual break-up of his marriage, Molyneaux returned to live with his sister Bridge and brother William, in Gunsborough. This remained his home for the remainder of his life.

Molyneaux earned a good income from teaching dance, but supplemented this with his other local trades. He enjoyed drinking alcohol, on which he spent much of the money he earned. Jeremiah Molyneaux died of a coronary thrombosis in the District Hospital. Listowel, on 23 February 1965, and was buried in Gale Cemetery, outside Listowel, on the Ballybunion Road. Listed under rank, profession and occupation on Jeremiah Molyneaux's death certificate was 'Labourer', not 'Dancing Master' as was listed on Múirín's death certificate some ninety years earlier. On 17 June 1973, eight years after his death, a memorial headstone was erected at his grave with the inscription: 'Jeremiah Molyneaux, Dancing Master'. Bryan MacMahon, local author and schoolmaster, gave the oration at the unveiling of the memorial headstone, and stated that 'like a stone cast into a pool, his little influence moved out in widening rings to places he never expected'. Also on the headstone is written: 'I láthair Dé go rabhad ag rince.'[57]

Contexts for Learning Step Dancing from Jeremiah Molyneaux

The Molyneaux step dance scholars' perceptions and understandings of step dancing were shaped to a great extent by who taught them to dance, together with where, what and how they were taught. They were also shaped by where they would, or would not, perform; this was culturally determined (discussed in more detail in Chapter 4). Jeremiah Molyneaux taught step dancing in a number of institutions in North Kerry. These included his dance schools, private houses and national schools.

Molyneaux's Dance School

Molyneaux held his first dance school in the kitchen of his cottage home in Gunsborough, a few miles outside Listowel, in 1903. To facilitate the dance school, the rest of the Molyneaux family left the house and paid a visit to the

---

[57]   'In the presence of God may he be dancing.'

Moriarty family, their next-door neighbours. The school was held for the duration of six weeks – the dancing master's quarter. He taught for three evenings each week, and local musicians played at the dance school.[58]

Young and old attended Molyneaux's first school from the surrounding nearby areas. Step dance scholars were taught by Molyneaux in 'the room';[59] the remainder of the gathering socialized and entertained themselves in the kitchen by dancing sets (sets of Quadrilles) and Reels (Four- and Eight-Hand Reels). Those who did not know how to dance sets were taught by John Flavin, Molyneaux's cousin and next-door neighbour.

Dance schools attended by the agricultural community of North Kerry were for the most part held during the winter months, when work on farms was slack.[60] When the dance school ended, Molyneaux moved on to another area, where another dance school was established; permission had first to be obtained from the local Catholic parish priest. A dance school was arranged by word of mouth, and Molyneaux generally walked to it or was sometimes given a ride on a horse and trap.

The majority of Molyneaux's dance schools were in the townlands of North Kerry, but he also taught in Athea in West Limerick (see Map 3.2). His schools were generally held in the kitchen and 'the room' of a house or farmhouse for the six-week duration of the dance school. Food and lodging were also supplied to Molyneaux by the people of the house free of charge. In exchange, Molyneaux taught step dances to the children in the house.

Each evening of the dance school, most of the people in the vicinity, young and old, men and women, from the ages of 14 upwards, gathered in the kitchen of the house used for the dance school. Following the pattern of his first school (see above), step dance scholars were taught by Molyneaux separately in 'the room', while the remainder entertained themselves with dancing sets and Reels (Four-Hand and Eight-Hand Reels) in the kitchen. The step dances taught and choreographed by Molyneaux were based on the dance material he had learned from Nedín Batt Walsh, but which he further developed and extended. The scholars were generally the younger people in the community, from teenage years to age 30; most of the elderly population present would have learned or picked up some basic step dancing in their youth from dancing masters, neighbours or relatives, and were thus in a position to assess and to talk about step dancers and their performances.

---

[58]   Ned Moriarty was one of these musicians; the others I was unable to trace.

[59]   'The room' was generally the good room in the house where visitors were brought.

[60]   From ethnographic research, the following areas were identified as having held Molyneaux dance schools: Molyneaux's house, Coolard, 1903 onwards; Denis Curtin's house, Woodford, 1913; Behan's house, Woodford, 1913; Sheehan's house, Kilmore, 1926; Ballyduff; Causeway; Tullahennel; Mountcoal (years not known); David Barron's cottage, Clashmelcon, 1932; Greenville and Leith, 1935; Kilflynn; Astee, and Dromnacarra.

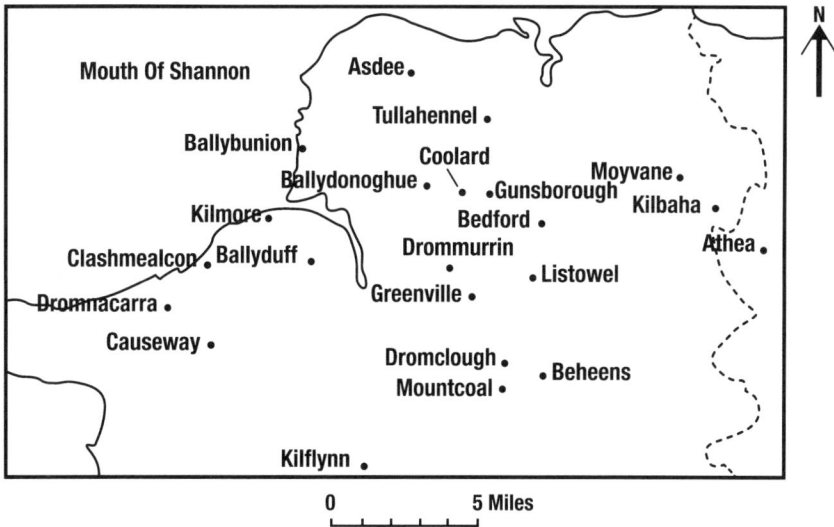

Map 3.2   Towns, villages and townlands where Jeremiah Molyneaux taught or held benefit nights

When a large crowd attended the dance school, Molyneaux used a 'floor manager' or a 'floorman'.[61] The floor manager had a number of functions. While Molyneaux was teaching the scholars in 'the room', the floor manager remained in the kitchen with those dancing sets and Reels and supervised the dancing on the floor. He oversaw the dances and ensured that everybody was given the opportunity to dance a set and a Reel, and that the same dancers were not monopolizing the dance space for the duration of the evening. He also supervised the behaviour of all present.[62]

For the duration of the dance school, Molyneaux used live music accompaniment. Whatever musicians could be gathered in the locality played for the sets and Reels in the kitchen, but Molyneaux taught step dancing to the scholars without a musician. Instead, he lilted or whistled an accompanying tune as he taught the step. No one particular musician accompanied him on his travels of North Kerry, which kept him away from his home for long periods, sometimes for as long as four years. The instrumental accompaniment in these dance schools differed from place to place, depending on the musicians who were available to play locally. The fiddle was commonly played, and sometimes Molyneaux succeeded in acquiring a melodeon player. The melodeon and fiddle were much favoured for dancing at that

---

[61]   John Flavin, a scholar and a cousin of Molyneaux, performed the role of floor manager in Molyneaux's dance schools held in his own home in Coolard. Paddy Cantillon, another dance scholar of Molyneaux's, also acted as floor manager for dance schools.

[62]   John Flavin (1983), ethnographic interview with the author.

time because they were regarded as strong instruments and could be heard above the sound of the dancers' feet.

In the step dance class, Molyneaux taught both male and female scholars the three basic step dance types: the Jig, Treble Reel and Hornpipe. According to the Molyneaux scholars, the step dance classes were progressive. In the first lesson, Molyneaux concentrated on the basic starting positions of the feet, which was a turnout of almost a 45-degree angle. He then illustrated how the upper body should be held upright and the arms held loosely at the sides of the body. According to the Molyneaux scholars, Molyneaux emphasized dance technique: feet and gestural positions, timing with the music, phrasing, rhythm, execution of steps according to the local aesthetic, upright posture and loose arms. These were the criteria upon which they were assessed, and how they assessed themselves and other step dancers. After this, he proceeded to teach the scholar the first dance step, 'The Rise and Grind' (also called 'The Rising Step'). This was a Light Jig performed percussively in Jig time ($\frac{6}{8}$ time), and for which he made up a rhyme which went as follows:

> *Out* with the right, and *out* with the left,
> *Out* with the right and *grind* with the left
> *Out* with the left, and *grind* with the right
> *Out* with the right, and *grind* with the left.[63]

This step of eight bars was then repeated symmetrically on the other side, starting on the left leg.

At the next lesson, if the scholar already knew the first Light Jig step, a second Light Jig step was taught, introducing some new element or motif. The system used by Molyneaux was a progressive one, and how long a scholar spent on Light Jigs depended on his or her ability. When Molyneaux thought that the scholar was ready, he then started on harder Jigs.

Treble Reels were taught after the Jigs. The first Treble Reel taught was the side-step, which commenced and also finished a Treble Reel performance. Two or three Treble Reel steps were then taught, which in performance were danced in between the two side-step renderings. The scholar was then ready to be introduced to the Hornpipe.

The first step of the Hornpipe taught was the Lead, and this was performed at the commencement and sometimes the completion of a Hornpipe performance; once this was mastered, Hornpipe steps were taught. Having taught the three basic dance types, Molyneaux then taught the traditional solo set dances – particular dances set to specific, but irregular, pieces of Jig or Hornpipe music. These were solo percussive dances, and were the exhibition pieces of the solo step dancer. They included 'The Blackbird', 'Saint Patrick's Day', 'The Job of Journeywork',

---

[63]   See Foley (1988b and 2012b) for Labanotated inventories of elements, cells, and popular motifs in Jigs, Treble Reels, and Hornpipes as danced by traditional step dancers in North Kerry. Step dances in these three categories are also provided in Labanotation.

'The Garden of Daisies' and 'The Humours of Bandon'; 'The Blackbird' was Molyneaux's favourite set dance.

All step dances taught by Molyneaux were percussive dances – that is, each movement was sounded out by the feet making contact with the floor, and all were performed in an earthy, close-to-the-floor style. Step dances were choreographed and performed to tune types of the same name, and similarly to the eight-bar structure in Irish traditional dance music, each step, was an independent compositional entity, consisting also of eight bars, and repeated symmetrically for a further eight bars.

Molyneaux taught steps visually, orally, aurally and by kinaesthetic imitation; nothing was ever written down or documented in any way. According to Paddy White:

> He would do it in parts for me. He wasn't very strict at all but he wouldn't have much patience if you weren't able to learn, to pick up the steps. He would be cranky when teaching. It was his way of living, you know.[64]

Molyneaux taught each step and its aesthetic a little at a time until gradually the whole eight-bar step was completed (see below).[65] The step had to be memorized and retained by the dancer as cognitive and corporeal knowledge. When teaching, Molyneaux used some terminology for specific motifs or movements, such as: batter, continuation grind, stamp and toe-fence.[66] This provided scholars with a common stock of movement terminology. I spoke about this with Sheila Lyons Bowler, one of Jeremiah Molyneaux's scholars:

C.F. When Jerry was teaching you to dance, can you remember specifically any of the terms that he used while he was teaching you?

S.L.B. Of course I can. The rock and the toe-fence. There was a single toe-fence and a double toe-fence. There was a front rock and a back rock; a drum – a single drum and a double drum, the toe, and lots of other steps. He had the raise, and click the heels. They have it in the modern stuff now which they do differently.[67]

Also, particular step dances were taught by Molyneaux according to gender, ability and Molyneaux's aesthetic judgement. Thus, each step dance or solo set dance had

---

[64] Paddy White, recorded interview, Siamsa Tíre Archive.

[65] Foley (1988b).

[66] See Foley (1988b; 2012b) for Labanotated inventories of movements.

[67] Sheila Lyons Bowler (1985), ethnographic interview with the author. The terms used here were used by the step dancers in North Kerry. They were also used by other step dancers and teachers. However, these terms are not universally used since, as a predominantly oral, aural, kinaesthetic and imitative dance practice, different teachers have used, and still do use, different terms. For instance, a batter is also known as a shuffle or a rally. See also Foley (1988b and 2012b).

numerous possible variations. Male scholars were generally given more complex movements in a step, while the steps of female scholars were generally made more graceful and simple. However, there were exceptions, and sometimes Molyneaux taught female scholars who had the ability the more difficult steps. Also, some female scholars imitated the more complex movements, since they regarded them as more challenging and flattering in performance.

Thus, within the Molyneaux system of step dance practice, step dances were individualized both by Molyneaux and the step dance scholars, giving them an implicit ownership (see also Chapter 4). Furthermore, Molyneaux privileged himself with retaining ownership of particular step dances for exhibition purposes. He did not teach these dances to anybody, although attempts were made by some of Molyneaux's scholars and others to get Molyneaux drunk in order to acquire a favourite step from him. Their strategy was that one scholar would try to get the first piece of the step from him; a second scholar would try to get the second piece, and so on until they would all between them have the step. They rarely succeeded. Molyneaux's choreographic skills at creating good steps were admired by the scholars of North Kerry; it is said locally that Molyneaux took many of these steps with him to the grave.

The fee for scholars attending the dance school was different from the fee for those who attended to dance sets and Reels socially. At the end of each week of the dance school, a dance was held on the Sunday evening in the same house where the dance school had been held. On this occasion, the scholars paid 1s. for one week's tuition, together with 4d. at the door for the owner of the house. Those who learned no step dances but who danced sets and Reels only paid 4d. on the Sunday evening to the owner of the house. On the Sunday evening, no step dances were taught. It was an evening of sets, half-sets, Reels and Jigs, and on occasion miscellaneous social dances, such as 'The Lady in the Boat', 'The Cat Rambled to the Child's Saucepan' and 'The Highland Fling'. Should the gathering be too big, then the assembly were given the choice of either sets and Hornpipe or Reels and Hornpipe, and all other dances were excluded.

When the dance school season was completed, Molyneaux held concerts in the spring to which he invited his best scholars from the surrounding regions. The prime function of these was to advertise the dance school for the following winter. A fee of approximately 2s. 6d. was charged at the door, with more from those who were able to afford it. Almost everybody from the surrounding areas attended. Molyneaux's scholars who were performing at these concerts did not pay at the door. Neither were they paid for performing. They gave a step dance exhibition, after which they received light refreshments. On these occasions, Molyneaux also gave a short step dance performance at the end of the evening.

When dance scholars finished with Jeremiah Molyneaux's dance school, they extended their repertoire of step dances by watching and learning from other step dancers in the area. Some of these included older scholars of Molyneaux, such as Liam Ó Duinín,[68] who taught in the region of North Kerry around the mid-1930s. However, Molyneaux was highly regarded, and enthusiastic scholars followed him to his other schools in different townlands to learn further material from him. Molyneaux sometimes returned to particular areas to hold further schools there. Scholars frequently took advantage of a chance encounter with Molyneaux on the road or in a neighbour's house to assist them with either filling in a bit of a step they had forgotten or perfecting a step.

The Benefit Night

Similarly to Múirín and Nedín Batt Walsh, Molyneaux also held benefit night concerts as the system of payment for himself and the musicians who had played for his dance schools (see above, and also Chapter 2). The venue for these was either the house in which the dance school had been held or a hall, if any was available in the vicinity. However, in Tullahennel, neither a house nor a hall were available, and Molyneaux held his benefit night concert in a grain barn. A hay float was used as the stage.[69] On these evenings, those who attended paid what they could afford at the door, which was any amount up to £1. However, more money was always contributed to 'The Dancing Master's Benefit', since it was believed that the dancing master had worked harder than the musicians. At a benefit night, Molyneaux collected approximately £20–30 at the door.

When held in a house, singers and musicians also performed between the step dance performances, and sets and Reels were danced by all the community to bring the evening to a close. However, when held in a hall, it was primarily scholars who performed their step dances to the accompaniment of local musicians. Sometimes, Molyneaux invited his better past scholars from nearby townlands to dance at these events. This assisted him in promoting his art and profession. One such benefit night concert was held in Ballydonohoe Hall in 1928. A bill advertising the event read: 'The Wonder Child Step Dancer'. People from as far away as Killarney (36 miles from Listowel) attended this concert to see Michael Carroll, then six years of age, perform solo. Since scholars in Molyneaux's schools of dance were generally teenagers and upwards, it was unusual to see a child perform step dance. Michael Carroll was taught privately by Molyneaux in Carroll's home. Michael, one of the Molyneaux step dancers I encountered in the field in 1983, performed a Treble

---

[68]   Liam Ó Duinín, a scholar of Molyneaux, registered as Liam Dineen, Kerry, with An Coimisiún in 1934; another Kerry teacher, Micheál Ó Sé, also joined. The previous year, other teachers from Kerry joined: Eileen Murphy, Killarney, and Brige Ní Shasnán. When Molyneaux's scholars wished to compete in registered competitions, they did so under Liam Ó Duinín or other registered teachers, since Molyneaux refused to become a registered teacher with the organization (see Chapters 5 and 6).

[69]   John Joe O'Donnell (1985), ethnographic interview with the author.

Reel and the first part of 'The Blackbird' set dance at the benefit night concert in 1928. At the end of the evening, Michael, together with an older step dancer in the area, Micky-Joe Sullivan, performed a Hornpipe together, while Molyneaux joined them on the left leg of the step for the completion.[70] Putting himself last kept the best for last. This climax generally brought the evening to a close.

The system of the dancing master's quarter and the benefit night system of payment had existed in North Kerry from the early decades of the nineteenth century, if not before, to the mid-twentieth century. Arthur Young mentions 'dancing masters of their own rank' existing in rural Ireland in 1776. Jeremiah Molyneaux represented the end of this system of dance tuition in North Kerry.

Private Houses

Together with dance schools, Molyneaux also taught in private houses to supplement his income. These classes were conducted at all times of the year, and it was for the most part the younger children in a household who were taught. Of the elderly step dancers I encountered in North Kerry, Sheila Lyons Bowler, aged 12 when she was taught by Molyneaux (see Illustration 3.3), Michael Carroll, taught at age six, and Liam Ó Duinín, taught at age 12, came under this category. Neither of them attended a dance school according to the benefit night system, but Molyneaux came to their homes. However, all performed at Molyneaux's benefit night concerts.

The fees for private tuition varied from pupil to pupil. According to Sheila Lyons Bowler, her mother paid £1 per class, which lasted from one to one and a half hours. Jigs, Treble Reels, Treble Slip Jigs and Hornpipes were taught, together with Molyneaux's solo set dances, such as 'The Blackbird', 'The Garden of Daisies', 'The Job of Journeywork', 'The Humours of Bandon' and 'Saint Patrick's Day'. Only one step or part of a solo set dance was taught at any one lesson. Sheila was the only one among the elderly step dancers I encountered who was taught Treble Slip Jigs. Today, the Slip Jig is predominantly regarded as a woman's dance with a light, graceful aesthetic, and is performed in light shoes or pumps. Interestingly, Sheila performed her Treble Slip Jigs with hard shoes which beat out the sound of the Slip Jig rhythm audibly. While this was in keeping with the visual, auditory and percussive nature of this dance tradition, it was unusual, both within Irish dance culture at the time and within the traditional step dance practice of North Kerry.

Michael Carroll was also taught in his home, and had free tuition. Molyneaux visited Carroll's house two or three times a week over a twelve-week period. Michael was taught one step on each visit. No fee was charged. Molyneaux made his own arrangements with the individual families in question, and tuition and fees he negotiated accordingly. Issues of reciprocity, family income and interpersonal relationships with families were all taken into account during this negotiation process.

---

[70]   Michael Carroll (1985), ethnographic interview with the author.

Illustration 3.3   Jeremiah Molyneaux and Sheila Lyons Bowler, Listowel, Co. Kerry, *c.* 1938. Used with permission of Bridie Trant, Listowel, Co. Kerry

Molyneaux, fond of drinking alcohol, sometimes included this as part of his trading. According to Liam Ó Duinín, Molyneaux gave him private classes in their public house in Ballyduff in exchange for pints of porter. Over the duration of one year, Liam learned Treble Reels, Jigs, Hornpipes and 'The Blackbird' set dance from Molyneaux; no money was exchanged.

National Schools

National schools were other venues where step dance was taught by Molyneaux. No step dancing was included in the national schools' curriculum at the time, and Molyneaux taught the children in the school who wished to learn after school hours. However, before Molyneaux could hold a dance class in a national school building, permission had first to be acquired from the local Catholic parish priest, who was often the manager of the school; this was often refused. Moreover, no dance classes were permitted to be taught in school buildings during Lent, Advent or during summer holidays.

The dance classes that Molyneaux succeeded in providing in the national schools were for short periods during the winter or spring; Molyneaux sometimes held his evening dance schools in these areas. Classes were taught once a week for one hour from 3 p.m. to 4 p.m; the fee was 4d. per pupil. The dances taught included step dancing, the Four-Hand Reel and the Three-Hand Reel. Generally, Molyneaux had no music for these dance classes, and he relied on his own lilting or whistling of dance tunes to accompany the dances. Should pupils wish to develop their step dancing skills further, then they learned from older dancers or Molyneaux was asked by the parents of these pupils to give private tuition in their respective homes. Alternatively, pupils waited until they were older and attended one of Molyneaux's dance schools as scholars.

When teaching in national schools, Molyneaux generally acquired board and lodgings from a local farmer near the school building, payment being in the form of dance tuition for the children of the house. For example, Molyneaux taught in Kilbaha National School around the spring of 1942 and stayed with the Hanrahan family.[71] Mr Hanrahan was also a step dancer in his younger days, and knew Molyneaux. Therefore, Hanrahan's farmhouse was used as a base or centre by Molyneaux for approximately six weeks. He walked from there to some nearby national schools to teach in the afternoons. These included, Kilbaha, Moyvane (three miles from Kilbaha) and Athea National School (two miles from Kilbaha, in Co. Limerick).

When teaching children in the hosting families, some male children in these houses were not inclined to learn dancing, and instead preferred to play Gaelic football. However, their fathers insisted on them learning step dance from Molyneaux, since they considered it to be an important social skill. All step dancers at the time were invited to parties, particularly the American Wakes, which were farewell evenings for those emigrating to America, and also to parties for those returning from America. Therefore, to be able to step dance implied that one's skill would be valued, and consequently in demand for all social gatherings. One of these children at the time stated:

> Molyneaux was a little bit eccentric. He was a dance teacher as far as my father was concerned. He was a guy to be looked up to as a dancer and as a teacher and he would have respected him as a teacher of dance. He was highly regarded as a teacher.

The dance school, the private houses, the national schools and some village halls were contexts for Molyneaux's step dance tuition. However, this tuition was allowed only at the discretion of the Catholic clergy.

Prevention of Dance Schools in North Kerry

Dance schools were held at the discretion of the local parish priests. During the six weeks of Lent and Advent, the Catholic clergy permitted no dance school to

---

[71]   Paudy Hanrahan (1985), ethnographic interview with the author.

be held in any parish in North Kerry. Neither were social dance events allowed to be held during this time in the country halls, which flourished during the 1920s and 1930s. In their place, concerts and travelling drama groups organized by the Gaelic Athletic Association[72] filled the parish halls.

The Gaelic Athletic Association's drama groups dominated the social life of the agricultural community during the weeks of Lent. With a branch of the organization in almost every townland, a programme was put together by each branch consisting of local musicians, dancers, singers and actors. The programme was generally a play with some music, singing, dancing and funny sketches. The drama groups toured individually to neighbouring halls during the six weeks of Lent, performing twice weekly in different areas. With the absence of dance schools and social dance events, these local dramas were well attended, and together with entertaining the rural communities, they supplied an important occasion for socializing for the scattered rural population.

The Role of Jeremiah Molyneaux, Itinerant Dancing Master in North Kerry

Step dancing was developed by itinerant dancing masters within the context of colonialism. Its outward manifestation was influenced by a Continental European aesthetic and kinetic vocabulary, an indigenous conceptualization of dance, and socio-cultural and historical circumstances. It was cultivated and taught in North Kerry by itinerant dancing masters, such as Múirín and Nedín Batt Walsh, and was regarded as an 'absolute system of education' within the civilizing process and an important and integral part of the social and cultural life of the region.

For fifty years (1903–53), Jeremiah Molyneaux continued the tradition of the itinerant dancing masters within the townlands of North Kerry and into West Limerick. He taught according to the dancing master's quarter and the benefit night system. For Molyneaux's scholars, Molyneaux's role was an important one. He transmitted step dance knowledge and skill which had roots in the eighteenth century and which had been developed and taught to their parents, grandparents, relatives and neighbours before them. Step dancing was valued. To the scholars, step dancing as taught by Molyneaux was 'dancing in the traditional way'. Through his choreographies, he culturally bridged the past and the present, and in transmitting this step dancing knowledge, he assisted his scholars in doing likewise. However, in his role as itinerant dancing master, Molyneaux also developed and extended this knowledge, as did his more experienced scholars. Molyneaux brought to the rural people of North Kerry, and particularly the step dance scholars, an artistic sensibility and aesthetic which historically referenced both the dance practices of the nobility in Continental Europe, England and Scotland, and indigenous Irish culture. Step dancing, as taught by Molyneaux, symbolically represented

---

[72] The Gaelic Athletic Association was founded in 1884 in Thurles, Co. Tipperary, to promote Irish sports, Gaelic football and hurling.

and embodied the history and culture of the people of North Kerry, and the step dancing body gave 'voice' to this history (see above).

Molyneaux was the last of a series of itinerant dancing masters of a region that took pride in its step dancers. Consequently, Molyneaux took his role as itinerant dancing master seriously. He spent much of his life in step dance, knew his own worth as a dancer and choreographer, and was aware of his place in the genealogical history of step dance in North Kerry. He was regarded by the people of North Kerry as the principal dance teacher of the region, and so much so that his name has become synonymous with its traditional step dance practice.

Life as an itinerant dancing master had its ups and downs. Molyneaux was respected as a dancing master, dancer and choreographer, and earned a good living from it. However, it was also an insecure and lonely profession. His dance schools and concerts were arranged by word of mouth and in an ad hoc manner. Since these schools took place, for the most part, during the winter period, he spent much of his life on the road during this time, spending long periods away from home. He was very dependent on the hospitality of the rural communities for his keep and transport.[73] Like the other itinerant dancing masters of North Kerry, he repaid in kind with dance tuition.

The dance schools and concerts, which Molyneaux established in different townlands, assisted both in structuring the lives of the scattered population of the region and in constructing a sense of community and identity; dance was an enabling tool for this construction. Through the transmission and regular practice of step dance and social dances of the day, these communities embodied and performed their shared cultural history, worldview and *habitus* (see Chapter 1). As Cohen states: 'People construct community symbolically, making it a resource and a repository of meaning and a referent of their identity.'[74]

Step dance had importance for the people of North Kerry. This importance was articulated by Bryan MacMahon, the Listowel schoolmaster and author, who in giving the oration at Liam Tarrant's funeral,[75] said the following:

> There is something in a step dancer that moves us most profoundly. I have often tried to analyse how it is that a step dancer moves us to the core of our being; I think I have chanced upon it. I have chanced upon it in a poem by Joseph Campbell when he pictures the step dancer as being from the waist up in love with death and from the waist down in love with life. He says 'The tall dancer dances with slow taken breath, in his feet lightening, and on his face death.' And again this could be truly applied to Liam Tarrant, one of the loveliest dancers we have ever known in a barony that is proud of its dancers. The dancer also

---

[73]   Apparently, Molyneaux once tried to learn to ride a bicycle, but unfortunately did not succeed. He therefore walked to his dance schools or was given a lift on a horse and trap by neighbours or other members of the agricultural community.

[74]   Cohen (1985), p. 118.

[75]   Liam Tarrant was a step dance scholar of Jeremiah Molyneaux. See p. 30.

plays a game of immortality, he defies gravity and returns again to it; and plays a mocking game with the ground, with the gravity that is forever pulling him down. So it is that the dancer is caught forever in our minds between time and eternity.[76]

The following poem illustrates how one step dance scholar of North Kerry is caught in the mind and heart of a North Kerry poet. The poet is Brendan Kennelly; the step dancer is Brendan's father.

I See You Dancing, Father
By Brendan Kennelly

No Sooner downstairs after the night's rest
And in the door
Than you started to dance a step
In the middle of the kitchen floor.

And as you danced
You whistled.
You made your own music
Always in tune with yourself.

Well, nearly always, anyway.
You're buried now
In Lislaughtin Abbey
And whenever I think of you

I go back beyond the old man
Mind and body broken
To find the unbroken man.
It is the moment before the dance begins,

Your lips are enjoying themselves
Whistling an air.
Whatever happens or cannot happen
In the time I have to spare
I see you dancing, father.[77]

---

[76] Bryan MacMahon, the oration at Liam Tarrant's funeral, 1974. I thank Fr Pat Ahern for providing me with a copy of the recording.

[77] Brendan Kennelly (2011), *The Essential Brendan Kennelly: Selected Poems with Live CD*, Newcastle upon Tyne: Bloodaxe Books; the poet kindly granted permission to reproduce the poem here. Permission to publish also received from Bloodaxe Books.

Chapter 4

Step Dancing as Embodied and Expressive Cultural Knowledge

In 1983, I met the Molyneaux step dancers for the first time. My role was as a collector of their step dances. However, my research interest gradually expanded to include their cultural knowledge of step dancing and the place of step dancing in their lives in North Kerry.

My own *habitus* was that of a trained Irish step dancer, having spent over ten years training in step dance. This included my having a strong sense of verticality and uprightness, a trained turnout of feet and an audience orientation. My *habitus* also consisted of an embodiment of particular dance types[1] and their respective movement patterns and aesthetics (see Chapters 5 and 6). This aesthetic included: good technique consisting of accurate foot positions and gestures; clearly articulated rhythms; accurate timing with the accompanying music; and erect posture. Other aesthetic characteristics included a sense of musicality, elevation, strength and grace when travelling in space.

When learning from the Molyneaux step dancers, I used my own body as a methodological research tool to embody, sense and store their dance knowledge. The Molyneaux step dancers danced in a different way to that in which I had been trained. The body was not held in the same erect posture; although erect, it appeared softer. Also, the arms were held loosely by the sides of the body. The gaze of the dancer was not always facing directly forward, sometimes it was looking towards the ground in a forward, low position. This gave a feeling of performing for oneself, and not for a formal audience. This internalized focus appeared to produce a sense of humility or modesty. Also, elevation was not part of the Molyneaux aesthetic. All step dances – Treble Reels, Jigs and Hornpipes – performed by the Molyneaux step dancers were hard-shoe dances, and were performed in a close-to-the-floor style. They all involved sounding out the rhythm of the music with one's feet. These characteristics directed the style of the performance.

In learning the step dances, I visually, aurally and kinaesthetically imitated the movements of each dancer. The process involved them breaking down each step into small units. As I imitated their movements, I felt gravity dictating this style of dancing. I was drawn to the ground with each beat of the accompanying music – generally, our own lilting voices. A step, a hop, a leap, a jump, a batter, a toe, a heel, a stamp, a drum, a toe-fence – all kept me, or brought me back in a fraction of

---

[1]   Reels, Jigs (Light Jigs, Single Jigs, Slip Jigs, Double Jigs) and Hornpipes. Solo set dances in Jig and Hornpipe time were also included.

a second, to the ground. The movement of each step dance was in the detail of the feet and the ankle. It was small, fast movements, where subtlety in the movement was highly valued. I was thinking, feeling and dancing these movement-sounds under my centre of weight. I was feeling and sensing these rhythmic movement patterns in order to understand how these movements fit the music, and also how they fit on my body. Some of the steps did not have regular phrases, so I found myself trying to fit the movements into particular points in the eight-bar musical structure, since this was a dance-music practice. There were very few travelling movements. Much of the movement happened under my centre of weight: time, rhythm and weight. My body felt grounded while I embodied and kinaesthetically practised this dance-music with my feet. The music flowed synchronically from the singing in my head through to my centre and to my feet. A step, some flow, grace; a correction, a joke, a repeat, a sense of achievement – all these contributed to my learning and embodying this dance-music practice, and all provided me with *hermeneutic arcs* of understanding of the Molyneaux step dance practice of North Kerry (see Chapter 1). I knew I could never understand step dancing in North Kerry as the Molyneaux step dancers understood it, since they had experienced it all their lives, but I could attempt to appreciate what it felt like to dance in this specific way. Furthermore, I believed that my embodiment of the dances would mediate the gap between me and the Molyneaux step dancers and it would also assist me in documenting, analysing and interpreting their dance. Finally, it might lead me to a new understanding of step dancing in North Kerry and the world that this dance form referenced.

All the Molyneaux step dance scholars I encountered during 1983–85 lived for the most part within a fifteen-mile radius of the town of Listowel and had lived in North Kerry for most of their lives.[2] They identified with the rural landscape and lifestyle of North Kerry, together with the nearby town of Listowel and the villages which they frequented for economic, commercial or social purposes. The majority of these dancers[3] were aged 55–90 and came from farming backgrounds (cattle and mixed tillage), all were Catholic, and all shared a common cultural and

---

[2]   The elderly step dancers of North Kerry I encountered and studied during 1983–86 were: Phil Cahill, Seán Cahill, Michael Carroll, Jack Dineen, Marie Finucane Kissane, John Flavin, Willie Goggin, Paudy Hanrahan, Jimmy Hartnett, Michael Kavanagh, Sheila Lyons Bowler, John McCarthy, Eileen Moriarty MacNamara, Jerry Nolan, John Joe O'Donnell, Willie O'Donnell, Liam Ó Duinín, Tom Joe O'Sullivan, Jack Stack and Michael Walsh (Mossie Walsh, another scholar of Jeremiah Molyneaux, was recorded in 2004). These dancers had learned step dance either directly from Jeremiah Molyneaux or from one of his scholars. Also, some of them learned steps from other teachers, such as Eddy Walsh, or from brothers, uncles, neighbours and fellow step dancers.

[3]   The word 'scholar' declined in usage in the region during the twentieth century; instead, the word 'pupil' was used more commonly; my use of these terms reflects the usage by the specific communities in question.

educational background. All the Molyneaux step dancers spoke English as their everyday language, and all would have had a good basic knowledge of Irish.

During the early decades of the twentieth century, dancing, together with music, football, handball, hunting and card-playing, were the main leisure-time activities for the rural people of North Kerry. Like most pre-modern societies, the social activities were local. Dance as a social activity, and an important integral part of North Kerry culture and society, assisted in shaping these dancers' sense of community, identity and place. This sense of community, in turn, was essential for the transmission of the indigenous performing arts of the community. Although social dancing dominated these social events, the Molyneaux step dancers frequently performed either solo or as part of a bigger group of step dancers. Some of these step dancers also performed in contexts specific to the performance of step dance (see below).

The step dances performed by the Molyneaux step dancers were embodied and expressive cultural knowledge. For the Molyneaux step dancers, the cultural knowledge they embodied and expressed consisted both of the more formal aspects of step dancing, which they generally learned from Molyneaux or other local step dancers, and contextual knowledge which related to where, when and how they would, or would not, perform step dance; this they learned through a process of enculturation.

The formal aspects of knowledge the Molyneaux step dancers embodied included knowing that the torso generally remained in its normal vertical, upright position, the arms remained loosely by the sides of the body, and the head either remained in its erect, forward-facing position, or was slightly lowered, with the dancer's gaze focused on the floor in front. This cultural practice placed emphasis on vertical control and uprightness in the dancer's upper body, thus placing a cultural value on standing tall, straight and upright. For the Molyneaux step dancers, however, the most important formal dance knowledge they embodied and performed was in the feet and legs, and consequently, it was these movements which carried most significance for them. These movements consisted of foot and leg movements such as weight transfers, batters, tips, toes, heels, stamps, cuts, jumps, hops, leaps, rocks, drums and toe-fences.[4] Particular combinations of these movements and others, structured within eight bars of the accompanying traditional dance music, produced a step, or step dance. These step dances were performed in a close-to-the-floor style with precision, discipline, neatness and rhythmic timing of the feet in dialogue with the accompanying music. Subtle detail of the feet and the manner in which the feet moved and flowed while dancing was characteristic of this dance practice. Leading with the ankle in some movements was considered important for stylistic purposes.

---

[4]   Foley (1988b; 2012b) for Labanotated inventories of elements, cells, and motifs in Treble Reels, Jigs and Hornpipes as performed by the Molyneaux step dancers. Steps in each category are also provided. A DVD accompanies the 2012b book.

When assessing or critiquing a performance, the Molyneaux step dancers looked for dance technique, rhythm, timing, phrasing, musicality, execution, posture, style and the quality of the choreography of the steps. In effect, they looked for an 'authenticity' or a step dance delivery that demonstrated this local dance knowledge. Molyneaux was their primary reference point. Molyneaux was the one against whom good step dancers were measured. This was also the case with Múirín in the nineteenth century (see Chapter 3).

Dance Music as Embodied Knowledge

The Molyneaux step dancers embodied and knew their step dances, and could identify and differentiate between the different step dances of their tradition. They corporeally and cognitively knew what differentiated a Treble Reel step from a Jig step and a Jig step from a Hornpipe step. And although the music was the primary indicator of what identified and differentiated these dance types, the combinations of specific foot movements into particular motifs also assisted in this differentiation. For example, they spoke of particular motifs named 'the full batter' in the Hornpipe and 'the continuation grind' in the Jig.[5]

Knowledge of traditional music, and particularly dancing to traditional music, was important to the Molyneaux step dancers. Rarely were step dances performed without traditional musical accompaniment, and in cases when musical instruments were not available, they performed to their own or others' whistling or lilting of the relevant dance-tune type. Therefore, knowledge was required of the structural, metrical and rhythmic interrelationship between step dance and the accompanying traditional dance music of Reels, Jigs and Hornpipes. This knowledge was embodied knowledge. The Molyneaux step dancers did not verbally articulate that the Reel was in $\frac{4}{4}$ time, or that the Jig was in $\frac{6}{8}$ time, but their bodies embodied, practised and performed this cultural knowledge. Also, they did not articulate that each step dance as a compositional unit was structured within eight bars of the accompanying music, but again they embodied this knowledge.

The Molyneaux step dancers knew the musical instrumentation which best suited their practice, together with their favourite tunes. They preferred to dance to instruments such as the fiddle, melodeon, flute, pipes and concertina, and their favourite Reel tunes to dance to were 'Miss McLeod's' and 'The Bedford Reel'. They also had favourite local musicians. These were experienced dance musicians who played at most of the local social dance events and were aware of dancers' favourite tunes and the dance aesthetic. They knew to play consistently steady music with a 'lift' and an energy that enticed the dancers up to dance. At social dance events (see below), these dancers and musicians related to each other in a dialogue fashion; they engaged in these dance-music moments and responded to each other's performances, often in the form of new variations or improvisations.

---

[5]   Foley (1988b and 2012b).

In keeping with Molyneaux's compositional technique, there was generally one foot sound to each note of the music. Step dancers therefore 'stepped' the music. All the traditional step dances choreographed, taught and performed by Molyneaux were conceptualized with the intention of expressing rhythmically, aurally and visually the dance tune that accompanied the dance. Therefore, ordinary everyday shoes were worn by the step dancers in North Kerry, allowing the feet to act as a percussive instrument while simultaneously producing interesting, visual, and choreographic foot and leg movements. In this way, each dancer beat out the rhythmic structure of the accompanying music, choreographically, rhythmically and sonically. In doing so, these step dancers embodied the sensibilities of both musician and dancer, providing rhythmical and visual expression of the music. Some of the step dancers played instruments, and most of the musicians did some social dancing, if not step dancing. Music and dance often co-existed within particular families, and younger family members informally 'picked up' music and dance material from older family members or from neighbours. Music and dance in North Kerry was thus integrated into the life of the community.

'Putting Style into It'

Together with embodying and knowing the formal aspects of the step dance practice, the general movement style was also important. The dancing body was centred and stable. A very limited, confined amount of space was used; the performer, for the most part, danced on the spot. According to the Molyneaux step dancers, a good traditional step dancer was capable of performing within four square feet. This placed an emphasis on a confined spatial aesthetic and the importance of small detailed rhythmic movements created with the feet in close contact with the floor. Neatness and lightness of foot was respected. Although individual step dancers sometimes travelled in performing their step dances for stylistic or performance purposes, the travelling movements were generally small, and usually in either a linear forward, backward or sideward direction. Sometimes, individual dancers might also dance in a small circle for stylistic purposes but the ability to move in a confined space was valued.

Knowledge of the Molyneaux step dance practice of North Kerry was also based on *how* one embodied the practice or performed it. The style and quality of performing these step dances were dependent on the personalities, musicality and dance competence of individual step dancers. The Molyneaux step dance style was a spatially confined, close-to-the-floor style of dance, and dancers moved individually within the confines of its practice. Some moved with ease and a sense of grace, while others moved vivaciously and rapidly, giving to the dance an abrupt and fiery appearance. With reference to Molyneaux's dance scholars, Jonathan Kelliher states:

they all add themselves to it – you can almost see the character. Paddy White is
soft spoken – he has his own little style, his own little bits; it's almost like a soft
easy way of dancing. Jack Lyons is more of a character. He'd kick the legs. It
[the dance] brings out a lot in them. The character becomes the dance.[6]

The manner of the performance was dependent upon the personality of the dancer,
but it was also dependent upon the context of its performance, which was either
a formal context such as a *feis* (see Chapter 5) or an informal social context (see
below).

From the Molyneaux perspective, a good step dancer moved accurately and
gracefully, with a strong sense of time, rhythm and music. Dancing in a 'wild'
manner was not admired. However, whatever the individual style of performance,
the personality, musicality and identity of the step dancer was embodied in the
dance and each dancer was expected to put something of himself, or herself, into
the dance. The Molyneaux step dancers referred to this as 'style', or 'putting
style into it', and they contributed to this sense of style by individually varying or
improvising step dances in performance.

A step dance performance, formal or informal, by the Molyneaux step dancers
consisted of those step dances which were considered by the step dancer in question
to be his or her best. Each step dancer had a particular repertoire of Treble Reels,
Jigs, Hornpipes and possibly solo set dances; much of this repertoire overlapped
with other Molyneaux step dancers. Therefore, when a performance was called
for, or when a step dancer spontaneously decided to give a performance at a social
event due to the desire to dance to good, lively music, each step dancer generally
had a particular ordering of two or three steps which, for the most part, had been
pre-arranged. Although step dancers generally continued to perform the same basic
steps over the years, each performance was coloured by varying, however slightly,
the basic movements of the steps. Once a step dance was varied, these variations
had the potential of being accepted into the step dance repertoire, thus extending
the number of possibilities to be selected for future performances by both the step
dancer who created the variation and those who observed it, liked it and recorded it in
their memories. However, these variations were themselves varied when observers
picked the variation up differently to the way it had originally been performed,
or when memory failed to recall the exact movements performed. Furthermore,
an observing step dancer might have selected only a particular movement from
a varied motif or phrase and subsequently constructed his or her own sequence
of movements around that specific movement. Consequently, what emerged was
a dance practice that was fluid, which illustrated how the people of North Kerry
valued individual expression and creativity within aesthetic parameters.

Variations in a step dance or a solo set dance also occurred for other reasons.
When teaching, Molyneaux altered and varied step dances to suit the gender and

---

[6]   Jonathan Kelliher (2004), Artistic Director of Siamsa Tíre, ethnographic interview
with the author.

the dance ability of his students (see Chapter 3). Phrases and motifs were taken from his step dance repertoire, and additional material was added to make up the eight-bar step dance and to suit individual step dancers' technical ability. Should particular scholars perform at his benefit night concerts, Molyneaux varied motifs or phrases in steps to impress the audience with his scholars, his teaching abilities and the virtuosity of the step dance art. Molyneaux held on to his best steps for himself, and taught diluted or simpler versions of them to his scholars.

In addition, step dancers had personal preferences for specific movements when personally varying a step dance, since they believed that they either performed these best, that they were more impressive, or they simply preferred them. Thus, during the Molyneaux step dancers' lifetimes, they experimented with bits of particular steps, changing and inserting movements they liked, or improvising during a performance. Sometimes, as mentioned above, step dancers varied steps in response to the accompanying music or musicians, or the familiarity and intimacy of a social context. Consequently, although there were common steps within the tradition, there were also variations and developments of steps which gave personal renderings, individual styles, and indeed an unspoken ownership of particular versions of step dances.

Step dancers also varied steps as a result of faulty memory. The Molyneaux step dancers did not like to leave a step unfinished. When they forgot a bit of a step while teaching or performing, they inserted other movement patterns to fit the structure of the accompanying music, thus creating and establishing personal variations of steps. Also, during a performance, old age sometimes prevented a step dancer from performing particularly swift movements, and again, modifications were made by the step dancer to adapt to these particular circumstances.

The ability to remember and to vary or improvise steps was therefore important to the Molyneaux step dancers. Competent step dancers knew the compositional structures of dance steps and had the ability to develop and vary them according to the aesthetic and performance criteria related to their step dance practice. Through desire, inventiveness and personal stylistic idiosyncrasies, they contributed to reinforcing, developing and shaping this region's step dance practice.

The Labanotated transcriptions at the end of this chapter are examples of how three of the Molyneaux step dancers, Michael Walsh, Jack Dineen and Willie Goggin, 'put style into' Molyneaux's Hornpipe Lead in one particular performance. As part of the Muckross House Collection, this performance took place in the Teach Siamsa, Finuge, North Kerry, in August 1983; the performance was video recorded.

This dance performance was structured as follows:

a. Hornpipe Lead (16 bars): 8 bars on the right leg and 8 bars on the left leg;
b. Hornpipe step performed by each dancer in turn (48 bars in total);
c. Hornpipe Lead repeated (16 bars).

On this occasion, the three step dancers hold hands in a line facing the camera as they dance the Hornpipe Lead step together (see Illustration 4.1). The Labanotated transcriptions illustrate how each dancer varies the Lead (a) between the right leg version and the left leg version, and also, on the repeat (c) at the end of the performance, the Lead is further varied, personally and interpersonally, by each dancer. The transcriptions illustrate these particular step dancers' renderings of the Lead and their preferences for specific movements, and also their individual interpretations of the accompanying Hornpipe music, 'The Home Ruler', played by myself on the tin whistle.[7] Other performances or other contexts may have produced different personal and interpersonal variations of this step dance performance.

Illustration 4.1   Molyneaux dancers: Michael Walsh, Jack Dineen and Willie Goggin with the author, Finuge, Co. Kerry, 1983. Used with permission of the Trustees of Muckross House (Killarney) Ltd

Masculine and Feminine Steps

One noticeable feature of traditional step dancing in North Kerry was that it was mostly a male prerogative; the majority of the step dancers were male. All the dancing masters in the genealogical step dance history of North Kerry were male itinerant dancing masters who spent much time teaching away from home. This reflected gender attitudes of the day in Ireland, which generally placed men in the public arena and women in the domestic arena. However, the fact that the dancing masters of North Kerry were male influenced the composition and transmission of step dance in the region.

Steps choreographed by Molyneaux were generally regarded as strong and masculine, particularly his more advanced steps, which included a lot of rhythmic and percussive detail consisting of drums, stamps, rolls and toe-fences (see Foley 1988b; 2012b). These were performed strongly and accurately by male dancers.

---

[7]   Audio-visual recordings of the Molyneaux step dancers are housed in Muckross House Library, Muckross House, Killarney. Together with the recordings, other step dances performed by other Molyneaux step dancers were documented and structurally analysed by me in my PhD thesis (Foley 1988b; 2012b). This structural analysis further illustrated the creative process at work through the documentation in Labanotation of personal and interpersonal variations of other step dances. Here, only one step dance, the Hornpipe Lead, is documented; see also Foley (2007c).

On the other hand, Molyneaux thought that too many of these movements were unbecoming for women, so they were kept to the minimum in women's more 'feminine' steps. Instead of drums and stamps, more batters, tips, toes, heels and cuts were inserted. However, as mentioned in Chapter 3, sometimes Molyneaux taught women who could master the more difficult steps, and some other women simply inserted the more 'masculine' movements themselves.

Molyneaux was regarded as a master at creating good, masculine steps, so much so that many male dancers walked miles to acquire one, or endeavoured to get Molyneaux drunk to acquire his most treasured ones, or indeed, stopped in the middle of their work to perfect one.

Cultural Significance of Steps

A genealogy of step dance history in North Kerry was maintained and developed not only through the performance of step dances, but also through storied steps within cultural memory. The step dancers told stories relating how they acquired a step and from whom, or maybe the context of performing or learning a step. Also, personalities from the past were remembered and recounted in stories. The following story about Jerry Nolan is an example of this. It was told to me by Seosamh Ó Bruadair, a friend of the Nolan family:

> Jerry, of course, was a great dancer, and Jerry liked to perfect his steps. He would often dance for me in his own kitchen if I was over there, and he liked to have the step just right. Jim [his son], would play a few tunes, and the father would dance. Now, long before I went to England, there was a parish priest in Ballybunion and two curates, and one of the curates was a Father MacDonnell. He was a small, wiry, hardy man; you might say in Irish, he was *beo, bríomhar, bathanta,* and he was the first to bring a Volkswagen around this district. Volkswagens had just come into Ireland, and like Father MacDonnell himself, the Volkswagen was a little *bríomhar, bathanta* car, too – it flew around. And at that time, it was the custom, and still is, for farmers to draw sand from the foreshore of Ballybunion with horses and carts at that time; now it is tractors and trailers. And one day, Father MacDonnell was coming from Listowel to Ballybunion. He met two horses with two loads of sand somewhere around Gale Cross – which would be about 3½ miles from Listowel, 6 from Ballybunion, and the horses having no guide, they kept to the centre of the road. Father MacDonnell had to pull well in with his Volkswagen to avoid them. The following Sunday, at Mass in Ballydonoghue, he gave this terrific sermon about meeting those horses with the load of sand and no guide, and how he had to pull into the dyke to allow the horses to pass. And, he said, about a quarter of a mile back the road, when the horses had passed him and he coming in the direction of Ballybunion, he met a young fellow … practising a Hornpipe in the middle of the road – a young scoundrel, a young blackguard. Well, it was years after that sermon that I found

out that the young fellow he had met on the road was no less than Jerry Nolan himself. It was a part of the tradition, when you look at it. If the horses or the priest had pulled into the dyke and the horses had top-sized, it could be put right. But if Jerry Nolan had not perfected the step, the step might be lost for ever. So that was a part of his tradition. People had plenty time for things like that, you see. Jerry Nolan's life was dancing – he lived for dancing and music.[8]

In North Kerry, fear of losing a step, particularly a valued one aesthetically speaking, was tied up with the respect people had for cultural knowledge and oral culture.. Step dancing was part of their cultural memory, history and identity. Step dancers therefore endeavoured to remember steps so that these steps, as cultural knowledge, could be passed on as part of their oral culture. This respect for tradition and cultural knowledge was not confined to step dancing. Tomás Ó Criomhthain in *An tOileánach*,[9] the autobiographical account of his life on the Great Blasket Island, off the West Kerry coast, tells of the poet Dunleavy, who one day interrupted and stopped the young Tomás:

'Well,' says the poet ... 'isn't it a pity for you to be cutting turf on such a hot day. Sit down a bit, the day is long and it'll be cool in the afternoon.' I didn't care much for what he had to say, but I was rather shy of refusing to sit down with him. Besides, I knew that if the poet had anything against me, he would make a satire on me that would be very unpleasant, especially as I was just about coming out in the world. So I sat down beside him. 'Now,' says the poet, 'perhaps you haven't got the first poem I ever made.'... Would you believe it – he started to recite every word of it, lying there stretched out on the flat of his back! ... I praised the poem to the skies, though it was vexing me sorely from another point of view – keeping me back from the profitable work that I had promised myself that morning should be done. The poet had put a stop to that with his babbling. 'The poem will be lost,' says he, 'if somebody doesn't pick it up. Have you anything in your pocket that you could write it down with?' ... It wasn't to oblige the poet that I fished out my pencil and some paper I had in my pocket, but for fear that he would turn the rough side of his tongue to me. I set about scribbling down the words as they came out of his mouth. It wasn't in the usual spelling that I wrote them, for I hadn't enough practice in it in those days. I wasn't too happy then; and no wonder: a man who had a sensible bit of work on hand in the morning and now it was laid aside for a pointless job! When once he'd opened his mouth, the poet had a jut on his jaw to send his voice out. I scribbled away at the words as best I could after a fashion that kept the poem more or less in my memory, and, besides, if a word should drop out here and

---

[8]   Seosamh Ó Bruadair (1985), ethnographic interview with the author.
[9]   'The Islander'.

there, the guide wasn't far from me, ready and willing to waste a bit of his life explaining it to me, even if the plough-team were waiting for him in the furrow.[10]

Step dancers, singers, musicians and Gaelic poets in Ireland spent much time preserving in their minds and bodies their artistic products and skills. The steps, poems, songs and tunes were integral to their cultural memory, history and identity. They believed that what was worth knowing was worth remembering. Also, they believed that knowledge could not be taken away from them as their land had been taken away from them and their ancestors under colonial rule. Step dancing was valued as part of their historical and cultural knowledge, and was therefore considered to be worth embodying, knowing, remembering and transmitting. What they considered to be good steps were treasured.

This may have been a reason why Molyneaux visited the Listowel writer and schoolteacher Bryan MacMahon some time before he died. MacMahon thought at the time that the visit was a social one. However, on reflection after Molyneaux's death, MacMahon believed that Molyneaux had come for him to write something down about him and his dances.[11] This would suggest that Molyneaux was very aware of the cultural knowledge that he had embodied, together with his own significance and place within the genealogical history of itinerant dancing masters in North Kerry.

A rivalry of memory and display of repertoire existed among step dancers in North Kerry, and Molyneaux was no exception. When speaking of Molyneaux and Jerry Nolan, Fr Pat Ahern, Founding Artistic Director of Siamsa Tíre, the National Folk Theatre of Ireland, had the following anecdote to tell:

> There's a story about the two of them, Molyneaux and himself [Jerry Nolan]. They had a contest one night, at the pub in Moyvane. Jerry was much the younger man ... they did it step-for-step, the old style. I'd dance a step; you'd dance a step, maybe better, and I'd dance another, maybe yet better; and poor Molyneaux conked out; he had to be revived. Jerry was still flying, as the younger man, more fit .... There was also a kind of a jealously there, too ... they prided in their own steps.[12]

In North Kerry, there was a hierarchy of steps. There were steps that most of the step dancers knew and which bonded them together and located and identified them as a specific dance community, and there were steps that very few knew. These steps were either retained by individuals as 'treasured' steps, or they were too difficult for most step dancers to perform. Molyneaux, for example, retained steps as 'treasured' steps for himself. This was partly due to the fact that his

---

[10] Tomás O'Crohan, *The Islandman* (1955), pp. 86–7 (pp. 92–3 in the original Irish). Published here by permission of Oxford University Press.

[11] Bryan MacMahon, personal communication.

[12] Fr Pat Ahern (2003), ethnographic interview with the author.

profession as dancing master relied on his reputation as being the best, and indeed that he had further knowledge to teach his scholars. Due to his 'ownership' of these steps, he was held in an esteemed position in the eyes of the step dancing community. It was said with pride of Molyneaux that he went to his grave with many steps that no other step dancer knew. Ownership of good steps was therefore analogous to having knowledge, skill and cultural capital. In North Kerry, this cultural knowledge was valued and respected by the rural people of the region.

Steps were also spoken about in great detail. Dancers spoke about beautiful steps, similarities in steps, variations in steps, how a step was or was not performed, and the movements that comprised a step. Good steps were regarded as being similar to poetry in their craftsmanship, mapping the acoustic space through visual and sonic interpretations of the music. Some of the Molyneaux step dancers used to say that when Molyneaux danced, it was as if he was writing with his feet.

This metaphor used by some of the North Kerry step dancers to describe the movement style of their dancing master informed to a degree the manner and style of its performance. The beauty of the feet in motion was what these dancers aimed to perfect through all the subtle details of the art. Fr Pat Ahern had the following to say:

> it was the beauty of the movement of the feet, it wasn't the rapid fire stuff you have in modern traditional dance. There were batters and so on, of course, but it was the way the feet interplayed with each other, if you like, and the movement of feet on the floor. Somebody used to say of Molyneaux that 'when he danced it was like writing on the floor' … it was almost like writing about your statement with your feet, do you know. But, I remember Jerry [Nolan]. Jerry had that very well; he had beautiful, beautiful movements of his feet. For Jerry, that dance was everything. It was his life, really. He became fanatically interested in it. I often think it was like a cult with him. And those people like Lyons and White, it was almost like a cult with them, do you know, the way that people would meet and talk about football, and matches, and great players and great catches, and the great scores, well, that was the kind of way that they talked about the dance, do you know, it was like … he would talk about such a one doing such a step, and how he picked it up, and 'he usen't do that now, he used to finish it differently, and this was the finish that he had'. And he would stand in the floor and show me the finish, 'but I had a different finish,' and he would show me the different finish, do you know, that sort of detail; and the pride in that. Being able to kind of boast about a step, and have a pride in a step, just because it was the step it was, you know, and for no other reason.[13]

The Molyneaux step dancers knew from whom they learned a step and recognized step dancers by particular renderings of steps. They took pride in their dance genealogy, knowledge and history. Steps made statements about dancers, and

---

[13]   Ibid.

in particular statements about who they were and where they came from. Steps embodied and represented their place, history and cultural identity. In the words of Dudley Patterson:

> Wisdom sits in places. It's like water that never dries up. You need to drink water to stay alive, don't you? Well, you also need to drink from places. You must remember everything about them. You must learn their names. You must remember what happened at them long ago. You must think about it and keep on thinking about it. Then your mind will become smoother and smoother ....[14]

Wisdom and knowledge of the Molyneaux step dance practice sat in North Kerry. It sat amidst the rural landscape and townlands of North Kerry where it had been cultivated and developed by a series of itinerant dancing masters for their predominantly farming patrons. These dancing masters, including Múirín, Nedín Batt Walsh and Molyneaux, contributed to the overall style of what is today called 'the old tradition' or 'the Munnix style': a style of earthiness; one that is close to the floor and which speaks from this place, North Kerry.

The earth and the soil were significant to these step dancers, and particularly so since they were or had been farming people. Land was their way of life, and they took pride in their holdings, especially since land had been denied to their ancestors during the colonial period. Land and place were historically and culturally significant. Since step dance in Ireland emerged and developed within a rural, agricultural context; since the Molyneaux dance steps were performed in an earthy, close-to-the-floor manner, I like to interpret this dance practice as a dance of the soil, with each dancer metaphorically 'writing' his or her signature on the soil of their place, North Kerry.

For the Molyneaux step dancers, dancing and talking about dancing contributed to their feeling of being alive and being alive to their local environment, culture and history. Dance contributed to their quality of life, and when dancing, they danced from their place, North Kerry. They knew the history, geography and ecology of the area. They knew their people and who was related to whom. They knew who taught them each step, or from whom they picked up a step. They remembered where they were when they learned a step, therefore placing the dance and dancing the place. They recognized people by the steps they danced, and they knew their history of dancing masters and respected them as the cultivators of their dance. Steps were of great metaphorical, compositional, socio-cultural and historical significance. They represented, in a sense, *meon na ndaoine*[15] of past and present generations, and like a poem, a tune or a song, each step was a representation of, and a link to, their cultural and historical past. The step dances or steps of North Kerry did not exist in a vacuum. They existed as an integral part of the culture, history and way of life of the rural people of North Kerry. Steps were therefore

---

[14] Feld and Basso (1996), p. 70.

[15] The mind or ethos of the people.

significant, and were memorized corporeally, kinaesthetically and cognitively within particular musico-rhythmic structures.

The Molyneaux step dancers of North Kerry formed a particular *habitus* which was iconic of rural North Kerry, and the step dancers who invested the time in perfecting their steps did so knowing that their step dances were part of the history and wisdom of that place, and each performance embodied and restated that history and wisdom, and their place within it. Being an agricultural people with a Christian ethos and worldview, this *habitus* of dance expressed their common rural values, beliefs and history: a history that had assimilated and adapted foreign as well as indigenous influences (see Chapters 2 and 3). The Molyneaux step dancers embodied this history. It was their way of *being* in the world, and their way of expressing who they were and where they came from.

Those dancers who excelled at it were perceived as heroes in their villages and townlands. Molyneaux was one such hero, as were Paddy White, Jack Lyons, Liam Tarrant and Jerry Nolan; their names were synonymous with their art:

> F. Pat.   And Jerry [Nolan] was a hero in his local village, you know, as a
>   dancer. He was a wonderful footballer as well, by the way. He was
>   regarded as a great footballer in the local team, but I'd say they loved
>   him more for his dance. The whole village took a pride in it.
>
> C.F.   Was he unique, do you think?
>
> F. Pat.   I think he certainly was in his village. There was nobody like Jerry.
>   And I can remember concerts at which Jerry would be a feature item,
>   and he was a bit of a showman as well. He would go up onto the stage,
>   and he would become a different person the minute he got on to that
>   stage. His face would go into a kind of a serious concentration; he
>   would stand ready to leap out, it was almost like a cat ready to spring
>   out on to the stage, you know. He would always come in two bars or so
>   before the end, you know, when the musician plays the introduction,
>   well just about the last two bars, Jerry would come in, and he'd end off
>   a little preamble. But he would leap in from the wings and leap onto the
>   middle of the stage and do this little step. And when Jerry would leap,
>   there would be a cheer from the hall. It was like … I often compared
>   it before to a football hero, Mick O Connell, coming onto the field to
>   play. It was that kind of cheer. He was a hero in the village.[16]

Dance Contexts as Cultural Knowledge

Together with embodying the formal knowledge required to be a step dancer, the Molyneaux step dancers of North Kerry also possessed contextual knowledge which related to where, when and how they would, or would not, perform step

---

[16]   Fr Pat Ahern (2003), ethnographic interview with the author.

dance; this they learned through the process of enculturation. According to Fr Pat Ahern, for the people of North Kerry, step dancing was:

> part of what they were as much as saving the hay, or feeding the cattle, or looking after the young calves. It was something they did as part of the rounds of their lives as much as going to Listowel Races was part of it. It wasn't something they did like, you went away and you took music lessons and dancing lessons as they do now. It was something that you imbibed as you went on, taken for granted almost, as part of what you did. Every second person did a bit of step dancing, you know.[17]

This cultural knowledge relating to where, when and how one would, or would not, perform these step dances was important for the Molyneaux step dancers, and it allowed them to practise step dancing appropriately within their society. The dance contexts and the social institutions which supported and fostered dance were named and located in particular places and dwellings, and these constituted part of the conceptual and cultural geography of the people of North Kerry. To quote Keith Basso, following Heidegger:

> dwelling is said to consist in the multiple 'lived relationships' that people maintain with places; for it is solely by virtue of these relationships that space acquires meaning.[18]

Dance highlighted these places and the people associated with them. Dance contexts and events thus provided sites for social interaction where 'lived relationships' were maintained and shaped in a social, cultural and meaningful way. These dance contexts were also framed temporal spaces which gave structure to the lives of these people and which provided sites for the construction, maintenance and negotiation of community, place and cultural identity.

For the Molyneaux step dancers, these spaces took the form of both informal, social contexts such as rambling houses, raffles and the Wren, and formal contexts for step dance performances such as benefit night concerts, spring concerts and *feiseanna*. Other dance contexts such as the summer-time crossroad dances and platform dances were not occasions when the Molyneaux step dancers performed step dance. Here, the Molyneaux step dancers danced social dances such as sets and Eight-Hand Reels, but they did not dance solo step dances.

---

[17]   Ibid.

[18]   Feld and Basso (1996), p. 54.

Rambling Houses

During the latter part of the nineteenth century and the early decades of the twentieth century, rambling houses were the principal informal venues for socializing among the agricultural communities in North Kerry. These rambling houses were named after the surname of the family living in the house, and these named places and their associations informed the cultural knowledge of those who participated at these events. Rambling houses were held throughout the year, but predominantly during the darker winter months, from November to February, when work on farms was slack. In these houses, the mode of socializing – card-playing, singing, music, dancing and story-telling – varied in accordance with the actual venue, the locality and those people of the community who gathered there. However, in the event of a dance school being held in an area, the dance school took priority, since most of the community attended it.

The following is an account of one such rambling house:

> Oh, every night, actually, the game of cards would be. There would be certain houses, you see, and they would say, 'Where are you going rambling tonight?' That was how it got the name. Well, Carroll's, Tom Carroll's – he's dead now – that was the house where we used to all gather. There would be ten or twelve of us altogether there, some playing cards, and more sitting by the fire. And there would be someone with an accordion and there might be a couple of Reels and Polkas danced, and there was more around that time that might be able to do the bit of step dancing as well, and we'd have a few steps.[19]

Some rambling houses were known for their music and dancing. This was due to the fact that members of these households together with local neighbours frequently played there. Dances were held in these rambling houses two or three evenings a week, with Sunday afternoons being the most popular. Local labourers and the general youth of the vicinity between the ages of 16 and 19, and numbering anything up to thirty, socialized and entertained themselves at the rambling houses. Sets and Reels were danced, and step dancers, singers and musicians performed. Sometimes ghost stories or emigrant stories were also told in between the dances.

Other rambling houses focused more on story-telling and singing. In some localities, there were mostly earthen floors in the houses at that time, and consequently, there was no dancing as these floors were not suitable. Time was spent talking, telling stories and singing. Only men, young and old, attended these rambling houses, which provided a venue for socializing, entertaining and opportunities for male bonding.

Rambling houses were not confined to rural regions. In the town of Listowel, Bryan MacMahon, the local writer and schoolmaster, frequented a rambling house. This was held in the kitchen of the local blacksmith, Dan Bunyan, and

---

[19]   John McCarthy (1985), ethnographic interview with the author.

Bryan MacMahon perceived this institution as an important educational centre of local folklore:

> There was a strong seam of folklore in the locality. The people did not call it folklore, they just thought it was something ordinary and not in the least to be wondered at. This seam was there for me to explore every night in the kitchen of the local blacksmith, Dan Bunyan. That gathering constituted another kind of school where I learnt but rarely taught. With the doors of the forge open by day, people were coming and going on various errands and leaving their news behind them. The smell of burning hooves, the rarest of smells in Ireland today, prevailed in the neighbourhood of the forge. By long tradition, the smithy has been a centre of revolution. In the last century copies of The Nation were read out by a literate man seated upon the anvil .... In the 'rambling-house' at night, especially in winter, twenty to more men gathered and began discussing politics, telling tales, and singing songs. No song emanated from outside Ireland was allowed. *Piseogs*[20] and salmon were topics regularly under discussion .... It was in this atmosphere I spent my nights for almost twenty years. At first I was by far the youngest person present.[21]

These rambling houses fulfilled a vital social function for the communities of North Kerry, and deepened their sense of belonging by bonding them together as a community. Some members found marriage partners at these social events. Local, national and international news were discussed, and through music, dance, song, stories or card-playing, these venues, in constructing a sense of community, allowed for music, dance, song and stories to be transmitted back to the community. Indeed, through these different actions, a sense of community was embodied and experienced, and dance was the perfect vehicle for making this sense of community *felt*.

Mutual Aid, Raffles, Gambles and Turkey Dances

Dance contexts were often determined by the seasons. According to Brody, 'Each part of the year demonstrated the basic continuity of the farm and its family, just as each activity involved the economic basis of the society.'[22] In North Kerry, dance involved the social and economic basis of society there.

---

[20]   Superstitious lore.

[21]   MacMahon (1992), pp. 23–24. My paternal grandfather, Eugene Foley, was a blacksmith in Inchinaugh, Glenville, Co. Cork. My paternal grandmother, Abbey Lane, was a concertina and fiddle player, and their home was also a rambling house where my father, Patrick Foley, among others, played traditional music for those who gathered there for social reasons. A lot of dancing, singing and story-telling also took place there (see also Chapter 1).

[22]   Brody (1982), p. 26.

Mutual aid is to be found in most peasant societies, and in North Kerry neighbours assisted local farmers at particular times of the year. Harvest, hay making, the digging of the potato crop, cutting the turf and the threshing of the corn were times of the agricultural year when the farmer was at his busiest, and many farmers in North Kerry received assistance from neighbours, old and young. The local Irish term for this was the *meitheal*.

To mark the end of a day's work or the completion of these co-operative occasions, the farmer receiving assistance provided food, drink and an evening of music, song and dance for the community. It was not only the workers who went to these dances. Others in the vicinity who heard that a dance was being held in a particular farmer's house also participated in the evening's entertainments. Food and drink were first given to the workers in the kitchen of the farmhouse, then the floor was cleared for a dance. Furniture was moved back to the walls, providing sufficient space for the dancing. The dances performed were again those which involved the whole community – sets and Reels. However, at the end of the evening, the step dancers among those gathered performed together either a Hornpipe or Treble Reel. According to Hugh Brody, this feature of 'the party accompanying the joint work' was found in most societies which had developed the system of mutual aid.[23] These events assisted in maintaining the sense of community important for the social and economic survival of the agricultural community. The experience of working together, dancing together and playing music together all contributed to the bonding of the community and to the sense of belonging. These events also provided sites where hospitality and reciprocity was actively maintained and continued. Within this environment, dances, tunes and songs were transmitted informally.

Also in the spirit of mutual aid, social dances were often held in particular houses during the winter in North Kerry, and particularly around Christmas time, to assist poorer families. Specific houses in the different rural townlands raffled turkeys, geese or goats annually. These events were known as raffles, gambles or turkey dances. The household that held the raffle was generally in need of money, so the main function of the occasion was economic. Raffles were held at different houses each evening, but in poorer households, two raffles were held to assist them throughout the winter. Most of the community were aware of the economic circumstances of the family in question. The terms gambles, turkey dances, turkey balls, turkey raffles or just raffles were all applied to this social institution, but the latter was the most common term.

Raffles included card games, which were played into the early hours of the morning. To participate at these card games, a player had to pay 1s. to the owner of the house when entering. This amount allowed a person to play one game of cards for a turkey or a goose or whatever was put up to be raffled by the house. Tea and food were provided by the owner of the house, and music and dancing took place simultaneously in an adjoining room, usually the kitchen. Since raffles

---

[23]   Ibid., p. 27.

were inclusive of the community at large, the dances performed were generally those communal social dances which allowed group participation. Therefore, sets and Reels were danced, with an occasional 'Highland Fling'.[24] Similarly to the rambling houses, step dancers present performed a Treble Reel or Hornpipe. These events were an integral part of the economic and social life of the rural communities in North Kerry.

American Wakes, Fairs, Patterns and Weddings

The Molyneaux step dancers also performed at American Wakes, fairs, patterns and weddings. With emigration from Ireland, particularly after the Great Famine (see Chapter 3), the American Wake was a characteristic feature of rural society in North Kerry. It was an evening of traditional music, song and dance hosted by the family which was losing a member to emigration. Although emigrants went to America, Canada, England and Australia, the farewell party was generally known as the American Wake, wakes being associated with the process of grieving a deceased person. Many emigrants who left rural Ireland did not return, hence the name. These occasions were sorrowful events, but they provided those emigrating with cultural memories, some of which were embodied through the dancing and the music.

Each American Wake event took place over a number of days. Generally, relatives, neighbours and friends came to the house of the person emigrating a day or two before departure, and shared with the family in bidding the emigrant farewell. A farewell party was held the evening before departure. On these occasions, local musicians, singers and dancers gathered with the community, and local communal dances – sets and Reels – were danced and the step dancers present also danced step dances. These were community events supporting the emigrant perhaps for the last time. The occasion was a microcosm of the community at large, where cultural values of support, hospitality and community were enacted. American Wakes were popular in some places in North Kerry until the 1960s. They were also popular for daughters leaving home to enter the convent or for priests going on a foreign mission.[25]

---

[24] 'The Highland Fling' was a couple dance, popular at rural social dance events.

[25] Gaughan (1973), p. 136. In my own family, there were also a number of American Wakes for family members emigrating to America. On one occasion, on the morning of their departure, my paternal grandmother, Abbey Lane, accompanied her daughters on horse and trap to Cobh, Co. Cork. She played her concertina on the quay in Cobh while her daughters danced a half-set to her music for the last time.

Fairs

Fairs were important occasions for step dancers to both perform and to advertise their skills. During the early decades of the twentieth century, fairs were held on particular days of the year in different areas of North Kerry. These were attended by the local agricultural community, and marked the agricultural calendar. Among those who gathered were musicians, who played on the sides of the streets, and step dancers. Around the early decades of the nineteenth century, it is said that Múirín performed 'The Blackbird' set dance at Ballyduff Lamb Fair, to the piping of McCarthy (see Chapter 3). Molyneaux is also reputed to have performed step dances at Listowel Fair during the early decades of the twentieth century. On seeing Molyneaux perform in The Square, Listowel, Bryan MacMahon, the local writer, was struck by the power Molyneaux had to draw all those nearby around him. According to MacMahon, people were awed by what he was able to do with his feet: 'He Christianized and pacified the people.'[26] The following anecdote further informs us how Jerry Nolan, a Molyneaux step dancer, also step danced at Listowel Fair:

> In Listowel at that time, before the coming of the cattle marts, fairs were held in the streets, open fairs – cattle fairs. And there was a big square in Listowel, and a small square, which were crowded with cattle. Now, the cattle fair was every fortnight, every Wednesday fortnight. And then there was two big fairs in the year. One on the 13th May, the other on the 28th October. And people that lived within ten miles of the town of Listowel – there was no tractors or trailers then – had to walk the cattle to the fair. And they would start out early and be at the fair before dawn would break, and perhaps have sold [their] cattle before dawn would break. Well, Jerry Nolan told me that one day in October – the big fair – he came to town with his father with, I suppose, three or four weanling calves, and they would be in at the dawn of day, as I say, or before it. And, the father went into a pub to get a drink for himself and left young Nolan, young Jerry, who was then about 15 years of age, minding the calves outside. But when the father came out, the calves were there, but there was no trace at all of the young Nolan. But he heard fiddle music somewhere in the small square, so he went over there, and in the middle of a crowd there was young Jerry Nolan hammering out 'The Blackbird'.[27]

---

[26]   Bryan MacMahon, personal communication with the author.
[27]   Seosamh Ó Bruadair (1985), ethnographic interview with the author.

Patterns

Together with fairs, patterns were also important contexts for the step dancers of North Kerry:

> 15 pie tents erected all along the village street – each pie cost 2d., whiskey 3d. a glass, stout – 2d a bottle. Pies sold in every house. A lot of drink, music played on the street and dancing. Tinkers, thimble riggers, 'maggie' men, and tramps. Cars of apples, oranges, and candy sold. Pigs' crubeens, boiled and salted were sold. Ginger bread – 1d. Fighting in the evening – sticks and stones were thrown. About 10 police cleared the town – custom now dead.[28]

The above description of Newtownsandes Pattern (Moyvane) is but one account of the many patterns which were held in the area of North Kerry at the turn of the twentieth century. The pattern was an annual event, and was associated with a local patron saint, hence the name 'patron' or 'pattern'. Originally, the prime object of the event was to offer devotions to the particular saint in question at a holy well. These holy wells were features of pre-Christian Celtic religion where prescribed rituals and devotions were practised by pilgrims who came to the sites seeking favours. During the penal laws of the seventeenth and eighteenth century, because of the restrictions on worship at holy wells, the devotional aspects of the pattern receded into the background. The pattern event continued, but it became disassociated from the holy wells.[29] The occasion became one of merriment, where stalls were erected as in the Newtownsandes Pattern described above, and sports, dancing, singing and occasionally faction fights[30] took place. However, patterns still take place today, where devotions are associated with them. Many of the Molyneaux step dancers have participated in them by praying and throwing money into the holy wells for cures and good health. It has been customary for a session of traditional music, singing and dancing to be held in a public house later in the evening, where sets and Reels have been danced and the Molyneaux step dancers have also performed step dances.

Weddings

Local weddings were other occasions when the Molyneaux step dancers had the opportunity to perform. After the wedding ceremony at the church, all the wedding guests gathered at the groom's house for a reception of food, drink and entertainment. Although it was predominantly social dances which were danced on these community-based occasions, the Molyneaux step dancers also danced solo

---

[28]   Nurse Stack, Irish Folklore Commission, Schools' Manuscripts, no. V 404, p. 357.

[29]   Gaughan (1973), p. 185.

[30]   O'Donnell (1975).

or in a group on request. These performances entertained the wedding guests and provided step dancers with opportunities to dance to good live music, to exhibit their dance skill, and to meet and converse with others.

The Wren

> The wren, the wren, the king of all birds,
> Saint Stephen's Day, got caught in the furze;
> Up with the kettle and down with the pan,
> And give us a penny to bury the wren.[31]

Of the informal ceremonial events in North Kerry that were held on specific days of the year, the most popular among traditional step dancers was the Wren (pronounced locally 'Wran'). This was the one informal event which automatically implied a step dance performance. The Wren ritual falls on St Stephen's Day, 26 December, and is still observed in some parts of North Kerry, such as Ballybunion and Ballylongford. However, it has undergone some modifications. Originally, the ritual took place over the twelve days of Christmas, but now it is confined to St Stephen's Day, and sometimes Christmas Night. Also, today the custom has become associated with the All-Ireland Wrenboy Band Competition held annually at the Harvest Festival in the town of Listowel.

According to local folklore, the Wren custom relates to the story of St Stephen, who upheld the Christian faith. When hiding from the pursuing Roman soldiers behind a holly bush, a wren on the bush drew attention by its whistling, and in so doing revealed the hiding place of St Stephen. Killing and burying the wren on St Stephen's Day was therefore a symbolic act in support of the Christian faith; and going from house to house was symbolic of supporting and disseminating the faith. However, this Christmas ceremonial ritual may also have had associations with pagan life-cycle rituals.[32] In North Kerry, the reasons given for 'going on the Wren' were because it was a part of the tradition and also that it was fun. The story of St Stephen was mentioned, but the origin of the ritual was not a major concern for the participants; it went without saying as a part of the taken-for-granted knowledge they had.

The Wren, with its ritualistic and symbolic elements, marked the mid-winter season with sociality, traditional music, song and dance. It was a time of year to which the youth of the townlands looked forward, while the rural households awaited the customary visits from these Wren groups. Going on the Wren involved different groups or batches of young people dressed up in disguise. Pyjamas were sometimes worn over clothing, and masks and high hats were also worn. Originally, it was young men – Wren boys – who took part in this ritual, but in

---

[31] John McCarthy (1985), ethnographic interview with the author.
[32] Parle (2001).

North Kerry, both male and female traditional step dancers, singers and musicians participated in the Wren. Each Wren group generally had a King, the leader of the group, and each carried a 'wren bush' and/or a wooden hobby horse. These Wren groups walked from rural townland to rural townland. On their journey, they visited farmhouses, and the first group to visit a house carrying the wren bush brought it good luck for the following year.

Each Wren group in its costumed attire recited the customary Wren verse above on entering a house. They entertained the people in every house they visited. They sang local, generally unaccompanied, traditional songs, played traditional music repertoire – much of which was associated with particular groups and localities – and danced. The instruments they played included accordions, fiddles and *bodhráns*. The dances performed were mostly step dances; step dancers therefore found themselves in great demand. The number of step dancers and the number of step dances performed varied from group to group and from area to area. On occasions, a half-set or a figure of a set was also danced. On leaving a house, each group received some money 'to bury the wren'. The reality was that the money collected was spent on buying food and a keg of porter for the Porter Ball which was held approximately a week later; a house in the locality was volunteered for the occasion. Social dances, such as sets and Reels, were performed at the Porter Ball until the early hours of the morning to the accompaniment of local musicians. These communal dances engaged and entertained the whole community. In between the sets and Reels, or at the end of the evening, a step dancer performed. However, sometimes no Porter Ball was held, as not enough money was collected to pay for food and drink, and on these occasions what was collected was divided amongst those who had gone on the Wren.

Although there may have been a lot of Wren groups in a particular area, there was no such thing as trespassing on another group's patch. Each group had its own particular route, but on occasions, one Wren group would meet another on the road, and should they be heading for the same house, the two groups would race to get there first. Whichever group reached the house first, they would then enter to entertain the household, during which time the second group waited outside. When the first group had finished and had left, the second group would then enter and entertain the same household. No group had a monopoly on a particular area.

The Molyneaux step dancers I encountered had all participated in the Wren ritual:

> The Wren boys gathered together in somebody's house and they got all dressed up in their outfits. They would have different kinds of old costumes and a face thing over their face. I can remember the old-timers with the screen of the window, a bit of a curtain, and there would be little holes for the eyes and a bit for the mouth, and you wouldn't know who the person was at all. And they used to have what they called a 'hobby horse'. This was made of timber, and there would be two men under him. It was a wooden frame, and it was really the shape of a horse's head. There would be a white sheet put over it, and it was

with strings that the horse's mouth would open and close. It was nails that were used for teeth, and children would be scared. They'd think that the horse was going to bite them. Musicians and dancers went around from house to house, and they'd play in every house. It was nearly all step dancing would be done in the houses. There might be 20 or 25 in the crowd altogether, and there would be probably three or four step dancers there. So you would dance in this house now, and I would dance in the house down the road, and some other one then, you see, and by the time you would be back again, you wouldn't feel it that way. When they'd come in, they'd start to play the music, maybe a Hornpipe or a Reel for the dancers. The *bodhrán* was used as well, but they were not as plentiful in those days as they are today.[33]

Jeremiah Molyneaux often performed with his local Wren group, and often acquired step dance scholars due to his dancing skills.

The Wren was an important 'fun' event for the rural communities of North Kerry, but it also assisted in supporting and consolidating each townland in the region as in a 'tribal' community. Through song, music, dance and costume disguise, these townlands were identified and made visible and audible.

The Biddy

St Brighid's Day, 1 February, honours St Brighid, the pagan Irish Goddess of fertility. On the eve of St Brighid's Day, a ceremonial celebration in honour of the saint was held in some areas of North Kerry during the early decades of the twentieth century – the Biddy. The Biddy featured groups of young men and women who disguised themselves and dressed up in similar attire to that worn for the Wren. Masks covering their faces were used by some groups, and were called 'hi-fiddles'. The Biddy boys carried a 'Biddy doll', supposedly an effigy of St Brighid. This annual ceremonial ritual on the eve of 1 February also referenced a pagan ritual of fertility. With the Christianization of Ireland in the fifth century, some existing pagan rituals and deities were appropriated by the Catholic Church and celebrated as part of the Irish Christian calendar. Brighid, the pagan Irish Goddess of fertility, was one such appropriation.

The Biddy was similar to the Wren. Each group of Biddy boys (some members of these groups were also female, but the majority were male) visited the rural houses in the vicinity and entertained with traditional music, singing and dancing. The same type of programme was performed on these visits as on the Wren. Again, money was collected by the group at each house, and was spent on food and drink for the Biddy Ball, a party with music and social dances.

Although the ritual of the Biddy was practised in the area of North Kerry, it was not as popular as the Wren. Of the elderly step dancers I encountered, only

----

[33]   John McCarthy (1985), ethnographic interview with the author.

two participated in the Biddy. In the Kilmore area, Jack Dineen went with the Biddy twice. They disguised themselves with 'old faces, top-coats and old hats', and in place of a Biddy doll they carried 'a face made in a turnip'. According to Sheila Lyons Bowler, in the Mountcoal area, they dressed up in 'straw skirts and hats' and carried a doll, any type of doll that was available. In this area, the Biddy boys were often referred to as 'straw boys' on account of the straw costumes worn. The same tunes, songs and dances – solo and group dances – were performed on the Biddy as on the Wren.

From the Molyneaux step dancers' point of view, the Wren was the more popular and more widely practised of the two ritual ceremonial events. This is illustrated by the fact that all the Molyneaux step dancers I encountered in North Kerry participated in the Wren during the early decades of the century, whereas only two participated in the Biddy.

Concerts

Concerts were the most common formal occasions at which the Molyneaux step dancers of North Kerry performed. These concerts provided the dancers with a platform to entertain, and to exhibit and express themselves through their step dance skills. Concerts included the benefit night concerts, the spring concerts held by Molyneaux in the rural townlands, the Gaelic Athletic Association's concerts which were held during Lent, and concerts which were held in aid of charity. The latter were generally in aid of a school building fund or a church fund. For these concerts, anybody in the community who was able to contribute to the evening's entertainment was welcomed. Musicians, singers and step dancers were much in demand, and since these were local social events, step dancers performed within the intimacy of, and surrounded and supported by, their relatives, neighbours and friends (see above and Chapter 3).

Feiseanna[34]

Feiseanna were other contexts at which the Molyneaux step dancers performed. *Feiseanna* were step dancing competitive events which took place at *aeraíochtaí*[35] and were held at different race and sports meetings in the vicinity. *Feiseanna* were organized by the cultural nationalist movement the Gaelic League, and took place annually in different localities in Ireland during the summer months (see also Chapters 5 and 6). The most popular *feiseanna* for the Molyneaux step dancers of North Kerry were those held in Abbeyfeale, Ballyheigue, Castleisland, Listowel, Newcastle West and Tralee. Of the Molyneaux step dancers I encountered in

---

[34]   'Festivals'; plural of *feis*.

[35]   'Field-days'.

North Kerry, only four performed at *feiseanna*, namely Marie Finucane Kissane, Sheila Lyons Bowler, Phil Cahill and Michael Walsh. The other step dancers did not participate at these *feiseanna*, either because of the distance they would have had to travel in order to attend, or simply because they did not wish to compete. (*Feiseanna* will be discussed in more detail in Chapters 5 and 6.)

Occasions When Dancers Did Not Perform

The dead and relatives of the dead were much respected by the rural Christian people of North Kerry. Should there be a death in a family, no member of that family danced, played music or attended a dance for twelve months afterwards. According to Jack Dineen, his sister died when he was approximately 17 years of age, and it would have been noted by the community had he gone to a dance or a dancing school. Hence, when Jeremiah Molyneaux arrived in the area to set up his dancing school at that time, Jack Dineen did not attend. He used to go to the door of the house where the dance school was being held to listen, but he never entered it. He learned to step dance at later dance schools and from his father. The ceremonial rituals of the Wren and the Biddy were not suspended in the event of a death, but the group in question did not call on the family of the deceased person.

Conclusion

Dancing in North Kerry was of social, economic, educational and historical importance. It bonded the scattered rural communities when work on farms was intensive and when it was slack. It assisted in supporting the mutual aid system prevalent in the region while also maintaining and developing its dance practices. The dance contexts discussed above thus supplied the people of North Kerry with familiar venues for socializing, and the act of dancing assisted them in constructing, embodying and shaping their shared sense of community, place and cultural identity.

The Molyneaux step dancers practised their art in both formal contexts specific to step dancing, and in social contexts where they participated both as step dancers and as social dancers; the step dancers negotiated their dance behaviour accordingly. A step dance performance at these social events focused the attention of the community on the art of the dancer and all that the step dance performance represented – a skilled, cultural, musico-movement system which had been generated and shaped by a shared social, cultural and economic history. It also focused the attention of the community in on itself, referencing its past and present, and temporarily creating a heightened and intensive sense of community.

Due to processes of modernity, as the twentieth century progressed, these rural social contexts became less significant to rural communities in North Kerry. New contexts and the advent of modernity necessitated new and different ways of being-in-the-world. Step dance would also change, as would the contexts, values and ideologies that supported it.

Glossary

Although it is customary to write Hornpipes in $\frac{4}{4}$ with groupings of quavers (see, for example, Breathnach 1977 and Roche 1982), Irish traditional musicians know that this is not how Hornpipes are played. Consequently, in transcribing and Labanotating the Hornpipes below, I use a $\frac{12}{8}$ metre in an attempt to capture more accurately the timing of the Hornpipe as danced by the elderly dancers. They could also have been transcribed in $\frac{4}{4}$ with groupings of triplets.

The Labanotation examples that follow are © Catherine E. Foley.

Example 4.0a	Glossary © Catherine E. Foley

THIS HEIGHT FROM THE FLOOR IS NOT ABSOLUTE. DEPENDING ON THE PERFORMER, STEP–DANCERS MAY COMPLETE THIS FORWARD GESTURE CLOSER TO THE FLOOR.

ARMS LOOSELY HELD

TORSO CONTROLLED SUFFICIENTLY

HARD SHOES ARE WORN

Example 4.0b   Glossary © Catherine E. Foley

Example 4.1   Hornpipe Lead (a), bars 1–8: Michael Walsh. © Catherine E. Foley

Example 4.2   Hornpipe Lead (a), bars 14–16: Michael Walsh. © Catherine E. Foley

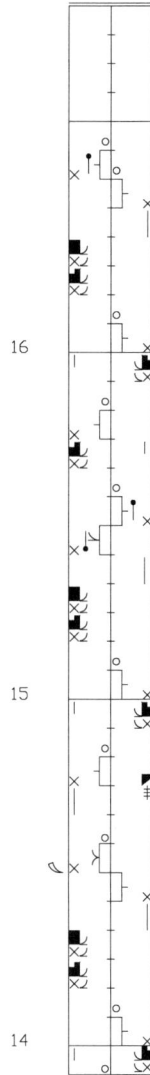

Example 4.3	Hornpipe Lead (a), bars 1–8: Jack Dineen. © Catherine E. Foley

Example 4.4   Hornpipe Lead (a), bars 14–16: Jack Dineen. © Catherine E. Foley

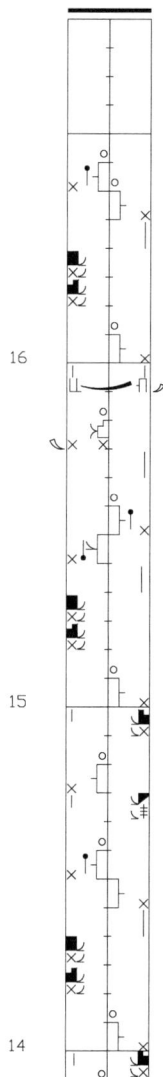

Example 4.5   Hornpipe Lead (a), bars 1–8: Willie Goggin. © Catherine E. Foley

Example 4.6   Hornpipe Lead (a), bars 15–16: Willie Goggin. © Catherine E. Foley

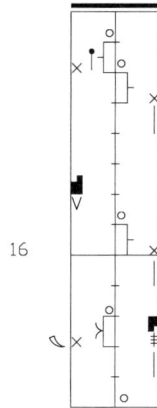

Example 4.7   Hornpipe Lead (c), bars 15–16: Michael Walsh. © Catherine E. Foley

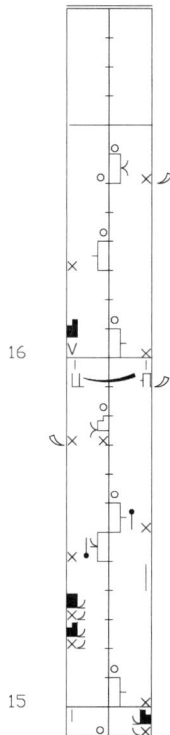

Example 4.8   Hornpipe Lead (c), bars 6–8 and 14–16: Jack Dineen. © Catherine
                E. Foley

Example 4.9   Hornpipe Lead (c), bars 6–8 and 14–16: Willie Goggin. © Catherine
E. Foley

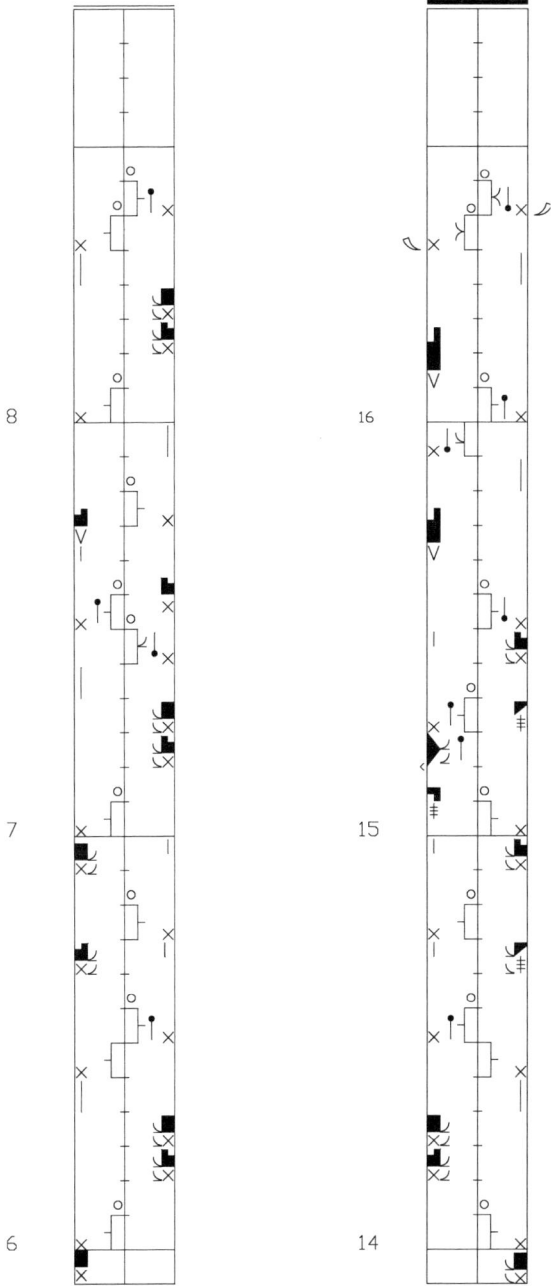

Example 4.10   Hornpipe: 'The Home Ruler'. © Catherine E. Foley

Chapter 5
Nationalism and the Invention of Irish Dancing

> Nationalist ideologies built out of symbolic forms drawn from local traditions ...
> tend, like vernacular ... to be socially deprovincializing but psychologically
> forced.[1]

While Jeremiah Molyneaux was learning, and later teaching, step dancing in North Kerry according to the dancing masters' quarter and the benefit night system (see Chapter 3), cultural nationalists in Ireland were endeavouring to establish Ireland as a separate cultural nation. Thus, at the end of the nineteenth century, and within the context of colonialism, these cultural nationalists set about constructing a programme that would assist in promoting an Irish cultural identity,[2] and step dancing would be included in this programme.

For these cultural nationalists, a cultural representation was required to establish an Irishness that was positive and uniquely Irish, and that was different from Englishness, and indeed any other culture. It was thus that Conradh na Gaeilge (the Gaelic League), an Irish cultural nationalist movement, was established in Dublin in 1893, and had as its primary agenda the de-Anglicization of Ireland. The Gaelic League selected various cultural practices as devices to assert this cultural nationalism, and although the Irish language and Irish-language literature were the primary interests of the Gaelic League, step dancing also played an important part in this cultural re-presentation.[3]

Between 1870 and 1914, traditions were being invented right across Europe, for various reasons which differed according to the ideological needs of specific countries. Broadly, however, they could be divided into two categories: (1) those traditions which were invented for political purposes and were, for the most part, associated with the formation of states and other political and socially organized bodies, and (2) those invented for social, non-political purposes.[4] However,

---

[1]   Geertz (1973), pp. 242–3.

[2]   The political and cultural quest for a separate nation did not commence in the closing decades of the twentieth century; Thomas Davis and the 'Young Ireland' movement had promoted the notion of a nation-state in the 1840s with their newspaper *The Nation*, first published in 1842.

[3]   This differed from East European countries, where it was the newly founded nation-states that appropriated cultural expressions for the same purpose.

[4]   Hobsbawm and Ranger (1985).

in certain countries, a combination of both political and social traditions were invented to meet these ideological needs. Movements, especially those fostered by cultural nationalist organizations, used methods such as ritual and ceremony for the purpose of establishing a nationalistic spirit. For example, Switzerland, with the formation of its modern state in the nineteenth century, altered and institutionalized cultural practices still in existence, such as folk song and physical contests, for 'the new national purposes'.[5] Cultural nationalist movements in Ireland similarly appropriated cultural activities for their ideological purposes.

In Ireland, the Gaelic Athletic Association, established in 1884, promoted Irish games and excluded all others. Overtly, it appeared to be an innocent sporting association; covertly, it was a means of inculcating in its members a unified *national* pride. From the outset, this association had nationalistic associations and aimed to achieve its objective by means of structured competitive games which stimulated local club, county and provincial[6] pride and a national patriotism. Within this shared, structured and national image of 'Irish' games, the Gaelic Athletic Association created and generated local and regional sporting rivalries through these structured competitive games. These competitions culminated at the All Ireland, the highest-ranking position within the Gaelic Athletic Association's hierarchical sporting structures. Through these structured games, 'Irish' sport was seen not only to unite the people of Ireland, but to express a sense of Irishness through sport while also providing a common interest, an Irish interest which promoted a shared Irish identity and destiny. However, it lacked an intellectual basis. With reference to this, the Irish socialist James Connolly made the following statement: 'revolutions are made with ideas, not hurley sticks'.[7]

The Anglo-Irish Literary Revival, a non-political movement, was also emerging on the scene, associated with names such as Yeats, Synge, O'Casey, Lady Gregory and Stephens. The movement endeavoured to develop a 'national literature', drawing from early legends and history of Ireland. It appealed at the time only to the intelligentsia, and not to the general public. The intellectual needs of this sector of Irish society were eventually provided for by the Gaelic League, founded in 1893 by Douglas Hyde, a Protestant scholar, and Eoin MacNeill, a historian.

The Gaelic League

> [W]e cannot understand nations and nationalism simply as an ideology or form
> of politics but must treat them as cultural phenomena as well. That is to say,
> nationalism, the ideology and movement, must be closely related to national

---

[5]   Ibid., p. 6.

[6]   There are four geographical provinces in Ireland: Munster, Leinster, Ulster and Connacht.

[7]   Connolly in Lyons (1973), p. 227.

identity, a multidimensional concept, and extended to include a specific language, sentiments and symbolism.[8]

The establishment of the Gaelic League[9] at the end of the nineteenth century owed much to the growing awareness in Ireland of imported English colonial and imperialist culture – a culture which cultural nationalists believed did not reflect the culture of Irish people. According to Douglas Hyde, this necessitated a cultural process which he referred to as 'de-Anglicization', that is: 'refusing to imitate the English in their language, literature, music, games, dress and ideas'.[10] It also necessitated an endeavour to establish an Irish cultural nation, different from England. This was in keeping with the new-look nationalism operating in Europe. To quote McCartney: 'According to this new nationalism, politically independent states should be raised up wherever there existed distinct cultural nations.'[11] The Gaelic League thus sought to demonstrate that Ireland was a distinct cultural nation. With this ideal in mind, the Gaelic League, with Douglas Hyde as its president, placed the Irish language as central in this cultural representation of Ireland. Consequently, the two objectives of the Gaelic League were: (1) the preservation of Irish as the national language of Ireland and the extension of its use as a spoken tongue, and (2) the study and publication of existing Irish literature and the cultivation of a modern literature in Irish.[12]

The Gaelic League was not the first organization to dedicate itself to the Irish language, but it was the first to promote Irish as a spoken language. This differed from the scholarly tradition associated with earlier movements, such as the Society for the Preservation of the Irish Language. Although primarily concerned with the Irish language and Irish-language literature, the Gaelic League also included in its 'de-Anglicization' process those social aspects of culture traditionally associated with rural people – traditional music, singing and dancing.

Initially, the Gaelic League was non-sectarian and non-political, but by 1915, the political and nationalist agenda of the Gaelic League became apparent, and Douglas Hyde resigned as President of the Gaelic League. However, for the first three decades of its existence (1893–1923), the Gaelic League functioned as a populist organization and had a huge impact in shaping Irish culture.

The Gaelic League was a culturally dynamic movement, and appealed particularly to middle-class people in Ireland who publicly identified themselves with this cultural endeavour. Indeed, it was common at the time to see men wearing kilts in nationalist colours of green or saffron and women wearing accessories such as Tara brooches. According to the modern Irish literature scholar and poet

---

[8]   Smith (1992), p. vii.

[9]   The Gaelic League, or Conradh na Gaeilge, was also referred to simply as 'the League' or 'An Conradh'.

[10]   McCartney (1984), p. 296.

[11]   Ibid. p. 297.

[12]   Ó Cúlacháin (1980), p. 6.

Seán Ó Tuama, the Gaelic League was a 'radical educational organization' whose philosophy centred on the development of 'the individual Irish personality' which 'could not reach its potential except in a community proper to it'.[13] The Gaelic League therefore endeavoured to construct that community – an 'Irish' community, based on a notion or ideal of an older, Gaelic Ireland. With the Irish language as its essential core, it attempted to construct this community through its educational programme, which could be regarded as the first adult education programme in Ireland.

The success of the Gaelic League in these early years can be measured by the growth of its branches all over Ireland. By 1897, there were 43 branches reported (seven of these were in America); but by 1901, there were 600 branches with a membership of 50,000 people.[14] The teachers of the Gaelic League were initially voluntary and untrained, but in 1904, the first training college for these teachers was established in Béal Átha an Ghaorthaidh, Co. Cork, and others followed. These teachers travelled around the country to the different branches and taught Irish as a spoken language, Irish reading and writing, and traditional music and dance. Together with these classes, public lectures were given, and social dance events were organized in the form of *céilithe*[15] (see below). *Feiseanna* were also organized, where local people competed in the different culturally specific areas of Irish literature, traditional music, song and dance. Thus, in endeavouring to assert an 'Irish' community and cultural identity, 'who we are' and 'what we are about', the Gaelic League selected the Irish language, including songs in Irish, traditional music and dance, in its Irish cultural re-presentation. According to the historian Gearóid Ó Tuathaigh:

> For Hyde and his fellow Gaelic League enthusiasts, it would be a catastrophe if the continuity of cultural tradition, articulated and given form principally through language, were to be ruptured. Such a cultural tradition encompassed thoughts, feelings, perceptions and wisdom, a distinctive world-view based on a unique set of values. The case made for cultural continuity, through the medium of Irish, and, therefore, for language revival, rested on a set of assumptions and propositions that combined elements of general humanism with specific tenets of cultural nationalism.[16]

Through its weekly newspaper, *An Claidheamh Soluis*,[17] the Gaelic League had a means to disseminate information to its membership. It covered events of importance for its members, including the publication of reports from the different branches of the Gaelic League, advertising upcoming branch meetings

---

[13] Ó Tuama (1972), p. 98.

[14] Mac Aodha (1972), pp. 20–30.

[15] Plural of *céilí*; *céilís* is also used.

[16] Ó Tuathaigh (2005), p. 47.

[17] 'The Sword of Light'.

and *feiseanna*, and printed tunes and Irish poems, Irish language vocabulary, letters and articles of general interest to its readership. Examples of these articles included 'The Value of the Irish Language and Irish Literature', which stated that the Irish language:

> summoned back the soul of olden times ... the customs, beliefs, and dreams of their forefathers; it preserved undying the image of Ireland clothed in the ancient Druid romances. Hence, the extinction of such a language would be to them an irretrievable loss – a gap in the continuity of their national being; the cutting of their intellectual life, the cutting off of their religious life; their sacred traditions and romances.[18]

The *Céilí*

The Gaelic League was not confined to Ireland. With a history of emigration to America, Canada, Australia, England and elsewhere, Irish immigrants in their adopted countries also formed branches of the Gaelic League. The Gaelic League in London was particularly active, and organized dance classes with Professor P.D. Reidy. Reidy was originally from Castleisland, Co. Kerry, and had taught step dancing in Co. Kerry and West Limerick prior to emigrating. Reidy's father was an itinerant dancing master who had learned from the Kerry dancing master O'Kearin. Consequently, the London branch of the Gaelic League acquired a strong reputation for dance, and more so after it established the first *céilí*, an Irish social dance event.[19]

The first *céilí* was held on 30 October 1897 in Bloomsbury Hall, London. This was as a result of an invitation Fionán MacColuim, the Secretary of the London branch of the Gaelic League at the time, received to attend a Scottish *céilí* on Easter Saturday 1897. MacColuim, who worked as a clerk in the India Office in London, observed the similarities between the group dances performed at the Scottish *céilí* and those taught by Reidy at branch classes. Consequently, the idea of holding an Irish *céilí* was set in motion, and as a result of the success of this first *céilí*, the event was subsequently popularized by the Gaelic League in Ireland and abroad.[20]

The Irish *céilí* became a social dance event where Irish people and others could interact socially and culturally, and could, through their dancing bodies, assert and express their identity and cohesion as an *Irish* community.[21] As Simon Frith states of music, but is equally applicable to dance:

---

[18] *An Claidheamh Soluis*, vol. 1, no. 38, 2 December 1899, p. 604.

[19] Foley (1988b; 2011; 2012b); Brennan (1999); Wulff (2007).

[20] For further details relating to the first *céilí* and its development throughout the twentieth century, see Foley (2011).

[21] See Foley (1988b; 2011; 2012b).

> Music constructs our sense of identity through the direct experiences it offers of the body, time and sociability, experiences which enable us to place ourselves in imaginative cultural narratives.[22]

The appropriation of dance and the construction of this social dance event by the Gaelic League was a manifestation of the fact that dance was perceived to be an important and powerful ideological tool which facilitated the shaping, sensing and experiencing of Irish culture and identity.

Within this context, *céilí* dancing was nurtured as Irish social dance, and a particular configuration and interpretation of Irishness was experienced through the dance, and indeed the whole dance event. Similarly to the *feis* and the *oireachtas*[23] (see below), the *céilí* was a whole dance configuration. It consisted of dancing *céilí* dances to live *céilí* band music, and all announcements were in Irish. However, these *céilithe* under the auspices of the Gaelic League were controlled dance spaces where discipline, control and co-ordination of movement were the norm. All *céilithe* were supervised, and this was facilitated by the institutionalization of both the *céilí* dances and the *céilithe* themselves. The *céilí* thus provided a site for the dissemination and implementation of the ideological agenda of the Gaelic League. In effect, the *céilí* took on all the attributes of what Hobsbawm defined as an *invented tradition*: 'essentially a process of formalisation and ritualisation, characterised by reference to the past, if only by imposing repetition'.[24]

The reference and link to the past was supplied by the actual dances. Two members of the London branch of the Gaelic League, James J. O'Keeffe and Art O'Brien, travelled to dancing masters in Ireland (two living in Glasgow, but who had originally come from Ireland) to collect social dances for publication; Reidy's dances were also collected. These dances had been practised in the rural counties of Ireland, predominantly in the south-west, and in particular County Kerry, and were believed to be old; they were published by O'Keeffe and O'Brien in *A Handbook of Irish Dances* (1902 [1944]).[25] For the Gaelic League, these dances were considered to be authentic Irish dances, and although danced only in some regions of Ireland, particularly Kerry, their believed authenticity prompted the Gaelic League in selecting, popularizing and institutionalizing some of them at the *céilí* dance event. These dances were round dances, long dances or country dances which had been adapted from English country dances by itinerant dancing masters in Ireland to suit their patrons (see Chapter 2). Other collections of Irish dances were also published, including *A Guide to Irish Dancing* by J.J. Sheehan (published earlier in 1902) and *The Irish Folk Dance Book* by Peadar O'Rafferty (1934).

---

[22]   Frith (1996), p. 124.

[23]   Literally 'deliberative assembly'; a major competitive step dancing event; plural *oireachtais*.

[24]   Hobsbawm and Ranger (1985), p. 4; see also Foley (1988b; 2011; 2012b).

[25]   This book was preceded by another Irish dance collection compiled by J.J. Sheehan (1902 [1986]).

Some of these collected dances were selected to form a canon of official Gaelic League *céilí* dances; they included, 'Ballaí Luimní',[26] 'The High Cauled Cap', 'Ionsaí na hÍnse'[27] and 'Baint an Fhéir'.[28] Other social dances performed in Ireland throughout the nineteenth century, such as sets (Quadrilles), were disallowed by the Gaelic League because of their perception as being foreign dances, not authentic Irish ones. The selected *céilí* dances were considered authentic and relatively easy to teach and to dance. Also, the names of these dances conjured up images of places in Ireland together with events of a historical and cultural nature; this further assisted in constructing images of 'home' and Ireland.[29]

The notion of authenticity was important to the Gaelic League, which tried to define what was and what was not Irish culture. This debate developed around a structure of binary oppositions which marked the cultural and ideological debate of twentieth-century Ireland: authentic/inauthentic, traditional/modern, pure/innovative, moral/immoral, rural/urban, and Irish/Other. In *Positions* (1981), Jacques Derrida speaks of binary oppositions as being in a structure of 'violent hierarchies' – one of the positions, both in actual and conceptual terms, becomes dominant, and it is only through inversion that this structure can be broken; the high becomes low, and the low becomes high. The revival movement of late nineteenth- and early twentieth-century politics in Ireland played out this structure of polarities. It prioritized the culture of the rural west of Ireland, and elevated the culture of the previously lowly in the system – the rural poor – to a superior position. In addition, the Literary Revival also championed rural values and culture in the construction of an Irish literature. Within the paradigm of binary oppositions available at the time, the alternative would have been one which demythologized the past and focused on a secular, pluralist future.[30] This alternative did not form part of the conceptualization of Irish culture for the Gaelic League. Within the cultural nationalist structures of binary oppositions, this alternative, predominantly associated with urban modern culture and its associated values, was an antithesis to its ideological agenda.

In the case of dance, group dances (*céilí* dances) associated with the rural west of Ireland (particularly Co. Kerry) were selected, prioritized and promoted by the Gaelic League. Although the selected *céilí* dances, believed to be pure and authentic Irish dances, assisted in contributing to the cultural nationalist dynamic during the struggle for Independence and later with the establishment of the Irish Free State, the selection process assisted in marginalizing other dances and other dance communities in Ireland. This process shaped and moulded perceptions of Irish dance practices in Ireland for most of the twentieth century.[31]

---

26   'The Walls of Limerick'.

27   'The Siege of Ennis'.

28   'The Haymaker's Jig'.

29   Foley (2011).

30   Kearney (1985); see also Foley (2007b).

31   Foley (1988b; 2001; 2005b; 2012b).

Irish Step Dancing[32] and the Gaelic League

The Gaelic League promoted solo step dancing through organized dance classes at different Gaelic League branches, and competitions at *feiseanna* and the *Oireachtas*, the national festival.

Historically, the *feis* was an ancient Gaelic assembly of Irish nobility, chiefs, politicians, judges, doctors, poets and bards, who gathered for the annual festival at Tara, the residence of the high King of Ireland. This event focused on politics and law-making, but it was also accompanied by much festivity, including entertainments and sports events. Ireland's 800-year colonization put an end to the *feis*, but it was re-invented at the end of the nineteenth century by the Gaelic League.

These cultural nationalist *feiseanna* were organized and hosted in different localities with strong Gaelic League support. They were generally one-day events that included competitions in various cultural practices. For instance, the *feis* held in the town of Macroom, Co. Cork, in April 1899 (believed to be the first *feis*) included step dance competitions in Reel, Jig and Hornpipe, a written essay on the life of Thomas Davis,[33] recitations, narration of folklore, Irish ballads and folksongs. Other *feiseanna* followed, including provincial *feiseanna* such as the Munster Feis, the Leinster Feis and the Connacht Feis. Like Irish games, these competitive events developed a hierarchical structure, with local, county, provincial and national levels. Again, these competitions were intended to inculcate pride in local, county, provincial, and ultimately, a national Irish culture.

Feiseanna were generally held as part of sporting fixtures or race meetings. These were held outdoors during the summer months, and competitive performance activities also took place on wooden platforms or flatbed lorries. Separate platforms were provided in the field for each performance specialization. For the step dance competitions, a traditional musician, generally a fiddler or a melodeon player, took his or her place at one side of the platform together with an adjudicator, allowing enough space for the step dancers to perform.[34]

---

[32]   Although the term 'Irish dancing' is the term used most often by competitive step dancers, teachers, adjudicators and others, I will use the term 'Irish step dancing' or simply 'step dancing' when discussing competitive step dancing to differentiate it from other forms of 'Irish dancing' such as *céilí* dancing, and also because the focus of the book is step dancing.

[33]   Thomas Davis (1814–1845) is associated with the Young Ireland movement and *The Nation*, a weekly newspaper founded in 1842 to assist Daniel O'Connell in the campaign to repeal the Act of Union. Davis, a young Dublin Protestant barrister, expressed in his writings Young Ireland's notion of Irish nationality: everyone who lived in Ireland, regardless of race or creed.

[34]   According to oral history, in the early years of the Gaelic League's step dance competitions, some adjudicators sat underneath the stage or lorry to adjudicate the

Irish was the official spoken language at these *feiseanna* – all announcements and results were conveyed through the medium of the Irish language. In effect, the event attempted to encapsulate a revived but idealized cultural representation of pre-colonial Gaelic Irish festivals. In participating at these *feiseanna*, individuals identified themselves with this cultural re-presentation of Ireland.

The *Oireachtas* was 'the great national festival of Gaelic Ireland'.[35] Similarly to the *feis*, the *Oireachtas* was again loosely based on the notion of the ancient Gaelic cultural festival, and according to Ó Fearaíl (1975), the idea to establish an *Oireachtas* was inspired by the Welsh *eisteddfod*. The first *Oireachtas* organized by the Gaelic League was held in the Rotunda, Dublin, in 1897.[36] The *Oireachtas* event established a modern model of a national, competitive festival, and it became the cultural showcase of the year for the Gaelic League, where the best traditional performers and Irish-language writers in Ireland could exhibit and share their cultural knowledge and competence. However, it was competitive, and winning at the *Oireachtas* was prestigious.

The Gaelic League established conditions for entry to, and participation in, *feis* and *Oireachtas* competitions: competitions in Irish prose, poetry, recitation, oratory, conversation in Irish, solo Irish singing, choral singing, instrumental traditional music and step dancing. Regarding the latter, there was one step dance competition at the Leinster Feis in 1899 – Reel and Jig, prize £1 – and two step dance competitions at the Munster Feis in 1900 – Irish Reel and Jig (Double) and Irish Hornpipe. Conditions for entry to the competitions included that professional dancers could not participate in Gaelic League step dance competitions;[37] in some cases, step dancers had to pass an Irish language examination before being allowed to compete in step dance competitions;[38] and in the early years of step dance competitions at the *Oireachtas*, dancers would not be awarded a prize should their dance costume not be made from Irish fabrics and materials. This indicated the nationalist mission of the Gaelic League at the time: the integration of all aspects of Irish culture, particularly the language, in order to build 'the individual Irish personality' and character.

The contribution of the Gaelic League to the 'inventing Irishness' project was huge at this particular point in Irish history. Its philosophy was educational, based on the development of the Irish individual personality within an appropriately constructed Irish community. The Gaelic League further linked this educational

---

competition, since the percussive sound of the step dancer's feet was perceived to be more important than what the dancer looked like.

[35] *An Claidheamh Soluis*, 20 February 1906, p. 164.

[36] There were two dance competitions which were open to both sexes; only male dancers participated. They performed the Hop Jig (Slip Jig) and the Single Jig; see Cullinane (2003).

[37] *An Claidheamh Soluis*, 9 December 1899, p. 622; *An Claidheamh Soluis*, 11 August 1900, p. 349.

[38] Mathews (2003), p. 181.

and 'intellectual awakening' to an economic awakening. The Irish language, the development of an Irish-language literature and the promotion of Irish cultural practices were linked in its propaganda to the development and promotion of Irish industry and agriculture. This is evident from advertisements in Irish newspapers such as *An Claidheamh Soluis*, *The Freeman's Journal* and *The Irish Peasant* during the early decades of the twentieth century in which people in Ireland were encouraged to support Irish industry. Concerning step dancing, this was made manifest, for example, in the Gaelic League's insistence that step dance competitors at the *Oireachtas* wear dance costumes made from Irish fabrics and materials. According to Matthews, directives like this 'betrayed the middle-class tendencies of the Gaelic League'.[39]

In re-assessing the contribution of the Gaelic League to Irish society during these decades, Breandán Mac Aodha stated that the Gaelic League:

> generated a social revolution in the superficial sense that for perhaps two decades it induced large numbers of young adults (perhaps at times as many as 75,000) to spend some leisure time in a new way.[40]

According to Mac Aodha, 'its success may have stemmed in part from a reaction to the superficial standards of the Victorian era'.[41] Although the Gaelic League was not the only nationalist organization aware of the importation of these Victorian standards, its particular cultural programme was, according to P.J. Mathews:

> a modernizing force within Irish society during the Revival. Yet, crucially, its programme for development was, for the most part, informed by a desire to follow an alternative path to modernization – on Irish terms.[42]

Although possibly motivated, inspired and informed by 'a belief in the dormant potential within pre-colonial Irish cultural forms',[43] the Gaelic League, in Kevin Whelan's words, 'deployed the past to challenge the present to restore into possibility historical moments that had been blocked or unfulfilled earlier'.[44] Therefore, imaginings of what might have been became integrated into the Gaelic League's populist project to regenerate a cultural Ireland based on a re-presentation of Irish symbolic cultural practices.

Mass support for the Gaelic League during this period was partly due to its claimed non-sectarian and non-political stance. However, there were tensions between the Gaelic League and the Catholic Church, since the Gaelic League

---

[39]   Ibid., p. 28.
[40]   Mac Aodha (1972), p. 22.
[41]   Ibid.
[42]   Mathews (2003), p. 28.
[43]   Ibid.
[44]   Kevin Whelan in Mathews (2003).

'was one of the first organized groupings outside the Catholic Church to exercise considerable control over social intercourse'.[45] In effect, this tension was as a response to the popularity of the Gaelic League and to the bigger question of whether the Irish language and its attendant traditional cultural practices or Catholicism was the primary indicator of Irish identity. Despite this tension, in the early years much support for the Gaelic League came from Catholic bishops and priests, who were instrumental in setting up the early branches of the Gaelic League, and although less strong, there was also support from Protestant and Unionist sources, particularly in relation to the revival of the Irish language. However, as mentioned above, it became difficult for the Gaelic League to avoid involvement in the developments in contemporary politics, and with the support of the nationalist party Sinn Féin, in 1915 the Gaelic League became a political and cultural nationalist movement. The Gaelic League exerted its influence both culturally and politically, and was significant not only for its dynamic and enthusiastic educational programme, but for its contribution to the development of national industry, and indeed the nationalist movement in Ireland.

Irish Step Dancing and An Coimisiún le Rincí Gaelacha

Following the War of Independence (1919–21) and the establishment of the Irish Free State in 1922, a positive and unified image of Ireland was required. Like all new nation-states, symbolic representations were required for the process of national identification, unification, loyalty and social organization. To this end, 'the invention of emotionally and symbolically charged signs of club membership rather than the statuettes and objects of the club' were required.[46] Thus, the universal nation-state symbols of a national flag, a national anthem and a national emblem were selected for the Irish Free State as part of this process:

> The National Flag, the National Anthem and the National Emblem are the three symbols through which an independent country proclaims its identity and sovereignty, and as such they command instantaneous respect and loyalty. In themselves they reflect the entire background, thought and culture of a nation.[47]

The new Irish nation-state asserted its identity against that which it was not. Irishness was not that which was perceived by the eye of the imperial and colonial Other. In effect, Irishness was different from Englishness. Historically, English identity was positively asserted and represented at the expense of negatively representing Ireland; England was perceived as the superior empire, with Ireland as the inferior 'Other'. As Stuart Hall noted: 'Identity … is a structured representation

---

45 Mathews (2003), p. 26.
46 Hobsbawm and Ranger (1985), p. 11.
47 Official Indian government commentary, quoted in ibid.

which only achieves its positive through the narrow eye of the negative.'[48] English writers had previously defined Englishness against that which they had perceived Irishness to be. Declan Kiberd writes:

> From the sixteenth century, when Edmund Spencer walked the plantations of Munster, the English have presented themselves to the world as controlled, refined and rooted; and so it suited them to find the Irish hot-headed, rude and nomadic, the perfect foil to set off their own virtues.[49]

With the formation of the Irish Free State in 1922, the language question became the responsibility of the new nation-state. The Gaelic League continued to promote the Irish language and Irish literature, but it would also find another focus in its cultural nationalist programme. This focus would be step dancing.

Generally, up until the 1930s, step dancing was taught by itinerant dancing masters and step dance teachers independently of the Gaelic League, although some teachers taught at branches of the Gaelic League and had close relationships with the organization. Some teachers were also associated with regional associations of step dance, established after the founding of the Gaelic League, such as the Cork Dance Teachers' Association,[50] The Dancing Teachers' Organisation of Kerry[51] and the Leinster Dance Teachers' Association,[52] primarily based in Dublin. However, *feiseanna* were generally organized by the Gaelic League throughout Ireland, and the need for a central organization to control step dance competitions became apparent as arguments and disputes over results at these events were widespread. One factor which contributed to these disputes was the fact that any member of the Gaelic League, even if not a step dancer, was eligible to adjudicate step dance competitions. This was unsatisfactory to a lot of step dance teachers, who disputed the results in many step dance competitions.[53] Also, the Gaelic League was concerned that some step dance teachers were also teaching jazz dance, while others were neglecting group or figure dances in favour of solo step dancing. In 1924, a 'steering committee' was jointly established by the Gaelic League and the Leinster Dance Teachers' Association. This committee was to look into the dance situation and to make recommendations. In 1928, a sub-committee was established by the Coiste Gnótha of the Gaelic League to further review the situation and to make recommendations. By 1930, the primary recommendation was that a body be established by the Gaelic League which would control, regulate and supervise step

---

[48]   Hall, S. (1991), p. 21.

[49]   Kiberd (1996), p. 9.

[50]   The Cork Dance Teachers' Association was founded in 1895 (see Cullinane 2003). .

[51]   It is not known exactly when The Dancing Teachers' Organisation of Kerry was founded (see Chapter 6).

[52]   The Leinster Dance Teachers' Association was founded in 1924 (see Cullinane 2003).

[53]   Peggy McTeggart, personal communication.

dance teachers, pupils and adjudicators. Thus, in 1930, Coimisiún an Rince was formed under the auspices of the Gaelic League to promote 'Irish' dancing; in 1943, it became An Coimisiún le Rincí Gaelacha – the Irish Dance Commission.[54] This organization, commonly known as 'An Coimisiún' or 'the Commission', remains today the largest hierarchical institutional structure in Irish dancing, overseeing all aspects of competitive Irish step dancing under its jurisdiction, both in Ireland and abroad. From here on, I will refer to this organization as 'An Coimisiún'.

An Coimisiún, under the auspices of the Gaelic League, implemented rules and regulations to promote, supervise and control Irish dancing. These rules and regulations, approved by the Gaelic League Congress, Easter 1931, called for the registration of teachers and adjudicators of Irish dancing; no individual was qualified to register as a teacher or adjudicator who attended, taught, adjudicated or directed dances other than what the Gaelic League considered to be Irish dances. The same rule applied to step dancers who wished to enter registered step dance competitions. This rule was in keeping with the Gaelic League's ideological agenda at the time. In 1931, at the Gaelic League's Árd-fheis in Belfast, it was declared that 'members who had anything to do with rugby, cricket or hockey or dances which were not "Gaelic" could not become a member of any committee'.[55] This was perceived by some within the organization to be an unhealthy trend at the time. According to MacGiolla Bhríde, then president of the organization, the Gaelic League was passing rules against a lot of things, and 'the individual member of the organisation has less freedom as a result'.[56] In 1933, members from the Coiste Gnótha of the Gaelic League met with the Minister for Posts and Telegraphs and asked for more Irish music and less jazz on Radio Éireann, then known as 2RN. In 1935, the Árd-fheis of the Gaelic League passed resolutions requesting a boycott of jazz music. Such were the endeavours of the Gaelic League in constructing a cultural and unified identity for Ireland.

Control, Power and Hierarchy

> [T]he history which became part of the fund of knowledge or the ideology of nation, state or movement is not what has actually been preserved in popular memory, but what has been selected, written, pictured, popularized and institutionalized by those whose function it is to do so.[57]

Under the auspices of the Gaelic League, an Irish dance configuration was culturally constructed. This configuration would gradually become a symbolic embodiment of Ireland, and would re-present Ireland culturally, shaping both

---

54   Cullinane (2003).
55   Ó Fearaíl (1975), p. 47.
56   Ibid.
57   Hobsbawm and Ranger (1985), p. 13.

the Irish people's views of themselves and their culture, and outsiders' views and perceptions of Ireland.[58]

Geertz states:

> Generalized, the "who are we" question asks what cultural forms – what systems of meaningful symbols – to employ to give value and significance to the activities of the state, and by extension to the civil life of its citizens.[59]

Step dancing as a solo dance-music cultural practice had been developed, transmitted and performed since the eighteenth century in some rural regions of Ireland (see Chapters 3 and 4). It had been developed along with the transmission and social practice of communal dances, and as such represented 'the way of life' and worldview of rural people. These notions of cultural history and tradition lent themselves to step dancing being perceived as a culturally symbolic and meaningful system rooted in antiquity, and consequently, it established a continuity and cultural link to the past. To Gaelic Leaguers, step dancing represented an important link with the past, so it was believed that step dancing had much to contribute to the cultural-nationalist vision and agenda.

The selected solo step dancing configuration was based on a style that had long associations with the itinerant dancing masters – a style of step dancing particularly common in the Munster counties of Kerry, Cork and Limerick. This dancing style placed emphasis on deportment, technique and repertoire of step dances. Consequently, a particular 'Irish' step dancing configuration was constructed by An Coimisiún which was influenced by Catholic moral teachings at the time, and which projected a controlled, disciplined, skilled and asexual step dancing body (see also Chapter 6).

An Coimisiún declared itself to be the authority and controlling body of Irish competitive step dancing and decided who was and was not eligible to teach it within the structures of the organization. Registered dance teachers were validated by the organization to teach and to adjudicate Irish dancing. Annual registration fees were required by teachers and adjudicators.[60] However, not all step dancers, step dance teachers or itinerant dancing masters registered with the organization. Some teachers and dancing masters continued teaching their own style of step dancing in their own regions independently of An Coimisiún; Jeremiah Molyneaux was one such dancing master.

Since an objective of the Gaelic League was to construct an 'Irish' community, group dances were also taught by registered dance teachers together with solo step

---

[58]   Foley (2001).

[59]   Geertz (1973), p. 242.

[60]   The annual registration fee for those wishing to teach Irish step dance at the time was 10s. In addition, those wishing to adjudicate Irish step dancing were also required to be registered, and the annual registration fee for adjudicating with An Coimisiún le Rincí Gaelacha was 2s. 6d. Certificates were given to all those who had registered; see Cullinane (2003).

dancing (see below). Like the process involved in selecting, disseminating and popularizing specific *céilí* dances for the *céilí* dance event, An Coimisiún selected and published *céilí* and figure dances for teaching, performance and competitive purposes. These dances were published in three booklets as *Ár Rincidhe Fóirne*, Volume 1 (1939), Volume 2 (1943) and Volume 3 (1969), and numbered 30 dances in total. These group dances eventually became the canon of Irish dances to be taught by registered teachers in step dance schools and to be performed at *céilí* dance competitive events (see Appendix).

In publishing *Ár Rincidhe Fóirne*, An Coimisiún published particular vocabulary and terminology (some bilingual in Irish and English) for describing the figures of the selected *céilí* dances. Much of this vocabulary had already been published in earlier publications by, for instance, O'Keeffe and O'Brien (1902 [1944]), and the common terminology and vocabulary of these published *céilí* and figure dances provided dancers and teachers with a shared common discourse, a scheme of knowledge, and a way of transmitting and communicating 'Irish' *céilí* and figure dance knowledge.

The institutionalization of these *céilí* dances narrowed the repertoire of communal social dances, and the standardized dances in time came to be perceived as *the* Irish *céilí* and figure dances. Aspiring and registered step dance teachers within the organization learned and taught from these prescribed booklets, which were, and still remain, the dancing teachers' 'text books'. Through these booklets, a canon of dances was preserved and disseminated throughout schools in Ireland and the diaspora. Teachers and step dancers alike came to share this common cognitive and corporeal knowledge which contributed to the construction of the nation as community.

In 1943, an official teacher's examination was introduced by An Coimisiún. This was the Teastas Coimisiún le Rincí Gaelacha (TCRG). The passing of this examination allowed one to register with An Coimisiún to teach Irish dancing; only students of registered teachers were eligible to enter *feiseanna* or *oireachtais* of An Coimisiún. Teachers were further required to be able to teach step dancing and the prescribed *céilí* dances through the medium of the Irish language. An adjudicator's examination (ADCRG) was also introduced for aspiring adjudicators with An Coimisiún. In establishing these examinations, An Coimisiún proclaimed itself to be a validating body and authority on Irish dancing. These examinations and qualifications are still requirements for aspiring teachers and adjudicators with An Coimisiún today.[61]

---

[61] The TCRG examination consists of five parts: a written examination based on the prescribed textbook volumes of *Ár Rinncidhe Fóirne*; a written examination based on knowledge of Irish traditional dance music; a practical examination based on candidates' dance competence and knowledge; a practical examination on candidates' ability to teach Irish dance, and an interview in English and Irish. Applicants from outside Ireland are not required to participate in an Irish oral interview; neither is it required of them to teach through the medium of the Irish language.

The authority of An Coimisiún was maintained throughout the twentieth century through a series of rules and regulations that were adopted by the organization in 1931. The rules covered the organizational structure and composition of An Coimisiún, registration of teachers and adjudicators, dance competitions and actual dances. Under the auspices of the Gaelic League, solo step dance competitions were categorized according to dance type, age and gender: for instance, Senior Males: reel, double jig, hornpipe, and two set dances; Junior Females: reel, single jig, slip jig, and two set dances[62] (see also below). These categories were later subdivided further to specific age groups and dances: Boys Jig Under 8; Ladies Reel Under 14, etc. Step dance competitions were also categorized according to competence: Beginners, Non-prize Winners and Prize Winners. These were later further categorized and graded: *Bun Grád*, *Tús Grád*, *Meán Grád* and *Árd Grád*.[63] Although some solo step dance competitions were mixed gender at local *feis* level, at *Oireachtas* level, solo step dance competitions were gendered. Also, particular assessment criteria for adjudicators were defined and categorized: time, deportment or carriage, execution and method and steps. These criteria were taught in the dance classroom and assessed by adjudicators in competition at the *feis* and the *Oireachtas*. These criteria apply also today.

Under the auspices of the Gaelic League, An Coimisiún became a hegemonic power structure in the field of Irish step dancing. However, there was criticism of the Gaelic League and its attempt to revive and popularize Irish dance. In his preface to *The Roche Collection, Volume III*, the music collector Francis Roche had the following to say:

> Up to the beginning of the present century, or for some time thereafter, the traditional style of dancing the Jig, Reel, Hornpipe and many social figure dance was in vogue amongst a considerable number of our people, and was still taught by a few of the old masters of the art, but as these retired or passed away a notable and regrettable change set in; the old style began to wane until, as time wore on, it became submerged in what has been called 'revival dancing' with injurious effects on our dance music. It was unfortunate that in the general scheme to recreate an Irish Ireland the work of preserving or reviving our old national dances should have largely fallen to the lot of those who were but poorly equipped for the task. For the most part, they were lacking in insight, and a due appreciation of the pure old style, and had, as it appears, but a slender knowledge of the old repertoire.[64]

As noted by Roche above, the so-called revival dancing of the cultural nationalist programme of the Gaelic League took precedence over the different traditional dancing styles in Ireland. An Coimisiún declared itself 'the core', while other dancing

---

[62]   Cullinane (2003).

[63]   'Beginner Grade', 'Primary Grade', 'Intermediate Grade' and 'Open or High Grade', respectively.

[64]   Roche (1982).

styles and practices were considered to be peripheral to its ideological agenda. Therefore, in its re-configuration and institutionalization of a particular step dance aesthetic, An Coimisiún constructed and projected a unified image of Ireland through the medium of step dance. This projection, embodied by step dancers, assisted in emphasizing the cultural unity of Ireland as a nation-state. With the embodiment of Irish step dancing tied to nationalist agendas, Irish step dancers performed and accomplished politics throughout both the de-colonial and the postcolonial periods.

Ireland was not the only country to incorporate body politics into its political agenda when asserting its cultural nationalist agenda. For example, in Spain, Franco used flamenco bodies to achieve a similar nationalist objective of projecting Spain as a unified nation. As Washabaugh states:

> Their bodies accomplish politics when they inadvertently resonate with and reinforce political energies consonant with existing political agendas. Such political actions of bodies making music are both more potent and more enduring than the political messages of songs, whether played forward or in reverse.[65]

Also, in India, the classical Indian dance form *bharata natyam* was appropriated for nationalistic purposes and came to embody the nation of India after its independence from England in 1947. Similarly in Ireland, with its appropriation of step dancing for ideological purposes, An Coimisiún and the Gaelic League acknowledged the power of step dancing bodies to accomplish political aims.

The Irish Step Dancing School, Age and Gender

The Gaelic League was stronger and more prominent in urban areas than rural ones. According to Art McGann: 'In the thickly populated centres organisation tended to be more finished, and aided by the Gaelic League branches, a definite revival set in.'[66] The first Irish step dancing schools emerged in the cities and towns of Ireland in the 1920s, and from the 1930s onwards, individual teachers were gradually establishing their own step dancing schools within the hierarchical structures of An Coimisiún.[67] As the century progressed, the towns and cities would become major centres for An Coimisiún step dance teachers, replacing the itinerant rural dancing masters of previous decades. Also, step dancing in these centres would no longer be an integrated aspect of society, but would become an optional leisure-time

---

[65]   Washabaugh (1996), p. 26.

[66]   McGann (1936), pp. 65–6.

[67]   These teachers included Lily Comerford, Cora and Ita Cadwell and Rory O'Connor of Dublin; Cormac O'Keeffe, Molly Hassen, Tommy Cullen and Peggy McTeggart of Cork; Joe, Úna and Mona Halpin and Máire Ní Ruairc of Limerick; Liam Ó Duinín of Listowel; Eilís Ní Tháilliúra, Irene Gould and Phil Cahill of Tralee; and Seosamh Mallon of Belfast (see Cullinane 2003.

activity available to the children and teenagers of a community. Consequently, the urbanization of step dancing in the twentieth century would see changes in both the age at which a step dancer learned and the gender balance within step dance practice. Different contexts of performance would replace the older contexts, and the function and meaning of traditional step dance practice would be transformed.

Since step dancing was originally associated with a rural way of life, it was considered by some, particularly the middle-class population of urban areas, to be inferior to dance forms such as ballet, which was perceived to be reflective of a 'higher' or Anglicized culture. In effect, step dancing was perceived as 'low art', while ballet was perceived as 'high art'. This perception was very much reflective of a postcolonial mindset in Ireland. Thus, it was predominantly children of rural migrants, working-class parents, or children of Irish nationalistically or culturally aware parents, who attended these step dancing schools.

The relative affordability of step dancing classes within the structures of An Coimisiún assisted children from lower-income families to attend. In this way, An Coimisiún provided communities with a social service. Students paid per class, not per term.[68] Also, there were family rates, which encouraged a number of siblings to attend. The emphasis on the younger age group, and indeed the younger body, influenced the development of step dancing throughout the twentieth century, but it also allowed for the cultural and political agenda of the Gaelic League to be embodied in the earlier years of childhood. This process enabled a particular community *habitus* to develop: a *habitus* that emphasized the nation as community.

Prior to the appropriation of step dancing by the Gaelic League, step dancing was performed in rural regions by the youth of the community. Although both male and female dancers from 14 years of age upwards attended the rural dancing schools in North Kerry, it was male-dominated. In addition, all the itinerant dancing masters of the region were male. With the institutionalization and urbanization of step dancing by the Gaelic League, the age group fell to between approximately four years of age and young adulthood, after which, with a few exceptions, these trained step dancers rarely performed publicly. Relatively few dancers continued until they were 18, and those who did so were committed step dancers who turned up regularly to their twice-weekly step dancing classes. Many dancers dropped step dancing classes after primary school at the age of 12. One reason was that they did not wish to commit themselves to the dance classes. Some chose to prioritize their formal secondary school education, and others, influenced by their peers who did not participate in step dancing classes, associated this genre of dance with childhood. Since there were no career prospects in Irish step dance performance at the time, many chose to stop taking Irish step dancing classes. Of those who continued, some would decide to train for their TCRG in order

---

[68]   According to Irene Gould, in the 1950s in Kerry, a two-hour step dance class was 5d. per pupil. However, when travelling out to national schools, the fee was 10d. per pupil, in order to cover travelling expenses; Irene Gould, personal communication. In the 1980s, a step dance class cost between 75 pence and £1 per pupil; in 2004 the fee per pupil per class in Ireland was between €5 and €10.

to qualify as a teacher of Irish step dancing.[69] It would not be until *Riverdance* in 1995, and the other commercial Irish step dance stage shows that followed, that a professional performance career in Irish step dancing would become a possibility.[70]

An Coimisiún's concentration on a younger age group, consciously or unconsciously, was an influential factor in the development of Irish step dancing in the twentieth century. The rural, traditional style of step dancing taught in North Kerry, for instance, during the early decades of the twentieth century was learned by teenagers and older 'scholars' in the dancing schools. These traditional step dances were earthy in style, and emphasized movements and beats created with the feet making contact with the floor, including batters, tips, heels, toes, stamps, drums and toe-fences.[71] Spatially, the required aesthetic was earthy and confined. However, the young age group and the athletic ability of younger dancers in the more urban dancing schools assisted in the development of kinetic vocabulary and a different accompanying aesthetic. In keeping with young dancing bodies, a more elevated and sharper style of step dancing emerged. The upright torso and the notion of verticality also became more pronounced. In addition, with the advent of larger dance stages for competitions in indoor halls, more travelling movements were introduced into step dances. In training, terms such as 'time', 'posture', 'lift' and 'move' came into frequent use in step dancing classes.

An Coimisiún also contributed to and reinforced notions of the ideal Irish male and female step dancer, and by extension, the ideal Irish male and female citizen. These notions were in line with Catholic teaching and culturally constructed notions of masculine and feminine traits in Irish society. From the Rules and Regulations of the Irish Dancing Commission for Provincial and All Ireland Championships in 1931, dance types were allocated according to gender. Male dancers were allocated Reel, Double Jig, Hornpipe and two set dances; female dancers were allocated Reel, Single Jig, Slip Jig[72] and two set dances (see Appendix).[73] Influenced by ballet, the pump or light shoe was introduced. Light-shoe step dances became associated with female dancers, which they performed in a light, graceful and airborne manner; and although female step dancers performed hard-shoe percussive step dances, male step dancers were more associated with them, which they were expected to perform in a strong and masculine way. The light-shoe Slip Jig was categorized as a female step dance due to the required graceful manner of its performance. Thus, in demarcating particular dances for male and female dancers, An Coimisiún was perpetuating and reinforcing what it considered to be conventional gender ideas

---

[69] My sister Pat and I were two of these step dance students.

[70] Foley (2001); see also Ó Cinnéide (2002).

[71] See Foley (1988b; 2012b) for Labanotated documentation of these and other traditional step dance movements.

[72] The Slip Jig is considered a female dance within the structures of An Coimisiún, however, young boys up to the age of ten are also taught it in some schools, to instil in them a sense of grace.

[73] Cullinane (2003).

and values in Irish society. These values were transmitted in the dance class and assessed by adjudicators at competitions.

Influenced by the Catholic Church, An Coimisiún was also promoting a heteronormative culture.[74] This was particularly evident in the *céilí* dances, where couples in group dances were ideally one male and one female dancer. Indeed, heteronormativity was considered to be integral to the construction of the nation, and the importance of family units was seen as central. According to David Cregan:

> While early nationalism based its identity project on reconfiguring the negative British imagery of Ireland, post-liberation Ireland began to devolve into its own essentialization of the nature of the 'true' Irish citizen … based on a Catholic morality rather than the broad based human rights of an emerging democracy.[75]

The promotion of community identities over individual identities was also made manifest in the dancing costumes. To make individual step dancing schools recognizable and identifiable at competitive events and performances, dancing costumes were introduced. Each school selected its own dancing-costume colours and created costumes in line with Gaelic League Irish dancing costume norms.[76] Combinations of green, saffron and *bánín* (off-white), the colours of the Irish national flag, were popular. These class costumes, with their recognizable colours and designs, were worn by all step dancers of the school for solo, *céilí* and figure dance competitions. This reinforced the notion of a community identity over an individual identity: a notion that was reflective of the ethos of the Gaelic League in its construction of a cultural nationalism. Initially, both male and female step dancers wore kilts due to the influence of the nationalist and political activist Pádraig Pearse. Later, a dance dress with lace collar and Celtic embroidery replaced the kilt for ladies, while male dancers continued to wear the kilt; later, trousers became a popular choice for men. As the twentieth century progressed, solo dancing costumes for competitions in solo dancing became the norm, thus also placing an emphasis on individual identities of step dancers; class costumes continued to be worn for *céilí* and figure dancing competitions. As the twentieth century progressed, step dancing costumes would develop further.[77]

Throughout the history of An Coimisiún, young female dancers have dominated this particular practice. Reasons for this include the fact that the kilt worn by male step dancers in competition was perceived negatively by many male dancers, who saw it as effeminate; this did little to attract male dancers to Irish step dancing classes. In addition, the act of dancing itself was perceived by many urban men to be unmanly, and consequently, few young male dancers took up Irish

---

[74]   Gareiss (2012).

[75]   Cregan (2009).

[76]   For information on the development of Irish step dance costumes, see Cullinane (1996) and Robb (1998).

[77]   Ibid.

dancing as a leisure-time activity. Those who did loved it and were prepared to tolerate whatever comments were directed at them. However, many boys chose to take part in sports such as hurling[78] and Gaelic football instead, which were well catered for by the Gaelic Athletic Association (GAA) Since the GAA did not cater so well for girls, they joined dance classes such as step dancing classes, which were affordable, physical and social. Also, in contrast to the dominance of male itinerant dancing masters from the eighteenth to the twentieth century, the majority of step dancing teachers within the step dancing organisation of An Coimisiún were female.

The step dancing teachers in the larger towns and cities in many cases combined their work as teachers with some other occupation or trade;[79] consequently, they taught part-time only. However, for some step dancing teachers, it was their only livelihood. Step dancing schools were established in individual teachers' homes or specific halls in communities where these teachers lived. Classes took place as an extra-curricular leisure-time activity throughout the year in the teacher's fixed dancing school premises. This coincided with the academic calendar of primary and secondary schools; classes were not held during school holidays. Usually, these classes took place two or three times a week, outside school hours, lasting two to three hours. During this time, solo dances and/or group *céilí* and figure dances were taught and practised (see the Appendix). Live musicians did not play for these classes; instead, teachers used a selection of recorded traditional dance music. At intensive times leading up to competitions or performances, some teachers selected additional afternoons or evenings for extra practice. To supplement this income, some teachers also travelled to rural national schools and to town and city national schools and convents. These national schools were usually visited once a week, as part of the school's physical education curriculum. As the disciplined configuration of step dancing by An Coimisiún met with approval from the Catholic clergy, these step dancing classes were welcomed in these schools, the majority of which were Catholic.

Communities in larger urban centres had a number of step dancing schools from which to choose. Competition became a means by which one teacher gained recognition over another. Therefore, a competitive spirit was inculcated in step dancing pupils in order to win at *feiseanna* and *oireachtais* for the prestige of both the step dancing school and the dancers themselves. Although a sense of rivalry and a competitive spirit had existed prior to the appropriation of step dancing by the Gaelic League, it was only with the Gaelic League's re-configuration and institutionalization of Irish step dancing that organized staged competitions became a primary context for step dance performance.

---

[78]   Hurling is an Irish sport played with a stick-like wooden bat called a *hurley* (made of ash) and a small ball called a *sliotar*.

[79]   Foley (1988a).

Transmission, Training and Discipline

Depending on the size of the school of dancing, step dancing class sizes and structures varied. Some teachers taught all age groups of different abilities during set weekly time periods; other teachers structured their classes according to age group or dance competence. However, whatever the size or structure, the focus of the class was on teaching and developing pupils' step dancing skills. Together with this, cultural values were also transmitted in the process of transmission and performance.

Step dance training concerned the discipline and skill of step dancing. The training associated with committed competitive Irish step dancers was long and meticulous; it was regarded as an art and a discipline.[80] Those step dancers who continued and competed at senior championship level, and those who were regarded as 'good', 'beautiful', 'lovely', 'great' Irish step dancers, had mastered this discipline and art.

According to the French philosopher Michel Foucault, 'discipline produces subjected and practiced bodies, "docile bodies"'.[81] It was, according to Foucault, the Classical age that discovered the body as 'object' and 'target of power'. Foucault references La Mettrie's book *L'Homme-machine*,[82] and in particular the 'technico-political' section, which included a 'whole set of regulations … relating to the army, the school and the hospital, for controlling or correcting the operations of the body'.[83] According to Foucault, *L'Homme-machine* concerns itself with the 'materialist reduction of the soul and a general theory of *dressage*'. At the centre of this notion is the idea that bodies can be 'subjected, used, transformed and improved'.[84] He contends that projects of docility were abundant throughout the eighteenth century. In the French army, particularly that of Louis XIV, there were well-trained regiments with long exercises and straight, meticulous lines.[85] Before that, Jesuit secondary schools and later primary schools were subjected to regulations for improvement in disciplinary behaviour, for classification and hierarchical structuring. Hospitals were also subjected to these regulations. These projects were designed to shape, order and discipline the lives and the behaviours of the people in these institutions.

The concentration on meticulous technique characteristic of disciplinary institutions was also a feature of the Irish step dancing schools, whose purpose was to produce Irish trained, disciplined and practised dancers. Step dancers' bodies were therefore shaped to suit the Gaelic League's political agenda and, through their training, step dancers came to share particular conceptions of their bodies.

---

[80] Hall, F. (2008).
[81] Foucault (1977), p. 138.
[82] 'The Man-machine'.
[83] Foucault (1977), p. 136.
[84] Ibid.
[85] Many Irish soldiers were in Louis XIV's army; see also Chapter 2.

Although step dancing had been taught formally by itinerant dancing masters within rural regions prior to its appropriation by the Gaelic League, the length of time spent in training was less, and step dancers commenced at an older age. With years of training from a young age, and assessed within hierarchical competitive contexts under the jurisdiction of An Coimisiún, Irish step dancers embodied the "Gaelic idea" and unconsciously became part of the political machinery for the Irish cultural nationalist movement. This concurs with what the anthropologist Sally Ann Ness suggests:

> The ... kinds of dance that have attracted the label 'classical' ... are the most tradition-bound, technically developed, and hierarchically institutionalized varieties of dance. Such dance genres typically require a relatively great quantity of practice in order for students to acquire mastery. Training for the most advanced levels also tends to begin at a very early age.[86]

The discipline of step dancing was transmitted in the step dancing class and assessed in competition (see Chapter 6). Each of the dance types transmitted in the dancing class had its own specific music structure, metre and rhythms, together with a kinetic vocabulary, aesthetic and steps. Similarly to Jeremiah Molyneaux's step dances, each step dance (excluding the solo set dances) was choreographed within the eight-bar structure, and rhythmic foot and leg patterns were choreographed with particular music metres in mind. The step dance elements used by Molyneaux[87] were also used in the more modern choreographies, but developed further and performed by younger bodies in a more virtuosic manner. Similarly to Molyneaux, in the early transmission process, specific movement motifs such as full-batters and threes[88] appeared to be regularly structured, musically speaking, with much repetition. As the repertoire increased in complexity, different or innovative motifs were choreographed, and these did not have to be regularly structured; rhythmic movement patterns and motifs were creatively choreographed based on combinations of old and new or innovative elements.[89] New vocabulary was thus developed, in keeping with the younger age group and younger bodies. Also, the accompanying music for hard-shoe dances gradually became slower. In lieu of Molyneaux's general method of choreographing a step with one foot sound to one note of the music, more rhythmically intricate foot and leg movements were inserted into new step dance choreographies; these challenges suited the younger step dancers and assisted in developing an Irish step dancing virtuosity.[90]

---

[86]   Ness in Noland and Ness (2008), p. 13.

[87]   See Foley (1988b; 2012b).

[88]   Ibid.

[89]   For a more detailed discussion of elements, cells, motifs and so on, see Foley (1988b; 2007c; and 2012b); also see Reynolds (1974).

[90]   See the documentary *Jig*, directed by Sue Bourne (2010); see also the six-part series *Rising Steps* (Stirling Productions, 2000).

In addition, contrary to Molyneaux's spatially confined space of four square feet for the performance of a step dance, floor patterns were included in the new choreographies of steps to suit the bigger stage venues for larger competitions. A different configuration of step dancing was thus developing.

The transmission process in these dancing classes was similar to Molyneaux's process, in that the methods utilized included visual, kinaesthetic and aural imitation with verbal or sung instructions. Throughout the transmission process, the teacher broke the step dance down into coherent motifs or smaller units. These were slowly demonstrated while students attempted to imitate and embody each movement. In this attempt, students used their minds, bodies and their senses: visual, aural and kinaesthetic. Each movement or section was then repeated until the student successfully embodied it and could dance it. These movements were not separated from the aesthetic of step dancing. Some teachers also used specific step dance terminology or "action vocabulary"[91] when teaching. This terminology was vocalized to accompany their own movements while teaching, or their students' movements when dancing. In this way, students learned to associate step dance terminology with specific kinetic movements. This combination of movement and vocalized terminology assisted in memorization and embodiment of this step dance practice. The following 'Easy Double Jig' is an example of this:

> Batter |batter hop back, batter |batter hop back,
> Hop |back 234, hop |back 234
> Hop |heel down heel down, 1|2 kick left heel,
> 1|2 kick right heel, Batter |batter hop back.

Once the step was learned and embodied, the student then performed it to music. These strategies of kinaesthetic imitation, aural vocalized terminology and the additional accompaniment of music combined to assist students in their embodiment of Irish step dancing. The assessment of this embodiment took place at the rituals of the *feis* and the *Oireachtas* and was assessed by registered adjudicators (see Chapter 6).[92]

Transmission of Cultural Values, Co-operation and Mutual Dependence

While teaching the skill and aesthetic of step dancing, cultural values were also transmitted during the process. These included discipline, uprightness, precision, strength, grace, modesty, self-presentation, competitive spirit, co-operation, mutual dependence, decency, respectability and morality. These values were

---

[91]   Ness in Noland and Ness (2008), p. 11.

[92]   Progressive grade exams (1–12) were also introduced by An Coimisiún in 1943 (see Culliane 2003) as a different form of assessment from the *feis* and the *Oireachtas*. Grade exams are still in existence today, but are not popular.

important to the Gaelic League (and the Catholic Church), whose philosophy centred on the development of 'the individual Irish personality' which 'could not reach its potential except in a community proper to it' (see above). The Irish step dancing class was one such community where values of co-operation and mutual dependence were important ideological tools. Although these values were made manifest within classroom behaviour, they were also inscribed in the dances taught in the classroom; these included solo dancing together with group dances: *céilí* and figure dances.

Within the group *céilí* and figure dances, perfection in execution of graphic patterns was a required aesthetic. These patterns included line formations, crosses, circles, squares, chain movements and interlaces; the proper execution of these patterns required group co-operation. According to the annual report of An Coimisiún in 1934:

> we will teach Irish dancing because it is part of the Gaelic Revival plan: we will use Irish dancing as a means towards instilling the Gaelic idea into our people: co-operation and mutual dependence are essentials of Irish dancing, and self and selfishness have no place in the Gaelic nation.[93]

The institutionalized *céilí* dances were well suited to meet the ideological agenda of the Gaelic League. The majority of the dances were choreographed for four, six or eight dancers, and could be performed by either all female dancers or male and female dancers in mixed teams. These dances required 'co-operation and mutual dependence' for their proper execution. Thus, in a co-ordinated manner, dancers' bodies moved in and out of prescribed positions, creating particular figures and spatial patterns inherent to the dance in question. These prescribed patterns were formed at particular points in the music, and all dancers were conscious of being in particular positions at precise moments. It was the execution of the dance figures and spatial patterns that mattered, aesthetically speaking. Hand and arm movements were integral to the execution of many of these patterns, and were performed by step dancers in a meticulous, disciplined, graceful and controlled manner. Foot and leg movements – including the basic characteristic motifs of the Reel, the 'threes' and the 'sevens' and the basic characteristic motifs of the Jig, the 'skip threes' and the 'skip sevens' – were also performed meticulously together. In these group dances, step dancers were required to perform in a uniform manner.

These *céilí* dances and the spatial patterns characteristic of them begged for an aerial view to oversee the perfection of these patterns. Dancers performed these dances in ways that kaleidoscopically constructed these symbolic patterns. All dancers within a dance team or group performed in a unified and co-operative manner within temporal, spatial and movement parameters. All dancers within the dance team performed as one unit, with no individual dancer standing out from the

---

[93]   Irish Dancing Commission in *The Teacher's Work*, vol. 24 (1934).

group. This process encouraged the notion of community and the ability to engage in teamwork.

These *céilí* dances allowed for the optimum of 'co-operation and mutual dependence'. The discipline needed and the unity of execution and performance of these dances required military precision, and since discipline and mutual dependence were required for perfecting these patterns, the step dancers corporeally performed 'the Gaelic idea'.

Step Dancing as a Vehicle of Thought and Sentiment

The apparent success of the cultural appropriation of step dancing by the Gaelic League was due not just to the adaptation of the notion of training, but also to the combination of training and 'tradition', within the context of a social, cultural and political institution. For economic reasons, many rural migrants had historically moved to the cities and larger towns of Ireland. Since the Gaelic League was strongly organized in these areas, Irish step dancing classes were a means of culturally connecting them and their children, emotionally and psychologically, to their immediate rural past.

Step dancing, as a culturally expressive movement system, was therefore a natural vehicle of thought, sentiment, feeling, philosophy and Christian morality. The socializing process involved in the step dancing class included the transmission of particular values and sentiments (see above) together with the more obvious benefits of socializing, having fun, and learning the aesthetic discipline of Irish step dancing. These values, promoted by the Gaelic League in its de-colonial and postcolonial endeavours, were acceptable to Catholic teachings in Ireland, where step dancing as a dance form was considered to be sanitized and respectable.

Hegemony and Homogeneity

An Coimisiún created a hegemony whereby it placed itself in a dominant position and at the same time gained the consent of many involved in *Irish* competitive step dancing culture. However, as Cowan reminds us:

> Gramsci did not conceptualise hegemony as a necessarily oppressive process. To the contrary, he saw the development of an alternative hegemony of the working class, under the leadership of those he referred to as 'organic intellectuals', as a precondition of social revolution. He saw the establishment of this new proletarian hegemony … as essential, moreover, in the formation of a just society.[94]

---

[94]   Cowan (1990), p. 13.

During the early decades of the twentieth century, the Gaelic League provided this leadership in Ireland. Through its rulings concerning organizational structures, dances, step dancers, teachers, adjudicators, dance events, *feiseanna*, *oireachtais*, clothing and music, An Coimisiún assisted in centralizing, homogenizing and institutionalizing Irish step dancing as a practice, and many step dancing teachers in Ireland succumbed to its control and leadership.

Improvisation or varying versions of step dances during performances were not part of An Coimisiún's representation of step dancing. Step dancers may have had the ability to improvise, but they were not assessed on this aspect of performance in competition, nor was improvisation expected. Although school styles and individual styles were discernible to the knowing eye of individuals within the organization who had developed an intimate relationship with step dancing and its competitive context, homogeneity and conformity became evident on a large scale. And although some regional and marginalized practices of step dancing might have declined anyway due to processes of modernity, by institutionalizing a particular configuration of step dancing and by developing a uniformity of practice, An Coimisiún assisted in narrowing and controlling the vision, practice and understanding of step dancing in Ireland. Isaiah Berlin states, however:

> One may wish to condemn nationalism outright as an irrational and enslaving force ... but it seems to me far more important to understand its roots. Nationalism springs as often as not, from a wounded or outraged sense of human dignity, the desire for recognition ....[95]

This 'desire for recognition' prompted the establishment of the Gaelic League. Under its vision and ideological agenda, step dancing was promoted and developed through An Coimisiún. Therefore, when step dancers performed in contexts invented and deemed appropriate to its practice by An Coimisiún, they unconsciously danced the nation.

---

[95]   Berlin (1991), p. 245.

Chapter 6

Step Dancing, Modernity and Change
in North Kerry

From the mid-1930s, processes of modernity in North Kerry gradually introduced different modes of social and economic interaction. Different venues for socializing, such as the public dance hall, the *céilí*, the public house, followed by the disco, the cabaret and the club, eventually replaced the older social institutions in rural regions (see Chapter 4). Although country dance halls were operating in rural areas of North Kerry from the beginning of the twentieth century, it was not until the late 1920s that bigger and better halls were built in nearby towns. Popular country dance halls in North Kerry were Bedford, the Six Crosses, Lixnaw, Ballyduff, Abbeydorney, Kilflynn and Causeway. In these halls, live band music was provided and couples danced Waltzes, Foxtrots and Quicksteps. These venues gradually replaced the more intimate rambling houses, raffles and the dance schools of the benefit night system. The latter, important to the educational, social and economic life of previous rural communities, were superseded by new contexts which facilitated different meaning and value systems and which assisted in constructing different notions of community and identity. As Hobsbawm argues, changing times required that 'social groups, environments and social contexts called for new devices to ensure or express social cohesion and identity and to structure social relations'.[1]

The availability of better transport, improved road conditions, better technological and communication systems and the increased option of third-level education and travel abroad provided choices for rural communities in socializing, work and education. Dance was no longer an integral part of rural society in North Kerry. The interests of the majority of the youth were less focused on practising or supporting the indigenous performing arts[2] as a wider range of interests and choices in leisure-time activities became available within an increasingly affluent and modern society. As one elderly step dancer stated:

> There were a lot of step dancers when I was young around the locality ... there isn't half as many now. Most of the old crowd they all had a few steps ... they had it either learned from their parents or uncles. It was the pastime and the

---

[1] Hobsbawm (1977), p. 263.

[2] That is not to say that youth within the perceived, older, close-knit-community system were all learning these indigenous arts, but that they were all exposed to them and shared in the community experience, either as performers or active members of the audience.

amusement they had mostly in their time. People don't have the same interest any more. My own nephew is into karate and rock and roll music. The Irish music don't mean a thing to him.[3]

From the 1960s, the youth who performed the 'traditional' arts did so out of choice, and for the most part learned within specific educational and cultural institutions, such as Comhaltas Ceoltóirí Éireann,[4] Siamsa Tíre, An Coimisiún or the individual step dance schools in the region which worked outside the structures of An Coimisiún. However, the social institutions of the rambling houses, raffles and porter balls declined, which consequently disrupted the process of local step dance knowledge and tunes being transmitted informally in homes. Although modernity and general material progress in the area would gradually have transformed these institutions, the Public Dance Halls Act of 1935, supported by the Catholic Church, assisted in accelerating their decline.[5] To quote Junior Crehan:

> a way of life was ended in the mid-30s by a number of events; and while it is hard to say that it would have continued in the same way for much longer it is safe to say that its end was quickened by those who, for different reasons, wanted to put an end to it.[6]

Dance and the Catholic Church

As mentioned in Chapter 3, the Catholic Church contributed to the civilizing process of its laity and was overt in condemning dance from the seventeenth century to the early decades of the twentieth century. According to Tom Inglis

> ...the church... was the civilizing force behind the embourgeoisement of the Irish farmer, and because it gained a monopoly of control over their bodies, secular civility became almost synonymous with Catholic morality.[7]

---

[3]   Anonymous (1985), ethnographic interview with the author.

[4]   Comhaltas Ceoltóirí Éireann (CCE), established in 1951, is a cultural nationalist organization which receives state sponsorship (Henry 1989). Its aims are to promote Irish traditional music in all forms; to restore the playing of the harp and uilleann pipes in the national life of Ireland; to promote Irish traditional dancing; to create a closer bond among all lovers of Irish traditional music; to co-operate with all bodies working for the restoration of Irish culture; to establish branches throughout the country and abroad to achieve the foregoing aims and objects, and to foster and promote the Irish language at all times.

[5]   Since house dances and raffles were understood to be public dances, they were also interpreted to be included in the Act which received Church support; see also Breathnach (1983) and Foley (1988b; 2012b).

[6]   Crehan (1977), p. 74.

[7]   Inglis (1987), p. 165.

In some rural areas of North Kerry during the 1930s, some parish priests were totally against people holding raffles, turkey nights or any community event where dancing was involved. According to one step dancer, 'a priest raided a crossroad dance in the middle of the noon day. We were dancing and he came behind and scattered women and all.' Also, around the 1930s, the parish priest in another area did not want raffles, all-night dances nor Wren nights:

> There was a curate … and when the dance would be in full swing, he would come in and you would see men and women scooting for the door as fast as they could …. It wasn't the dance I think they were so much against, it was company-keeping. That was the worst thing that they were against, and one followed the other.[8]

According to my informants, during the early decades of the twentieth century, the rural people of North Kerry respected and feared the local parish priests. These priests were perceived as powerful since they were generally also the managers of the national schools. Consequently, the Catholic Church and the parish priests played an influential role in shaping the ethos of these schools at the time. Great importance was placed on Christian teaching and learning in the national schools, and a strict moral code was imposed within these schools by the clergy: a code which was imposed equally outside the school. For example, social dance events were perceived by the clergy as places that threatened this moral code of behaviour, and consequently, when rural people of North Kerry gathered for a social dance, they feared being caught by the priests. The following story is an instance of a raid on one such social dance:

> They were running every night from Father [X] …. There was one girl in the crowd, I knew her well, and she had, I suppose it would be like polio; and she young. And, she used to carry a crutch, you see; the leg was kind of deformed. But in the road she could run with any of the men or the women. But the priest was an awful hardy young man at that time and he had a whip. And he was coming after them, the whole crowd, and when he was getting too close, they left the road and they went into the field. And it happened that the field was a ploughed garden, and of course, the one with the crutch, she couldn't go, the crutch went down and she was anchored. The priest came up and he drew the whip, 'twas dark, like you know, and drew the whip across her legs and she was in an awful state. But when he found out who she was, he apologized, and went after the other crowd.[9]

In 1923, the Archbishop of Dublin stated:

---

[8]   Anonymous (1985), ethnographic interview with the author.
[9]   Anonymous (1985), ethnographic interview with the author.

Dancing has become a grave danger to the morals of … young people, not only in the city but in the country parts of the diocese and parents were warned that God would demand a strict account of them if, by their want of vigilance, they allowed their children to be led astray from the path of virtue. It was a matter of notoriety that the dances often were of a kind imported from other countries and were, if not absolutely improper, on the border line of Christian modesty.[10]

The so-called imported dances were 'importations from the vilest dens of London, Paris and New York, direct and unmistakeable incitements to evil thought and evil desires',[11] and these imported dances were differentiated from the 'clean, healthy, national Irish dances' (see Chapter 5). Indeed, objections to dancing were not only felt on the mainland of Ireland, but also on the islands. Eibhlis Ní Shúilleabháin, in *Letters from the Great Blaskets*, recounts the following in her entry for 7 July 1936:

Great change have come on the island lately, there was a Mission here, preached by two Redemptorist Fathers. They were here for a week. They blessed everyone and every place, and they left written hard rules for the visitor that come here, no mixed bathing allowed. White Strand for women alone to bathe and bask. There is a sign post near this strand and written on it is 'Women'. Near the gravel strand is another post 'Men'. Below at the pier top too is all about the strand rules and information is written in Irish. No dance in any house day, or night, no one out later than 10.30 and all visitors and all members of the family in at that time for the Holy Rosary. Of course we are keeping the rules as the parish priest wishes us to do so nor neither they would not bless the boats nor sea unless they were promised to do …. No boy or girl here is allowed to walk at night with any of the visitors nor either in the day time.[12]

These notices were strategies of the Catholic Church at the time concerning the moral behaviour of its laity. Keeping men and women apart as much as was possible was at the core of its mission. Since social dance events were popular with rural communities and brought men and women together, they were condemned by the Catholic hierarchy. Young people found to be behaving in a way that was not acceptable to these parish priests were slandered before the eyes of the community from the pulpits in the churches. Although dance in Ireland was condemned by the Catholic hierarchy for its perceived potentially immoral and unacceptable behaviour, it may also have stemmed from a fear on the part of the Church of a threat to its over-riding control of its laity at that time. In spite of the above objections from the Catholic Church, social dance events continued in more remote places where supervision by the clergy was less prevalent or non-existent, and this allowed for traditional music, step dance and social dances to be

---

[10]   Breathnach (1977), p. 43.

[11]   Ibid.

[12]   Ní Shúilleabháin (1936), pp. 44–5.

transmitted and practised in these areas. However, in 1935, the Catholic Church's influence was finally made widespread in an Act passed by the Irish state assisted by three hundred years of pressure from the Catholic hierarchy: the Public Dance Halls Act.

The Public Dance Halls Act[13]

In 1935, the Public Dance Halls Act was passed in Ireland. According to the bill introduced by the Minister for Justice in 1934, the Act was intended 'to make provision for the licensing, control and supervision of places used for public dancing, and to make provision for other matters connected with the matters aforesaid'. The Public Dance Halls Act thus required all public dances to be licensed, and should anyone hold a public dance without a licence, then that person incurred a fine. Public dances were interpreted to be 'dancing in which members of the public actively participate'.[14]

According to this bill, any person wishing to hold a 'public dance' should apply for a licence to a 'licensing area' – 'a district court area prescribed by law for the purpose of the transaction of licensing business'.[15] Annual licensing district courts were also established for the hearing of applications for 'renewals of licences' that included the sale of 'intoxicating liquor'. Certain provisions were laid down for applicants who wished to attain a licence issued by the district justice to hold a public dance. These provisions included:

1. the character and the financial and other circumstances of the applicant for such licence;
2. the suitability of the place to which such application relates;
3. the facilities for public dancing existing in the neighbourhood of such place at the time of such application;
4. the accommodation for the parking of vehicles in the neighbourhood of such place;
5. the probable age of the persons who would be likely to make use of such place for public dancing;
6. whether the situation of such place is or is not such as to render difficult the supervision by the *Garda Síochána*[16] of the management of and proceedings in such place;
7. the hours during which the applicant proposes that public dancing should be permitted in such place.[17]

---

[13]   Public Dance Halls Bill (1934).
[14]   Ibid.
[15]   Ibid.
[16]   The Police Force.
[17]   Public Dance Halls Bill (1934).

Health and safety issues were also taken into account when applying for a licence, thus objections to particular social dances were also made on the basis of these issues.

Objections to the holding of a public dance, and therefore to the acquisition of a licence to hold one, were made at the hearing of the application before the district judge. Generally, all applications for public dancing licences were made at the annual licensing district court, and at no other time. Exceptions to this rule were applications where no other licence was in existence in the area at the time of applying, and applications for a defined period not exceeding one month. Another provision required that the applicant place a notice in the local newspaper one month prior to the application being heard at the district court;[18] this allowed sufficient time for any objections which might have arisen. Should an application for a licence be refused for whatever reason, applicants were able to appeal the decision and take their case to the circuit court.

The passing of the Public Dance Halls Act had an impact on all types of public and social dances. In rural areas, applications for licences included not only dances in halls, but also rambling house dances, raffles, porter balls, crossroad dances and platform dances. These social institutions had played an important role in the social and cultural life of the people of rural Ireland (see Chapter 4), but since these dance contexts were interpreted to be 'public dances' under the Public Dance Halls Act, many of these social institutions declined. The Act required a formalization and legalization of hitherto informal and spontaneous social events. Also, the threat of incurring fines was a disincentive to hold a house dance, a raffle and so on. Therefore, in North Kerry, social institutions such as, the raffles, Biddy nights, Wren nights, turkey balls and house dances in general declined. In the Clashmealcon area of North Kerry, dances were still held in private houses where no money was taken at the door, but they were no longer as frequent. Consequently, much of the local dance, music and song repertoire declined in its informal transmission and practice, and revivalist organizations such as An Coimisiún (see Chapter 5) and Comhaltas Ceoltóirí Éireann would assist in promoting and disseminating Irish dance and music as national expressions of cultural identity.

Demographic Trends and Dance

Demographic trends also contributed to the decline of rural social and cultural institutions. From the aftermath of the Great Famine, statistics show how the population in rural areas of North Kerry steadily declined. In 1841, statistics record a population of 434 in the townland of Clashmealcon; in 1851 it had decreased to 260, and by 1981 it had a population of only 175. This decline in population was a general trend in rural areas of North Kerry. This trend, according to Brody, was

---

18   Ibid., Sections 2 and 3.

found in 'the majority of villages and communities which, in vestigial form, spread still from Bantry Bay to Tory Island'.[19] With the end of subdivision of farms after the Great Famine, young men and women found themselves either emigrating, or moving to the larger Irish towns or cities for employment. Thus, it was only the one son, generally the eldest, who inherited the farm, while in many cases his parents remained living on the farm. Referring to Kilmore, Jack Dineen states:

All that village back, between darling boys and girls, was full, and now there is only one in every house, no one in another house, an old man like myself in another house. Isn't it a fright? Where there used to be 11 of us. They all went for foreign lands, New York, America.[20]

So common was the occurrence of emigration that American Wakes were frequent (see Chapter 4). The Listowel writer John B. Keane, himself an emigrant to England, wrote the song 'Many Young Men of Twenty Said Goodbye' with emigrants in mind. In his book *Self-portrait*, he recalls his own departure to England:

When I boarded the train at Listowel that morning, it seemed as if everybody was leaving. It was the same at every railway station along the way. Dún Laoghaire, for the first time, was a heartbreaking experience – the goodbyes to husbands going back after Christmas, chubby-faced boys and girls leaving home for the first time, bewilderment written all over them, hard-faced old stagers who never let on but who felt the worst of all because they knew only too well what lay before them.[21]

Social and demographic trends as illustrated above contributed to changes in rural social and cultural institutions. Those who left the rural areas moved to America, Canada, Australia, England, Scotland and also to Irish towns and cities. They embodied and brought with them their personal memories and cultural practices, some of which were further disseminated in their new adopted places.[22]

Changing Times and Step Dancing

Although the social and cultural organization of rural life in North Kerry was changing, some step dancers continued to transmit and practise their step dances. The step dancer was traditionally associated with a rural way of life, so much so that John B. Keane stated that very few in the town of Listowel learned to step

[19] Brody (1982), p. 73.
[20] Jack Dineen (1985), ethnographic interview with the author.
[21] Keane (1964), p. 32.
[22] The work of the Gaelic League in London during the closing decade of the nineteenth century is an example of this; see Chapter 5.

dance because of this association with the country and with rural life.[23] However, this concept changed as the twentieth century progressed and when step dance was institutionalized and urbanized by the Gaelic League and An Coimisiún (see Chapter 5).

Jeremiah Molyneaux continued to teach step dancing in North Kerry as part of the dancing master's quarter and the benefit night system until 1953. He and his scholars continued to perform socially wherever the occasion arose. Also, as part of the Gaelic League's cultural nationalist programme, Jeremiah Molyneaux and a number of his scholars performed at some of the Gaelic League *feiseanna*. However, most of Molyneaux's scholars in North Kerry did not compete at them. For those who did compete, the most popular annual *feiseanna* at the time in North Kerry were Abbeyfeale, Castleisland, Listowel, Newcastle West and Tralee. To enter a step dance competition at these *feiseanna*, Molyneaux's scholars simply submitted their names before the competition on the day. Once entered, they waited until their competition was called, and availed of the opportunity to enter other competitions in traditional music, singing or field sports events. Alternatively, they socialized with others at the event. All announcements at these competitions were in Irish.

In North Kerry, there were generally three step dance competitions at these *feiseanna*; male and female step dancers competed against each other, but male step dancers outnumbered female ones. There were three awards: an award for the best step dancer at performing the Jig, Reel and Hornpipe (see the Appendix); an award for the best step dancer at dancing a solo set dance ('The Blackbird' and 'The Garden of Daisies' were the most popular solo set dances in North Kerry), and a championship award for the best overall step dancer who performed Jig, Reel, Hornpipe and a solo set dance. All competitors wore their 'Sunday best' clothing in competition and wore ordinary everyday leather shoes.

Paddy White, one of Molyneaux's scholars, noted how Jeremiah Molyneaux won a number of championships at these *feiseanna*. Paddy himself won the County Kerry Championship at Listowel Feis in 1914; he was 20 years of age before he ever competed. No *feis* was held in North Kerry during the political upheavals of 1916–23. However, after the Irish Civil War (1922–23), *feiseanna* were again organized, and the first one in North Kerry was held in Tralee in 1926. Phil Cahill, another Molyneaux scholar, competed at the Tralee Feis in 1927, aged 30, and was awarded the County Kerry Championship. In 1935, aged 39, Phil competed for the last time in Tralee, and again he won the County Kerry Championship. Of interest is the age these traditional step dancers were when competing – a factor which changed as the twentieth century progressed and as step dance became appropriated, organized and institutionalized by An Coimisiún and also later by other step dance organizations.[24]

---

[23] John B. Keane, personal communication.

[24] Although An Coimisiún is the largest international step dance organization, Comhdháil na Múinteoirí le Rincí Gaelacha (generally referred to as 'An Comhdháil') is

As mentioned in Chapter 5, the Gaelic League was stronger in urban areas, and this greatly influenced the development of Irish step dancing throughout the twentieth century. Teachers were appointed by the Gaelic League to teach in town centres and schools, and this was also evident in North Kerry. Although Jeremiah Molyneaux never taught for the Gaelic League, some of his scholars did. Phil Cahill and Liam Ó Duinín, taught *céilí* dancing through the medium of Irish in Tralee for the Gaelic League. Phil Cahill taught in The Theatre Royal, Tralee, in 1928, and was paid £1 per hour; he taught the selected *céilí* dances, such as 'The Walls of Limerick', 'The Siege of Ennis', 'The Waves of Tory' and 'The Rince Fada'.[25] Phil, Liam and Sheila Lyons Bowler also taught in national schools and convents in many parts of Kerry.

During the early decades of the twentieth century, as part of the Irish cultural nationalist revival, step dancing was taught during the school day in some national schools and convents in North Kerry. As with Jeremiah Molyneaux, permission had to be received beforehand from the principal and manager of the school in question; the manager of the school was usually the parish priest. Being part of the cultural nationalist revival, step dancing was generally accepted by the majority of the clergy as clean, healthy and respectable, so step dancing was allowed to be taught in some schools. These classes were held once a week. However, it was the individual step dancing schools, established in the bigger towns and cities, in Ireland and abroad, which were to influence to a greater extent the development of Irish step dancing throughout the twentieth century (see Chapter 5).

---

the second largest Irish step dance organization. Prior to the establishment of An Coimisiún, various Irish dance teachers' associations existed in Ireland (in Kerry, Cork and Dublin). However, in 1969, some long-standing An Coimisiún-registered Irish step dance teachers decided to break from An Coimisiún and the Gaelic League to develop step dance independently from the Gaelic League. Thus, these teachers formed a separate step dance organization which they officially called An Comhdháil. This departure became commonly known as 'the split', and effectively created two separate step dance organizations, still in existence today. It was at this point that Oireachtas Rince na Cruinne emerged. Effectively, this means that generally step dancers belonging to An Coimisiún do not compete against step dancers in An Comhdháil competitions, and vice versa; these organizations work independently of each other. Teachers in An Comhdháil are predominantly based in Ireland and the UK. Other step dance organizations in Ireland include Cumann Rince Náisiúnta (CRN), the Festival Dance Teachers of Northern Ireland (FDTA), and Cumann Rince Dea Mheasa (CRM; similarly to An Comhdháil, teachers in this organization are based in Ireland or the UK, but they hold *feiseanna* that are open to all step dance teachers, schools and organizations around the world). Organizations outside Ireland include the World Irish Dance Association (WIDA), mainly on mainland Europe, and the Nordic Irish Dance Association. The popular magazine *Irish Dancing* advertizes and features articles and photographs of step dancers, step dance shows, results of major step dance competitions, and step dance costumes, relating to all step dance organizations internationally. It also features advertisements concerning music and musicians.

[25] *Ár Rinncidhe Fóirne.*

Although Jeremiah Molyneaux and his scholars continued to dance at both rural and town social events, new contexts replaced the old ones for the performance of traditional step dancing. These contexts were, for the most part, *feiseanna*, exhibition performances at weddings, concerts for charity, tourist events, informal social gatherings, *fleadh cheoils*,[26] *céilithe*, and pubs where there was live traditional music. Although traditional step dances continued to be taught by Jeremiah Molyneaux and some of the Molyneaux step dancers of the region, it was to a lesser extent than before. Molyneaux taught as an itinerant dancing master in the rural regions of North Kerry until 1953, when he held his last dance school according to the dancing master's quarter and the benefit night system. This brought to an end fifty years of teaching according to the system which he had inherited from Múirín and Nedín Batt Walsh. In the meantime, three of Jeremiah Molyneaux's scholars, Sheila Lyons Bowler, Phil Cahill and Liam Ó Duinín, taught traditional step dancing in different areas of Kerry; however, none of these step dancers practised as itinerant dancing masters according to the dancing master's quarter and benefit night system.

From 1940 to 1987, Sheila Lyons Bowler taught traditional step dancing in national schools, convents and halls in North Kerry:

> C.F. When did you finish with Jerry Munnix?
>
> S.B. I suppose I was 15 or 17. I took up teaching dancing then myself in different places around my own parish, Raheen and up around Kilflynn and Abbeydorney. I took classes all around. I went as far as Abbeyfeale, Debon Road.
>
> C.F. And what did you need in those days to be a dancing teacher? Did you need to be certified to teach?
>
> S.B. I was a dancing teacher with what was called the Dancing Teachers Organisation of Kerry, and I had to do a bit of an exam for that. It was more or less to test your music to see if you could distinguish one tune, like a Reel from a Jig, from a Hornpipe. And dance a few steps. I got a certificate then for that.
>
> C.F. And to qualify for this certificate, did you have to have won, let's say, the Kerry Championships? Or did you have to have won a Munster Championship or what?
>
> S.B. Oh, yes! Well, I had the Munster. At that stage, I had got the Munster and I had seven Kerry Championships won in a row …. So, I'd say you would have to have won the Kerry Championship or the Munster, if possible.[27]

---

[26] Traditional Irish music festivals; these were organized by the cultural nationalist organization Comhaltas Ceoltóirí Éireann, established in 1951 to promote and foster traditional Irish music, song and dance in Ireland and the diaspora; see also Henry (1989).

[27] Sheila Lyons Bowler (1985), ethnographic interview with the author.

The Dancing Teachers Organisation of Kerry was established in connection with the Gaelic League, and was the validating organization for certifying teachers in the county of Kerry prior to the establishment of An Coimisiún. Sheila Lyons Bowler became certified with the Dancing Teachers Organisation of Kerry in 1939; she did not register with An Coimisiún. She taught traditional step dance as she had learned it from Molyneaux to young local step dancers, male and female, aged for the most part between six and 14. Sheila taught for almost fifty years in North Kerry, her last step dancing class being in 1987. Her students performed at local concerts, particularly those organized by the local branch of the revivalist movement Comhaltas Ceoltóirí Éireann, and competed at two *feiseanna* per year: Feis Mhuire, Ballyheigue, in Kerry, and her own class *feis*. Sheila's students performed in the traditional Molyneaux step dance style. She saw differences in style between what she was teaching and what was being performed at An Coimisiún *feiseanna*. The latter she regarded as 'modern'. According to Sheila:

> The modern stuff is off the floor or you are more or less timing the music in the air. While his [Molyneaux] dancing was all on the flat, on the floor. He had every beat coming out.[28]

According to Sheila, the two styles of step dancing were not compatible on the same stage in competition. For example, Molyneaux's Reels were hard-shoe Treble Reels performed close to the floor in a small spatial area, while the Coimisiún style was light-shoe Reels, performed in a more airborne style, and took up a greater area. Consequently, Sheila decided to continue to teach the style she had been trained in. One of Sheila's students, Kay Carmody, was teaching during the early phase of my fieldwork in the 1980s in Causeway and taught some of the traditional material she learned from Sheila. She also taught set dancing. Similarly to Sheila, her students performed at local concerts and competitions.

Phil Cahill and Liam Ó Duinín, two other scholars of Jeremiah Molyneaux, also gave step dancing classes. Similarly to Sheila Lyons Bowler, Phil and Liam taught in many rural national schools in North Kerry; Liam also taught in Castleisland, and in Dingle in the West Kerry Gaeltacht. In addition, Phil taught step dancing privately in his own home, but these classes were small, with approximately four students per class. However, Liam Ó Duinín's first step dancing class was not in Kerry, but in Victoria, Australia:

L.OD.   I finished with Jerry Munnix at the age of 17.

C.F.   Did you then go and teach dancing yourself?

L.OD.   I did! My first experience of teaching dancing was in Victoria, Australia!

C.F.   When did you go to Australia?

L.OD.   I went to Australia when I was about 17½ to 18 years of age!

---

[28] Ibid.

C.F.   What did you work at over there?

L.OD.   I worked in Australia as a barman in the Victoria Hotel, and on my
          half-day off I'd go out to the convent in Shepperton and teach the
          children how to do some Irish dancing …. They were very interested,
          and their parents would be all Irish. I was five years in Australia when I
          decided to return home. I conducted dancing classes then after coming
          back from Australia, and I have been continuing with that until very
          recently. But now I have given it up completely.[29]

Students of Liam and Phil continued to teach in the region of Kerry, but again, none of these taught according to the itinerant dancing master's quarter (see Chapter 3); instead, they taught step dancing as a leisure-time activity on a weekly basis. Eileen Lade, taught by Liam Ó Duinín, later taught in Listowel, Tralee and national schools and convents in the County of Kerry. Jimmy Hickey, a student of Liam Ó Duinín, taught and continues to teach traditional step dancing full-time today. He gives classes in many national schools in North Kerry and the borders of North Cork and West Limerick. Jimmy Hickey also teaches in Listowel. The students of Hickey's school of dance do not compete in *feiseanna* organized by An Coimisiún. Although solo step dances, together with other dances, are taught in Hickey's school of dance, the students are taught solely for social, cultural and educational purposes.

Irene Gould, a student of Eileen Lade, Timmy Lynch and later Phil Cahill, taught in Tralee and national schools and convents in Kerry. Irene was the first step dancing teacher in Tralee to complete the TCRG qualifying examination with An Coimisiún. According to Irene, when she competed at Ballyheigue Feis, around 1951, Phil Cahill saw her perform and asked her father if he would permit her to go to him for step dancing classes. Irene had been a student of Eileen Lade, but when Eileen left Tralee for England, Irene then joined Timmy Lynch's school of Irish dancing, where she trained. At Phil Cahill's suggestion, Irene subsequently left Timmy Lynch's class to attend Phil Cahill's dancing classes. Phil taught in his home in Leith, approximately twelve miles from Listowel and five miles from Tralee. Irene lived in Tralee, and every Sunday afternoon she cycled to Cahill's house for her step dancing class from approximately 3.30 to 5.30 p.m. Sometimes her father, who was interested in all aspects of Irish culture, cycled with her. According to Irene, there was no fee.

Irene's dancing class with Phil Cahill, where sometimes the only pupil was herself, was held in the kitchen of Cahill's farmhouse. Nora Cahill, Phil's wife, played the concertina and usually played for the classes. Reels, Jigs and Hornpipes were danced, but Phil never taught Slip Jigs, as being a man, he had never been taught them by Molyneaux. Slip Jigs were considered the most graceful of all step dances, and were therefore regarded as a woman's dance (see the Appendix). Prior to this, however, Irene had learned some Slip Jigs from Eileen Lade in Tralee.

---

[29]   Liam Ó Duinin (1983), ethnographic interview with the author.

Figure dances and *céilí* dances were not taught by Phil either at these classes, but on occasions, if eight dancers were present, a Polka set (a Quadrille) was danced.

According to Irene, when teaching a step dance, Phil whistled or hummed the accompanying tune, taking a section of the step dance at a time until the full step was completed. Phil danced each section, and Irene imitated his movements. When the step was learned, Nora Cahill would play the concertina for them. The steps taught were mostly Molyneaux's steps, and Phil altered the steps for Irene as a woman. According to Irene Gould, there was a distinct difference between men's steps and women's steps. Although it was the same basic step dance that was being taught, anything rhythmically complicated in the step was simplified for women. Furthermore, movements with stamps were altered to toes or heels, to maintain a graceful flow in the women's execution of these step dances. This aesthetic was in keeping with gender perceptions of the day (see Chapters 3 and 4).

Around the 1950s, only three or four *feiseanna* were held annually in North Kerry. Usually, these were one-day events associated with sports meetings, and included other competitions in Irish singing, traditional music, running, long jump and high jump competitions (see also Chapter 5). Ballyheigue Feis was the biggest of the year, and it was the only local place where a championship competition was held. At this *feis*, a platform was especially erected for the dancing competitions, and two or three wooden steps enabled dancers to ascend onto it. Irene usually wore a green and amber costume (colours associated with the national flag of Ireland) and performed all dances in hard shoes.

These *feis* competitions started at approximately 2 p.m. and were completed by 6 p.m. In each dance category, there was a competition for children under 10 years of age, another for those under 14 years of age, and another for the senior dancers. All competitions were open: there was no segregation according to ability or gender. The majority of those competing were local, but on occasions, some step dancers on holiday from England and America also participated. Generally, Irene cycled to these competitions, but those who had no bicycles travelled on a seaside excursion bus. Irene Gould never competed outside Kerry. Together with *feiseanna*, Irene also performed at concerts in the town of Tralee and nearby rural halls.

An Coimisiún in North Kerry

In December 1954, Irene Gould received her TCRG and qualified as an Irish step dancing teacher with An Coimisiún. Jeremiah Molyneaux had finished teaching according to the dancing master's quarter a year earlier. Irene was one of the first step dancing teachers to qualify with An Coimisiún in the town of Tralee.[30] Phil Cahill tutored her for the qualifying examination, which she sat in Dublin. Subsequently, she established an Irish step dancing school in her home in Tralee, which she taught in a little house at the back of her garden. The step dancing

---

[30] Eilís Ní Tháilliúra, Tralee, registered with An Coimisiún in 1933; see Cullinane (2003).

class of two hours' duration was 5d. per student. However, when travelling out to national schools, the fee was 10d. per student in order to cover travel expenses; Irene's father drove her to these schools and was very supportive of Irish culture. Irene also taught in halls in areas of West Kerry, such as Dingle, and west of Dingle, where she taught through the medium of Irish:

> I taught through the medium of Irish there because the children would not understand my giving them instructions through English. So I had to brush up on my Irish and learn quite a few small little phrases to explain the different steps. I think I managed fairly well. The only thing is that I would probably get stuck on a word and I would have to explain it in English to the senior students and they would give me the Irish word for it and they in turn would explain it to the little ones.[31]

Irene Gould also taught in national schools in Abbeyfeale, Ahasla, Anascaul, Asdee, Ballyferiter, Brosna, Camp, Castlegregory, Castleisland, Dunquin, Lispole, Lisselton, Maharies, Minard and Ventry. These classes were all held once a week, thus supplying these communities with classes on a continuous basis. The dance school of the rural itinerant dancing master, based on the dancing master's quarter and the benefit night system, no longer applied.

Step dance students in these national schools competed once a year. This was Irene Gould's class *feis*, and another step dancing teacher from Tralee adjudicated it. This *feis* was generally held between two of Irene's dance classes, and no specific dancing costumes were worn. A local musician was usually employed to play for the *feis*, but if no musician was available, a record player was used. The competitions were generally in the solo Reel, solo Jig and a figure dance, such as a Four-hand Reel (see Appendix).

When interviewing Honor Flynn, a student in Irene Gould's dancing class in the town of Tralee, she had the following to say:

> H.F.   It was the only thing we did apart from skipping, swings, spinning tops and all that. But our dancing was Wednesday evening and Sunday morning. Because Irene worked, you see, she worked in the office in a garage and she had a half-day on Wednesday, so we had dancing Wednesday evening and Sunday mornings after Mass. We'd be all gone off to early Mass and we'd be down in her house for 11 [a.m.]or 12 [noon] and we'd be there until 2 [p.m.]. They came from all over the town up to Irene's house. I was lucky because I lived quite near her. We actually adored her. She was strict and she wouldn't take any nonsense, but we looked up to her so much.
>
> C.F.   And was it a very small class?
>
> H.F.   I'd say the most she ever had was 18 to 20.
>
> C.F.   And what was the ratio of boys to girls in that class?

---

[31]   Ibid.

H.F.   In those days, actually, we had about five or six boys and they were all very good.

C.F.   Where did she teach?

H.F.   Well, it wasn't a shed, really, but it was a little house. It was a workshop which belonged to her father. He was a marvellous craftsman. He was a cabinet maker, carpenter, and he used it. She had little stools all around, and the floor was small.

C.F.   What music did she use?

H.F.   A gramophone that you wound up, that's what we started off with, records, like 78 records, and we'd be dancing away and next thing it would go hmmmm, hmmmm, and you'd be slowing down and then you'd know who had good rhythm and who didn't .... And the next thing she'd start winding and we'd all start speeding up again, you know .... I remember the first day then that she got the electric one, there was fierce excitement altogether. All these knobs and it would play four or five records ... but anyway, I remember the one well with the wind-up, the gramophone.[32]

Irene Gould's class was held twice weekly, on Wednesday afternoon after national school hours and Sunday morning after Mass. Both boys and girls attended, but there were not as many boys as girls. Jimmy Smith, now a teacher of Irish step dancing with Rinceoirí na Ríochta in Tralee, left Irene Gould's class at 12 years of age because of the scarcity of boys at these dance classes, but returned at 14 to step dance classes with Honor Flynn because he loved it. Jimmy continued competing at *feiseanna* until he qualified as a teacher with An Coimisiún in the 1960s.

Irene Gould's Tralee class consisted of tuition in step dances and *céilí* dances, the latter being a combination of those she learned from Phil Cahill and those selected from the Coimisiún series of booklets *Ár Rinncidhe Fóirne* (see Chapter 5). According to Honor Flynn, Irene Gould taught the traditional step dances that she had learned from Phil Cahill, and although she also created her own, these were always based on the traditional style of North Kerry.

Feiseanna and concerts were the two formal occasions where Irene Gould's students performed. During the late 1950s and 1960s, approximately five *feiseanna* were held per year, at Ballyheigue, Dingle, Kilflynn, Killarney and Listowel. Three open step dance competitions were available: two solo competitions, and one figure dance competition. By this stage, light shoes or pumps were worn for soft-shoe dances, and hard shoes were worn for the hard-shoe, percussive ones. Competitors were predominantly local, but at Ballyheigue Feis some outsiders on holiday in the area might also attend and participate in the competitions. Irene Gould's school competed predominantly in the region of North Kerry, and individual dancers of the school only competed elsewhere should they be on holiday there. According to Honor Flynn:

---

[32]   Honor Flynn (2004), ethnographic interview with the author.

Most of them would have been Gaelic League *feises*. You had a big *feis* in Killarney in those days, that was a Gaelic League *feis* as well, but that was the only *feis* where we'd see dancers from Cork and Limerick.[33]

Honor said they were 'dazed' by what these outsiders could do with their feet.

Gould's school of dancing also participated at local concerts on St Patrick's Night and Easter Sunday night in Tralee, and also at those concerts attached to Macra na Feirme ('The Farmers' Association'), and the Irish Countrywomen's Association. For these performances, Irene Gould choreographed 'invention dances'. These were group figure dances which were newly choreographed by Irene for her dancing school. Some of these invention dances were based on old Irish myths, such as Tír na nÓg,[34] and special theatrical costumes were made specifically for these exhibitions. The Easter Sunday night concert was regarded by these students as being one of the most important dance events for the dancing school. However, Irene Gould's school also performed at concerts during Lent:

At that time there wasn't any television and there were no dances allowed during Lent. This was around the 1950s, early '60s. I was involved with a group from the Light Opera Society here in Tralee, and we used to get together at the beginning of Lent and we'd book various halls. I can remember a Father Moriarty who was Dean here in Tralee later … but he was a parish priest then and he was building a church in Lyracrumpane and we used to do concerts for charity for him. We were involved in charity concerts for everything and anything: school building funds, Macra na Feirme, the ICA. I used to take some of my students, and dance myself …. The hall would consist of the local school house, which would consist of two rooms, and we went to places like Lyracrumpane, Derrinduff, Asdee and various other places. We'd be very lucky if we got into Listowel Hall, but basically it would be in the school, and as I say, that would consist of two rooms and there wouldn't be any electric light, but there would be a Tilley lamp and the stage would be a portable stage. You'd have to climb up on a few desks to get up on the stage, and maybe in the middle of somebody singing 'Galway Bay', the caretaker or someone would come on stage and say 'Excuse me! Carry on singing!' And, they'd pump up the Tilley lamp. The one room would not be big enough to facilitate all the local community, so women and children would be allowed in to see the concert and the men would stay in the room next door. They'd play cards or talk about the weather or the harvest or whatever. Occasionally, when the comedian would crack a joke, they'd run to the doorway to see what was going on. They'd take turns to stand at the doorway and see bits of the concert. We had singers, dancers and comedians. They were very good, innocent, funny times.[35]

---

[33]   Ibid.

[34]   The Land of Youth where, according to Irish mythology, one never grew old.

[35]   Irene Gould, (1985) ethnographic interview with the author.

Although the step dancers of Irene Gould's dancing school competed at *feiseanna*, dancing at specific social events was also important in enhancing both their social and performance skills and experiences. All of these events structured their year, which for the better dancers was centred on the dance calendar. Irene's students enjoyed going to the *feiseanna* in Kerry which provided them with 'a day out'. Going to a *feis* was not for them about just competing in step dance; it was about the whole dance event and the memorable social and cultural experiences that this event offered:

> I remember the highlight of our year of dancing would be the *feis* in Dingle. Irene would take us down the pier. We'd bring a packed lunch with us and we'd go into one of the boats and we'd open or lunches and have our lunch in the boat. And that is what we used to look forward to. We used to look forward to that more than we'd look forward to dancing. We used to have a great day in Dingle. Dingle was our favourite *feis*.[36]

Over the years, Irene Gould kept in contact with her teacher, Phil Cahill:

> I loved Irish dancing, and Phil's house was steeped in the tradition of Irish dancing and that's where I felt I could really sit down and talk Irish dancing to my heart's content and know that the people there understood what you were talking about and that they were quite happy to talk about it for hours on end and get up and dance and sit down and talk. And it would just turn into a very enjoyable evening. Nobody had to force us to do these things; we did them because we liked to do them.[37]

When Irene Gould acquired a car, around 1962, on occasion she brought her better students to Cahill's house. According to Irene: 'It was a novelty to go to Phil Cahill's house for the evening. The students would be fascinated realizing the fact that I too had a dancing teacher.'[38] Phil Cahill taught Irene's students traditional steps which they performed in the earlier competitions when they were young. And although Irene Gould was a registered teacher with An Coimisiún, she did not take her school to competitions in areas outside the county of Kerry.

Irene Gould stopped teaching step dance in the rural national schools in 1967, and around 1970 she stopped teaching in Tralee. Some of Irene's students had by this stage decided to teach step dancing part-time in their homes; these included Honor Flynn, Jimmy Smith and Patricia Hanafin. According to Honor Flynn:

> My class wouldn't have been big either because I did something like Irene did. I worked as well. I worked in the National Insurance Company, and I taught

---

[36] Honor Flynn (2004), ethnographic interview with the author.

[37] Irene Gould (1985), ethnographic interview with the author.

[38] Ibid.

more or less the same days as Irene: Wednesday evenings and Sunday mornings. But when I started teaching, Irene was still teaching, and I never took a pupil from her …. I never took anyone's pupils. And the Kerry teachers made a pact. We were all friends …. We are best friends, and we have been best friends all our lives …. We always helped each other out.[39]

However, in 1962, Honor Flynn wished to take her step dance students to compete at the well-known Feis Maitiú, Cork. Since she was not a registered teacher with An Coimisiún, her students were not allowed to compete. Subsequently, Honor, together with Jimmy and Pat, trained for their TCRG – the teacher qualifying examination with An Coimisiún:

> C.F. Why was the TCRG important? Why was it important to you at that time to get a TCRG?
>
> H.F. We were all competing at *feises* around the county [Kerry] here, that were little *feises*, Ballyheigue Feis, and things like that, where you had an off-shoot of something that was happening in a village and they'd just have a little *feis*. But when we realized that there was a bigger world out there and that we couldn't take part in it because it was run under the rules of the Commission, we decided that if we wanted our pupils to progress in the dance, and just try and bring the standard up a little bit more, then we needed to get our TCRG, and that was the main purpose in those days, just to get that.
>
> C.F. So you must have really liked the dance that you saw outside of Kerry?
>
> H.F. We did, I suppose. We thought that it was much more difficult than what we were doing, and we wanted to learn more of that kind of dance.[40]

Consequently, Honor Flynn, Jimmy Smith and Patricia Hanafin took their qualifying examination with An Coimisiún and registered with the organization. To this end, Honor Flynn and Jimmy Smith travelled weekly to another Irish step dancing teacher, Ciss Cullinane in Cork, in order to learn the dance material to qualify with An Coimisiún. Once qualified and registered with An Coimisiún, these teachers were then in a position to take their students to compete at the registered competitions of An Coimisiún, and on seeing what was winning in competition, they modified and developed step dances for their students in order that they could compete satisfactorily, and hopefully successfully, at the *feiseanna* and *oireachtais* of An Coimisiún.

These teachers believed that the traditional style of step dancing that they had learned in their youth could not compete successfully against the more 'modern' Coimisiún style of step dancing in bigger centres such as Cork and Limerick. They believed that what these 'modern', competitive step dancers were doing

---

[39]   Honor Flynn (2004), ethnographic interview with the author.
[40]   Ibid.

was completely different to what they were doing, and they liked what they saw. Different aesthetic expectations within the structures of An Coimisiún required step dancers to use larger spatial movements on stage. Also, the style of dancing was higher off the ground. In lieu of the traditional structural principle of one movement per note, there were now many movements and sounds to one note in the Coimisiún's modern, percussive dances, which resulted in the music of the Double Jig and the Hornpipe being played much slower. The slow tempo was only suitable for, and flattering to, the 'modern' Coimisiún step dancers. Thus, in order for their students to compete successfully, these teachers travelled to *feiseanna* and *oireachtais* and picked up 'modern' techniques and movement vocabulary by watching competitors perform; they also exchanged steps with other teachers. Gradually, they created new and more 'modern' steps for their students in line with An Coimisiún's aesthetic. When Irene Gould visited one of her teaching students some years later, she had this to say:

> I.G.   I was absolutely fascinated with the advancement in dancing in the number of years since I had stopped, and I thought that they were absolutely fantastic. I loved what they were doing, but I myself could not have done it because I was into the more traditional style and this had gone a little bit more modern.
>
> C.F.   How would you describe this 'modern'?
>
> I.G.   Well, the treble beats, the very slow music, doubling up the beats to fit in as many beats as possible to fit the slower time. That wasn't the way that I learnt it. So that's what I found fascinating. They were able to do so much more with their feet.[41]

This exemplified for Irene Gould the style of step dancing which had come to define the Coimisiún style, where slow music was required for the more virtuosic percussive dances.

Also by this stage, *feiseanna* were no longer only associated with outdoor *aeraíochtaí*;[42] they were now also held indoors in community halls or halls in towns and cities. This meant that *feiseanna* were no longer confined to the summer season; *feiseanna* could now be held all year round. Consequently, *feiseanna* and *oireachtais* became more frequent, and teachers and step dancers participated more often at these events. This became particularly apparent from the 1970s, when An Coimisiún established its first Oireachtas Rince na Cruinne (World Irish Dance Championships) for An Coimisiún-registered teachers only.[43]

---

[41]   Irene Gould (1985), ethnographic interview with the author.

[42]   Sports fixtures.

[43]   In 1969, some teachers within An Coimisiún left the organization to promote and develop step dancing independently from the Gaelic League. Those teachers who left formed a separate organization called An Comhdháil; it still functions today as an independent organization.

From the 1980s, there was a noticeable increase in the number of *feiseanna* and *oireachtais* registered with An Coimisiún, culminating each year in Oireachtas Rince na Cruinne.[44] There was also an increase in the number of teachers registered with An Coimisiún, and today more than half of these teachers live outside Ireland. This period also witnessed an international increase in the number of competitive step dancers and a noticeable homogeneity and virtuosity in kinetic vocabulary – traditional and innovative. Some of these innovative movements were introduced by teachers and their experienced and successful competitive pupils, who either rhythmically, spatially or kinetically developed step dance material, or having seen movements they liked in other dance forms, such as ballet or musicals on television, subtly adapted these movements into steps; if successful in competition, these movements subsequently became part of the step dance vocabulary. A common international kinetic vocabulary gradually developed which was facilitated by both an increase in travel and attendance at *feiseanna* and *oireachtais*, and an increase in invitations to step dancing teachers in Ireland to teach outside their own schools of dancing, and indeed their own country. This kinetic vocabulary included grounded, earthy movements together with aerial movements; sounds made with the feet either in contact with the floor or in contact while in the air. Some of the vocabulary included air clicks – front and back – heel clicks, double clicks, triple clicks, entrechats, high jumps, butterflies, bicycles, swivels and high leg raises, together with the traditional movements of threes, sevens, rocks, batters, toes, heels, stamps, cuts, cross-keys, drums and so on.[45] Far more travelling movements were also used, to adapt to the larger stages in competition venues. During this time, there were also developments in dance shoes, particularly the hard shoes, and in lieu of leather-soled shoes, fibre-glass heels and toes were introduced, allowing for new movements. More money was also being invested by parents and students in attending more classes for training, and more *feiseanna* and *oireachtais*, to meet, compare and compete with rivals before Oireachtas Rince na Cruinne. All of these factors contributed to the development of a greater athleticism and virtuosity.

Due in part to these developments, An Coimisiún institutionalized a certain solo traditional set-dance repertoire in the 1970s in an attempt to preserve some traditional dances (see the Appendix and Chapter 5). Four solo set dances were declared by An Coimisiún to be traditional set dances: 'The Blackbird', 'Saint Patrick's Day', 'The Garden of Daisies' and 'The Job of Journeywork'. All aspiring and registered step dancing teachers were required to know and be able to teach these specific traditional solo set dances; these would then be performed at An Coimisiún competitions. Particular versions of these traditional solo set dances

---

[44]   The introduction of the Dance Drama Competition at the Oireachtas Rince na Cruinne championships extended the scope for Irish step dance choreography for teachers.

[45]   These terms are those that I have heard used by step dance teachers and dancers. Other terms are also used, but there is no universal standard of terminology. For instance, the batter is also known as a shuffle or a rally. See also Ní Bhriain (2008).

were selected and popularized through workshops, the TCRG examination and competitions. This institutionalization process consequently marginalized other versions of these solo set dances, and also other solo set dances.[46] In North Kerry, this institutionalization also applied. The following extract from an interview I conducted with Honor Flynn exemplifies this:

C.F.   ... what dances would your students dance if they enter the traditional dance competitions under the Coimisiún?

H.F.   Well, the traditional Hornpipe that they do is the traditional Hornpipe that I learned myself, so it would be the real old, old Hornpipe. There wouldn't be that much lifting in it or anything like that, no jumping up high, no big jumps; and of course, if it was the traditional set, it is nearly always 'The Blackbird', or the younger ones would do 'Saint Patrick's Day', but it would be nearly always 'The Blackbird'.

C.F.   Which 'Blackbird' would they do?

H.F.   Well 'The Blackbird', now, and all these traditional sets were standardized years ago, I suppose twenty years ago, and we were more or less told to have workshops to learn the Commission one.

C.F.   So who taught you?

H.F.   We went to workshops, and we were taught by people like the Nolans and maybe some of the older teachers like, you know, Brenda Springer. These people are in the dancing for years. Also, Phylis O'Regan from Cork. Now they would all have had a lot of the Cork traditional stuff that was very like Kerry, and of course, John [Cullinane] himself. And we learned a lot at workshops, Sunday workshops; and they were standardized.

C.F.   Where were these workshops?

H.F.   They'd be in Mallow, maybe in a hotel, or in Cork in a hotel. And we'd all go .... And we taught them steps as well, and they loved it, but the Commission wanted the kids to dance the same sets, you know, but we still have our own sets as well, but we don't really teach them that much now except for Siamsa [Tíre] or something like that, because they don't use them.

---

[46]   When Peggy Roche of Chicago performed her father Pat Roche's version of the traditional set dance 'The Blackbird', An Coimisiún did not recognize it. Peggy had to learn the official, institutionalized version of it (personal communication). Indeed, from a personal ethnographic perspective, the same applied with the step dance organization An Comhdháil. I remember training for my TCRG in 1977, and I also had to learn the institutionalized versions of these four solo set dances. An Coimisiún has attempted to address this issue in recent years by adding three other 'traditional' set dances ('The King of the Fairies', 'Jockey to the Fair' and 'The Three Sea Captains') to its list, both for competition and for aspiring teachers. The four institutionalized set dances, however, remain the most popular traditional set dances with Irish step dancers and Irish step dancing teachers on an international basis. In 2013 An Coimisiún announced that different traditional versions of the solo traditional set dances are now also allowed to be performed in competition.

C.F. So if you were going to teach a 'Blackbird' for your students to compete in the Coimisiún competitions now, or you were going to teach them 'Saint Patrick's Day', for instance, would you teach them the standardized 'Saint Patrick's Day' that they would dance in competition?

H.F. I would!

C.F. The Coimisiún one? Batter down, batter down, batter down, batter down?

H.F. I would! Because I would not want to confuse them at all when it's for competition.

C.F. Is it the same with 'The Blackbird'?

H.F. Yea!

C.F. And there are certain set dances that have been standardized, aren't there?

H.F. Yea!

C.F. Can you tell me what ones they are?

H.F. 'The Blackbird', 'Saint Patrick's Day', 'The Garden of Daisies', 'The Job of Journeywork', and of course, you have 'The King of the Fairies', the Cormac O'Keeffe one; that's coming on stream now. A lot of our kids now have learned that, we never had that now, really, only in the last few years …. But if they have a choice, you know, it is always either 'The Blackbird', sometimes they do 'The Garden of Daisies' now all right, but otherwise it is the basic 'Saint Patrick's Day' and 'The Blackbird' that I teach mostly.[47]

Within the structures of An Coimisiún, competition is a major motivation for teachers, parents and children, and since these competitions are structured throughout the Coimisiún year, teachers' time is focused for the most part on these competitions. Doing well in competition is considered important, and teachers concentrate on teaching the material required for competitions. The standardized 'Blackbird' is only one version of this solo set dance, and although An Coimisiún has changed this ruling in more recent years to include other local versions, its standardized traditional sets are still the most popular. In the 1980s, I collected three Molyneaux 'Blackbird' set dances from one Molyneaux step dancer in North Kerry. These versions were choreographed by Jeremiah Molyneaux according to the different competence levels of his step dance scholars. Although Molyneaux and Molyneaux's scholars prized his more advanced 'Blackbird' set dance, the younger generation of step dancers in Rinceoirí na Ríochta (see below) do not learn to dance it except if they are dancers or actors with Siamsa Tíre (see Chapter 7). According to Honor Flynn, the teachers of Rinceoirí na Ríochta take pride in teaching the 'national' or Coimisiún style of Irish step dancing, and they acknowledge that they have sacrificed their traditional style in order to compete successfully and to contribute to the wider international developments in step dancing into the twenty-first century.

---

[47] Honor Flynn (2004), ethnographic interview with the author.

Rinceoirí na Ríochta

In 1984, the individual schools of Honor Flynn and Jimmy Smith merged to form Rinceoirí na Ríochta.[48] Patricia Hanafin continued to teach step dancing, but independently of An Coimisiún:

> H.F.   Well, Jimmy was my pupil. First of all, he was Irene's pupil until he was maybe 11, and then he left dancing, and when I started teaching at 17, he came to me at 13 or 14, and he stayed with me then until he started teaching himself. Now, he did go to Anthony Nolan[49] before his exam to get help from Anthony and to progress more … but when he started teaching, then we used to make up stuff together, even though we were under the Flynn and the Smith school, we taught an awful lot of the same material. We had the same mind about things.
>
> C.F.   And there was no kind of competition between the two schools?
>
> H.F.   Not at all! So it was a kind of natural progression that we would amalgamate the classes.[50]

Rinceoirí na Ríochta is a registered school of step dancing with An Coimisiún and has approximately 150 students. It is run by four teachers. Honor Flynn and Jimmy Smith, the founders of the school, are the principal teachers. Jimmy teaches Irish step dancing full-time, and is also a registered adjudicator with An Coimisiún. Honor has semi-retired from teaching, but continues teaching the beginner class of the school; both also teach in more rural areas outside Tralee. Jimmy Smith has taught in national schools in East Limerick, West Cork, Dingle, Kenmare and Listowel, and Honor Flynn has taught classes in Dingle and in some national schools outside Tralee. With the availability of transport, students from the more remote rural areas can attend these classes and can have the opportunity to compete at registered An Coimisiún competitions. The other two teachers of Rinceoirí na Ríochta are Tríona Breen, a past student of Jimmy Smith, and Miriam O'Sullivan, a past student of Honor Flynn. When not teaching at the school, Tríona teaches Irish dance to children in a local pre-school, and since she has also performed in two of the commercial Irish step dance stage shows, *Spirit of the Dance* and *To Dance on the Moon*, she also trains dancers in the stage shows in Killarney during the tourist season in the summer. Miriam is a qualified national school teacher in West Kerry, and teaches full-time in a national school during the week. She teaches a weekly Irish step dancing class for the West Kerry branch of Rinceoirí na Ríochta in Dingle. The students are both male and female and are generally

---

48   'Dancers of the Kingdom'.

49   Anthony Nolan is a step dancing teacher in Limerick; he is registered with An Coimisiún.

50   Honor Flynn (2004), ethnographic interview with the author.

aged between five and thirteen. Although there is an open policy in the school for children from all ethnic backgrounds to come and learn, the majority are Irish.

The main class of Rinceoirí na Ríochta takes place on Saturday afternoons from 2.30 to 5.30 p.m. in the Pipe-band Hall, Tralee. Children and teenagers, male and female, learn new step dances and practise old step dances for competitions, concerts or cabarets at this class. However, competition is the primary focus of the dance class, which is structured according to ability and the categories of competence within An Coimisiún competitions: beginners (*Bun* and *Tús Grád*), intermediate (*Meán Grád*) and advanced open championship dancers (*Árd Grád*). The structure of the class is similar each week. The class commences with a warm-up session led by Honor and Jimmy, who face the line of dancers. The focus of this warm-up is on posture, timing and basic foot and leg positions and movements. This is followed by a session of teaching and practising specific step dances with the *Bun* and *Tús Grád* pupils, followed by the *Meán Grád*, and finally the experienced *Árd Grád* dancers.

The solo dances that are taught include the Light Jig, Single Jig, Slip Jig (female dancers only), Reel, Double Jig, Hornpipe, traditional solo set dances and contemporary solo set dances (see Appendix). However, not every dancer learns or knows all of these step dances. The *Bun* and *Tús Grad* dancers concentrate on steps in the Light Jig and the Light Reel; the *Meán Grad* dancers work on steps in the Light Jig, Single Jig, Light Reel, Slip Jig (female dancers) and traditional solo set dance, while the *Árd Grád* do all of these, except to a higher and a technically and rhythmically more demanding standard, together with steps in the Double Jig, Hornpipe and solo set dances, such as 'Kilkenny Races' and 'Bonaparte's Retreat' (see the Appendix). These set dances are choreographed by the teacher or advanced students to specific pieces of music of the same name and are regarded as the most rhythmically and technically complicated step dances. The close relationship of the choreographed dance movements to the set dance music is important; therefore interpretation of the music is important. Some of the movements and rhythms that comprise these dances form what the anthropologist Clifford Geertz calls 'deep play' for the dancers.[51] These are challenging movements. They are the movements that one can see the advanced dancers practising as they wait to dance, be they sitting or standing. They practice to the music in their heads and bodies. When physically dancing, they test themselves, or are tested by their teachers, in attempting to get these technically challenging movements and rhythms right within the context of the full set dance. When this is considered to be correct, it is then performed to the accompanying music, when it is further assessed and corrected, verbally and corporeally, if required. For the dancers and the teachers, this play with rhythm and music, foot and leg movements and technique, within a prescribed aesthetic, becomes increasingly deep in these set dances. Emphasis is constantly placed on the upright posture, hands by the sides of the body, timing with the music, foot and leg positions, and ability to step dance and travel smoothly through space.

---

[51]   Geertz (1973).

Although *céilí* dances and other group dances are also taught in class, solo dancing takes up most of the class time. Of these solo dances, the set dances are considered to be the showpieces of individual dancers. Together with illustrating the skills of the dancers, they also make manifest the creative abilities of the teachers to choreograph what are considered to be good set dances.

The dancers dress casually for class. Some wear the class tracksuit, which is black with some Celtic embroidery and the school name, 'Rinceoirí na Ríochta, Trá Lí', embroidered on the back of the jacket. These dancers openly publicize their belonging to this step dancing school. Others wear trousers, or sports shorts and T-shirts; some may be seen to wear the Kerry football jersey, again publicizing a belonging to the County of Kerry, but through sport. Football is very important to the people of Kerry and it comes as no surprise to find some of these dancers donning the football jersey. Place, community and belonging is important to the dancers in class and they illustrate this through their shared dance practice, their belonging to Rinceoiri na Riochta, and to Kerry. Step dancers' parents with their toddlers and babies are also welcome into class, and some remain throughout the whole period, chatting to each other in the background. Breaks in between dances allow both the teachers to announce and discuss upcoming competitions and events, and step dancers to chat to their friends. New solo dancing costumes and sometimes trophies awarded at a recent dancing competition are also brought to class to show the teachers and fellow dancers. The atmosphere is warm, friendly and structured, illustrating both a pedagogical and social side to the class.

Similarly to other step dancing schools registered with An Coimisiún, competition is the major performance context for Rinceoirí na Ríochta, and the most important and prestigious competitive event within the structures of An Coimisiún is Oireachtas Rince na Cruinne (the World Irish Dance Championships, or simply 'The Worlds').

Ethnography of Oireachtas Rince na Cruinne 2003

Oireachtas Rince na Cruinne brings together different communities of step dancers from around the world. Since the closing decades of the twentieth century, these communities are no longer confined to Ireland and its diaspora; they now also include dancers from Japan, Africa and East European countries. Furthermore, these dancers may or may not be of Irish ancestry. An Coimisiún has grown internationally, and the success and global acclaim of the Irish step dance shows *Riverdance* and *Lord of the Dance* have assisted in this growth.[52]

It is Easter Week, April 2003, and Oireachtas Rince na Cruinne is being held in the Gleneagle Hotel, Killarney, Co. Kerry. This is the 33rd Oireachtas

---

[52]   Foley (2001).

Rince na Cruinne, so its establishment is relatively recent.[53] These step dancing championships are generally held annually, and always for a week, usually Easter Week. For most of this step dancing community, this event marks the end of the year's work. Typically, these events have been hosted in the Republic of Ireland, but in 2000 they were hosted in Belfast, Northern Ireland, to mark the millennium; in 2002, they were held for the first time outside Ireland, in Glasgow, Scotland; and in 2008, they were hosted in Philadelphia, for the first time in the United States. For the most part, however, Ireland remains the primary location for this prestigious step dance event.

The choice of location in Ireland is dependent upon the facilities available to stage and host the event. Between 3,000 and 4,000 competitors participate, and many of these are accompanied by friends and family members. Teachers, adjudicators, musicians, administrators and others interested in witnessing or participating in the event also attend. Accommodation facilities together with travel infrastructure are also considered when selecting the venue for hosting these events. Holding Oireachtas Rince na Cruinne in an area therefore brings many social and economic benefits.

Step dancers who participate in these competitive events are generally aged between ten and the mid-twenties. They come not only from Ireland, but from the diaspora and beyond. Families that travel to Ireland frequently extend their stay for touring purposes or to make contact with relatives. Some step dancers from outside Ireland make the trip as a result of hard fundraising work on the part of their dance school, their teachers and their parents. Parties not involved in step dance do not attend Oireachtas Rince na Cruinne; it is a subculture for step dancers and those associated with the Irish step dancing world.

Since Oireachtas Rince na Cruinne 2003 is held at the Gleneagle Hotel, Killarney, for convenience many choose to stay at the hotel for the full week. Others stay at other nearby hotels or bed and breakfasts. The week is all-consuming for both performers and teachers; this is made manifest in the celebration of Mass in the venue for Catholic members of the Irish step dancing community on the Saturday evening. It is *the* event of the year. It is the event towards which both dancers and teachers have worked and practised, where dancers and teachers can keep abreast of any step dance innovations within their dance community, where dancers can see and meet their dance friends and their competitive rivals, and

---

[53]   The first *Oireachtas Rince na Cruinne* was held in 1970. This coincides with what is generally known as 'The split'. This refers to the 'split' that occurred when some teachers within *An Coimisiún* decided to establish their own Irish step dance organization which would not be under the auspices of the Gaelic League. This organization became known as *An Comhdháil*. Consequently, in 1969, there were two organizations of Irish step dance: *An Coimisiún*, under the auspices of the Gaelic League, and *An Comhdháil*, which was organized and directed by the dance teachers themselves. This 'split' continues today. Other organizations, such as CRN and the Festival Dance Teachers of Northern Ireland also exist, and run their own competitions.

where teachers and adjudicators have the opportunity to renew acquaintances and revitalize their Irish step dancing network.

Step dancers at Oireachtas Rince na Cruinne[54] are generally experienced and sophisticated dancers. They have trained for years, have competed at numerous competitions, and they know the etiquette of these competitions. For some, this may be their first Oireachtas Rince na Cruinne. To compete at this event, a step dancer must first qualify at a prior regional or national level. Once qualified, they then pay a dance fee to An Coimisiún through their teacher in order to register for one or more competitions at these championships; this occurs prior to the actual event.

It is Sunday 20 April 2003, and I park my car in the already packed car park of the hotel. On entering the hotel, I am aware that I am entering a quite specific subculture. Vendors stand with their colourful merchandise displayed on stalls erected around the foyer of the hotel. This merchandise includes all kinds of Irish step dance goods: dance shoes[55] from the different commercial dance shoe makers: hard shoes and pumps, poodle socks, sock glue, buckles, tanning gels, glitter make-up, tracksuits, brooches, jewellery, costumes, wigs, hair accessories, tiaras, laces, cassettes, CDs, video recordings, DVDs and books. Step dancers and others are looking at the different merchandise; this is an opportunity to purchase specific Irish dance items.

Since the advent of the Irish step dance stage show *Riverdance* in 1995, and the other step dance stage shows that followed, these vendors and their stalls have become an integral aspect of the bigger step dance events, the *oireachtais*. The 1990s in Ireland coincided with what is termed the Celtic Tiger era: a period associated with economic prosperity. The vendors and their merchandise are indicative of this prosperity. Irish competitive step dance culture has thus developed to include the more commercial aspects of the dance form, to meet the changing demands of Irish step dancers within the more affluent, modern and globalized Celtic Tiger Ireland.

Although step dancers are assessed on their performances and dance technique within step dance competitive contexts, presentation on stage is also important. Dancers and teachers are aware of the current dress code. Male step dancers generally wear either kilt, shirt, tie and blazer, or trousers, shirt, tie and waistcoat (cummerbund is optional). Female step dancers wear step dance dresses. Costumes may be either class costumes or solo costumes; the latter have developed hugely since the 1970s. Class costumes are worn by all dancers of a school on stage when performing *céilí* dances or figure dances; solo costumes are worn for solo competitions. Since female dancers far outnumber male step dancers at these competitive events, female solo step dancers not only need to conform

---

[54] There are different levels of Irish step dance competitions held throughout the year, and indeed throughout the world, in order for step dancers to qualify for Oireachtas Rince na Cruinne: regional levels (in November) and the All Ireland level (in February).

[55] Step dancing shoe companies include: Pecelli, Inishfree, Capezio, Fays, Blarney, Hallachan, Halmor and Katzs. Step dancers each have their own favourite brands.

to a contemporary dress design, but they also need to differentiate themselves from other female step dancers in competition. Although individual dancing styles facilitate this differentiation, adjudicators require other means by which they can remember specific competitors within large, solo, step dancing competitions. The dancing costume is one such means. Since there can be eighty or more competitors in the female senior ladies' competition at Oireachtas Rince na Cruinne, being remembered by the adjudicators is significant.

These female solo step dancing costumes are very individual in colour and design, and are a means by which dancers can assert their own individuality while conforming to a norm. To contain and maintain control over this aspect of competitive step dance culture, An Coimisiún established a decency committee in the 1990s, after *Riverdance*. With the demand for female solo step dancing costumes, an Irish step dancing costume industry has developed, and the costume manufacturers are aware of current fashions. Individual female step dancers, assisted by their parents and teachers, select the colours and designs for their solo costume. These solo costumes cost over €1,000 new, but they can also be bought second-hand at some vendors' stalls and also on the Internet. The expense and the highly ornate design (including feathers, sequins and glitter) has been criticized by some parents and teachers; however, for the moment, they continue to be worn in competition. Indeed, once a female Irish step dancer wears a solo dancing costume at an Oireachtas Rince na Cruinne event, she then sells it and replaces it for the following year's competitions. In Irish step dance culture at present, a female dancer will not be seen at two World Championships in the same solo dancing costume.

Wigs of curls or ringlets are also a current characteristic of the female Irish step dancer's costume. These are available at the vendors' stalls or may be bought on-line, and are relatively expensive. According to the step dancers, these wigs are useful since they do away with the trouble of having to curl their hair. Wigs, or curled hair, function to give bounce and volume to the performer while on stage; this draws attention to the dancer. In addition, wigs assist in giving an appearance of total uniformity to the group when performing *céilí* or figure dances, an important requirement in teamwork dances (see Chapter 5).

For the uninitiated, these female solo step dancing costumes, wigs, tanning gels and so on appear 'over-the-top' and 'beauty-pageant' like. However, if we look to the culture from which this particular fashion has emerged, we may well see how it reflects the mentality of Celtic Tiger Ireland, when Ireland was experiencing economic prosperity. It reflects what Tom Inglis refers to as a cultural shift from self-denial to self-indulgence.[56] However, some people I spoke with mention influences from America due to the current large representation of American teachers with An Coimisiún.

Young women in full dance costume pass me by and wear brightly coloured, ornate dance dresses, wigs and make-up. They are dressed to belong to this subculture. As I walk through the venue, I recognize different accents, including

---

[56]   Inglis (2002).

Irish, American and English. People are coming and going. I see dancers practise oblivious to others around them. Some practise in full costume, while others practise in sports shorts, T-shirts and wigs. Some dancers practise on their own, some with their teachers, and others practise in groups. One particular group of eight dancers is dancing 'The Trip to the Cottage', a *céilí* dance, and their teacher is giving them their final instructions before they go on stage for their competition. This group is mixed, four male and four female dancers, and it is practising for the Senior Mixed Céilí Championship, which is scheduled for 7.30 p.m. (only eight-hand dances are currently permitted at the *céilí* dance championships at Oireachtas Rince na Cruinne). The teacher is reminding the dancers of their spacing, their positions and their timing with their arms and hands. She is lilting the accompanying music while simultaneously vocalizing instructional key words emphatically as they move. In a corner of the room, a female dancer is practising a solo set dance, oblivious to the other practising dancers, and keeping time to her own music – music in her head and in her body. People pass by and look, but do not stop to watch; they are accustomed to this competitive environment with its associated rituals of behaviour.

Doing fieldwork at home means that it may not be long before I encounter familiar faces. I meet some *feis* musicians and teachers I know, including my own step dancing teacher, Peggy McTeggart, and we decide to go to the café for a cup of tea and a chat. Later, we enter the 1,500-seater concert hall where the step dance competitions are being held. The lights of the auditorium are dimmed and the focus is on the stage. The senior ladies are in the middle of their championship, and are preparing to perform their final step dance: the solo set dance. This is the 'recall' for the championship competition. The senior ladies have all performed a hard-shoe dance in the first round and a soft-shoe dance in the second round of the championship. Generally, they either perform the hard-shoe Double Jig or Hornpipe for their first round, and the soft-shoe Reel or Slip Jig for their second. The actual dance type to be danced is decided and made known to all by An Coimisiún in advance of the Championships. Having performed in the two rounds, the highest-ranked dancers in these dances, according to the adjudicators, are called back or 'recalled' to perform a solo set dance of their choice. This is the required third round of the championship.

I make my way towards the tiered rows of seating, and I find a free seat a number of rows behind the three adjudicators, who are seated at small individual tables in front of the stage. The competition is the Senior Ladies Dancing Championship Over 21, which has an entry of 98 ladies. The hall is full of step dancers, teachers and relatives of the competitors. All eyes are fixed on the stage as the first lady walks purposefully and alone to the centre of the stage. I watch intently as she turns and faces the silent audience and the adjudicators. In her upright posture she turns her feet outwards and points her turned out right foot on the ground in front of her turned out left foot. This brings back memories of my own training and competitive years: the turned out feet, the tautness of the right extended leg, the upright verticality, the adrenalin and the waiting in anticipation of the right moment to commence. Her number and the name of her selected set dance, 'The Drunken Gauger', together with the metronomic speed at which she will perform it, are announced over the audio system for all to hear.

The music of 'The Drunken Gauger' commences on the piano accordion, accompanied by the piano. This is typical of the music instrumentation at these step dance championships. The music is slow. This is to allow the dancer time to percussively beat out the intricate rhythms and movements of the set-dance choreography. After the usual introductory bars (the first part or 'A' part of the set-dance music), when the dancer stands still, she proceeds to dance her hard-shoe, percussive set dance. The set dance is reputed to be the showpiece of the step dancer; there is no hiding. The dancer dances both with the music and in syncopation to it, but the timing and intricate rhythms and movements are complicated, accurate and crisp. Gestures are exacting, with precise angles, some high, straight, frontal leg movements and travelling spatial movements. These movements are combined in a way that enhances the accompanying set dance music and brings interest, excitement and contrast to the choreography. However, in all this, timing,rhythm, phrasing, positions of the feet and legs, technical competence, posture, grace, fluency, musicality and the choreography of the set dance are being assessed and commented upon in writing by the adjudicators. Similar to the adjudicators, I am also absorbed and engaged in assessing the performance for myself. The dancers are assessed and marked according to a points system. They are marked according to time, posture, step, dance execution and overall effect. This includes the actual step dance choreography: how it is choreographed, performed, and presented on stage (see Chapter 5 and below). Watching this performance, I am conscious of my muscles tightening and feeling a kinaesthetic empathy with the step dancer. I am watching, hearing and feeling every move that she is making. I find myself holding my breath as if I am performing. I feel the tension. I am concerned that she may miss a beat or slip, but to my relief, all goes well.

At the end of this set dance choreography, which lasts for approximately two minutes, the step dancer returns to the position from which she started, to the sound of applause, and again she points her turned out right foot on the ground in front of her body. I am relieved that she has represented herself well, and that after her year of training building up to this moment, all has gone well for her. She waits for a few seconds in this position to allow time for the adjudicators to write further comments and to review their marks. She awaits the sound of the bell, a symbol that she has the adjudicators' permission to leave the stage. She bows to the adjudicators and to the musicians, and leaves the stage with the same erect posture. The next dancer is ready, and takes up her position and stance in the middle of the stage. Similarly, she waits for the announcement of her number, the name of her selected set dance and the metronomic speed at which she will dance it, and for the sound of the music of her selected solo set dance to commence.

When all the competitors have performed, the next competition is announced, and people await the results of the competition in anxious anticipation. The marking sheets are collected from the adjudicators, and the stage is prepared for the awards ceremony. A tiered, hierarchical podium is placed on the middle of the stage. In the meantime, people come and go; dancers get in and out of dance costumes; they practise steps or parts of steps at the back of the hall; older dancers help younger dancers tie their shoes. Some people browse through the programme, and parents or teachers do a final check that a dancer is presentable for the next competition. Eventually, marks from the adjudicators for individual competitors are displayed on a computerized screen for all to see. Accumulated marks for individual competitors are ranked, and the name of the winner and school of dance to which the winner belongs is announced to screams from fellow dancers, family and teachers. She walks to the sound of recorded music, in full dance costume, to the highest position on the podium. She receives her trophy to applause from the audience. The teacher also comes on stage, and is also rewarded with a trophy. The ranking continues, announcing the name of each dancer and their teacher. The second- and third-placed dancers also stand on designated steps on the podium, while the remaining ranked dancers stand on stage near the podium according to their ranking in the competition. The ranking is visible for all to see. The dancers stand for a few minutes to the applause of the audience, and some photographs are taken; some dancers are emotional and tearful. They leave the stage in their trained, upright postures having been ranked and rewarded for their hard work.

These dancers express and perform *Irish* culture. Although the 'Gaelic idea' was a promotion of co-operative teamwork on a national level (see Chapter 6), it also encouraged individual dancers to take part in a competitive play of skills where one's dance competence and skill was displayed and ranked. Thus, within the competitive context of the *feis* and the Oireachtas Rince na Cruinne, it is the 'symbolic capital',[57] prestige and status of the individual dancer, together with the dancing school to which the dancer belongs, that is at stake. With years of training, discipline and practice, solo competitive step dancers exhibit their competence to their peers, their parents and relatives, their teachers and the adjudicators. Within the heightened and intensive context of competition, step dancers are therefore involved in a state of 'deep play'[58] which is publicly assessed. Therefore, in participating in dance competitions such as Oireachtas Rince na Cruinne, step dancers challenge their own bodies and their very person. It is the role of the adjudicators at these competitive events to decide which step dancer, or step dancers, best embody what it means to be an *Irish* step dancer. They do this through a system of ranking.

Ranking: Rewards and Punishments

The *feis* or Oireachtas Rince na Cruinne is primarily about competitive presentation of step dancing competence. Success in competition assists in rewarding the work

---

[57] Bourdieu (1977).

[58] Geertz (1973).

and reputations of teachers and their step dance students. Therefore, competition and developing standards on a regional, national and global basis are major incentives in competitive step dance practice. Preparation for these competitions takes place in the Irish step dancing class; assessment by specialists – the adjudicators – is at the *feis* or the *oireachtais*. Graded according to age, standard and gender at *oireachtais*, the step dance competitions are adjudicated by registered adjudicators within the organization. Rules regarding actual dances, tempo of music, dance costumes, shoes and ethics are known and are adhered to by all involved within the hierarchical structures at these dance events. And although some rules have been verbally articulated to dancers by teachers in the dance class, it is through the ritual behaviour at the *feis* and the *oireachtais* that rules and the accepted behavioural norms of these dance events are learned.

From the dancer's perspective, rules relating to practice and behaviour on stage are primarily learned either from the teacher in the classroom, or from observation and experience at *feiseanna* and *oireachtais*; thereafter, power is handed over to the adjudicators, who assess stage performances through the process of ranking and awards. Dancers who perform, behave or dress on stage in a way that is not acceptable to the adjudicators are not placed in the rankings. The adjudicator's role is therefore perceived as a significant, powerful and political one within the organization.

The notion of competition has both positive and negative connotations. Step dance competitions are perceived to prepare step dancers for the competitive environment of the 'real world'. According to Ness: 'It is difficult to imagine a value more core in western cultures than the value placed on being able to achieve a single, identified goal... .'[59]

Competitions in Irish step dancing are goals for many competitive step dancers and, although they have raised technical standards in the practice, they have also assisted in homogenizing it. In addition, ranking in competition rewards some and punishes others. According to Michel Foucault:

> The distribution according to ranks or grade has a double role: it marks the gaps, hierarchizes qualities, skills and aptitudes; but it also punishes and rewards. It is the penal functioning of setting in order, and the ordinal character of judging. Discipline rewards simply by the play of awards, thus making it possible to attain higher ranks and places; it punishes by reversing this process. Rank in itself serves as a reward or punishment.[60]

Foucault's double-edged system of gratification/punishment lies very much at the heart of Irish step dance competitions. He speaks of 'the art of punishment' in relation to discipline. He states that it brings five distinct operations into play:

---

[59]   Ness in Noland and Ness (2008), p. 18.
[60]   Foucault (1977), p. 181.

comparison, differentiation, hierarchization, homogenization and exclusion. These clearly operate within the Irish step dance competitive context.

Step dance competitions are by their very nature a 'field of comparison'. Dancers are compared and differentiated by adjudicators, teachers and dancers themselves. Their performance on the day is measured against others, and in accordance with Foucault, the 'art of punishment' measures 'in quantitative terms and hierarchizes in terms of values and abilities, the level, the "nature" of individuals. It introduces through this "value-giving" measure, the constraint of a conformity that must be achieved.'[61] This process is made manifest at Oireachtas Rince na Cruinne, for example, in the ranking of Irish step dance performers in a hierarchical manner and in the homogenization of competitive Irish step dance performance practices. Solo step dancers accommodate, for the most part, the accepted kinaesthetic vocabulary of the day; however, it may be negotiated by highly skilled performers, and even then very subtly. Informed step dancers and teachers are all aware of those impressive novelty movements that won last year's Oireachtas Rince na Cruinne championships, and which they have inserted in steps for this current year's championships. This homogenization has contributed to a sense of community and belonging, but it has also assisted in the measurement process.

Dancers are measured according to time, carriage, steps and execution – all elements that are measurable. Indeed, the process of homogenization in competitive Irish step dance and *céilí* dance repertoire facilitates this measurement and assessment. Consequently, this has led to 'the constraint of a conformity' within competitive step dance practice. Creativity does occur within the genre, and step dance consistently develops, but it does so under these constraints.[62] Yet this 'constraint of a conformity' is what defines and gives meaning to competitive Irish step dance practice.

Step dancers with An Coimisiún do not improvise in competition; they generally do not diverge from the blueprint of their prepared dance. They are examined and adjudicated according to how correctly they have mastered the dance they have prepared and are performing according to a formalized and institutionalized aesthetic and technique. Anything measured to be 'too far out' is not placed in the ranking; it is not considered 'normal' practice, and the dancer is punished by not being placed. Competition thus normalizes, and similar to Foucault's discussion of the examination, the Irish step dance competition is about the power of the 'Norm':

> The examination combines the technique of an observing hierarchy and those of a normalizing judgement. It is a normalizing gaze, a surveillance that makes it possible to qualify, to classify and to punish. It establishes over individuals a visibility through which one differentiates them and judges them. That is why, in all the mechanisms of discipline, the examination is highly ritualised.

[61] Ibid., pp. 182–3.
[62] See Ní Bhriain (2010).

> In it are combined the ceremony of power and the form of the experiment, the
> deployment of force and the establishment of truth ....[63]

Competitive Irish step dance events are also highly ritualized. They provide sites
where hierarchies of rank can be contested, but only in accordance with 'the
constraint of a conformity': a conformity in dance technique, dance genres, dance
repertoire, posture, musical accompaniment, codes of dress, performance and
behaviour.

Irish step dance competition involves conforming to the power of the 'Norm'.
This 'Norm', however, is not static, and in step dance competition it has been
developed and regulated by An Coimisiún, under the auspices of the Gaelic
League, throughout the twentieth century. In so doing, it has validated to itself and
others that what it has represented is authentic and that it is the keeper, protector,
promoter and disseminator of 'the truth'. An Coimisiún exercised this hegemonic
power through the hierarchical institutional structures of the organization and
through the competitive structures at *feiseanna* and *oireachtais*.

Step dance competitions also provide sites where emotions are played out:
joy at winning, sadness at losing. These sites facilitate the teaching of acceptable
behaviour in relation to winning and losing. Although a step dancer may not win
a step dance competition, the dancer is expected to congratulate the winner, as the
winner is expected to congratulate those who are ranked lower. These competitions
are important sites in the transmission of moral and behavioural education.

An Coimisiún Today

An Coimisiún remains today the largest, hierarchical, institutional structure
regulating competitive Irish step dancing. It oversees all aspects of competitive
Irish step dancing under its jurisdiction, both in Ireland and abroad. It has achieved
this position through its institutionalization and promotion of Irish step dancing
as a unified, national dance practice and cultural expression, and by putting in
place certain measures to attain this. These have included the construction and
registration of cultural events to promote the practice (the *feis and the oireachtas*),
the implementation of rules and regulations, the introduction of a teacher's
qualifying examination (TCRG) and an adjudicator's qualifying examination
(ADCRG), and the prescription and institutionalization of specific *céilí* dances
in its text booklets, *Ár Rinncidhe Fóirne* (see Chapter 5). All the above have
assisted in constructing and promoting a unified, co-operative and international
community of Irish step dancers, teachers, adjudicators, musicians, administrators
and others. These individuals contribute to and share, to varying degrees, a
particular community *habitus*.

---

[63] Foucault (1977), p. 184.

Although the names *feis* and *oireachtas* may conjure up images of perceived glorious times past in Gaelic Ireland, this history is not known to the general step dance population who come to the *feis* or Oireachtas Rince na Cruinne to dance and to compete, and who, for the most part, have little knowledge or interest in its history.[64] It is the dancing and the belonging through the act of dancing that matter. Thus, the ritualistic context of Oireachtas Rince na Cruinne provides a site where this specific dance community can share and celebrate its relationship to one, step dance performance and its particular conceptualisation of the body; and two, iconographic content at the event. Step dancing acts as the glue in constructing and maintaining a sense of community, and the Oireachtas Rince na Cruinne event assists in constructing, reproducing, maintaining and shaping the identity of the group and the identity of individuals within the group.

Step dancing is an embodied practice, and whether consciously or not, in the act of participation, culture is embodied, expressed and experienced. Oireachtas Rince na Cruinne is organized by An Coimisiún under the auspices of the Gaelic League, therefore the ideological agenda of the Gaelic League cannot be ignored, although the latter decades of the twentieth century has seen a weakening of its nationalist agenda. Therefore, although step dancers are generally not aware of the ideological agenda of the Gaelic League, by participating at *feiseanna* and *oireachtais*, they mediate and perform politics.

Since the 1970s, there has been a growing internationalization of Irish step dancing. Oireachtas Rince na Cruinne and the promotion of Irish dancing at home and abroad by An Coimisiún have assisted in this dissemination. In addition, the global acclaim of the Irish step dance shows *Riverdance* and *Lord of the Dance*

---

[64] A Gaelic *Oireachtas*, called *Oireachtas na Gaeilge*, continues today in Ireland, but it is separate from the Irish step dance competitions of An Coimisiún. Today, *sean nós* ('old-style') dance competitions are held at *Oireachtas na Gaeilge*. *Sean nós* dance competitions were held for the first time at *Oireachtas na Gaeilge* in 1978. The inclusion of *sean nós* dance that year was to recognize and revitalize the region of Connemara through its dance (see Brennan (1999)). Since then, *sean nós* dance competitions are integral to the *Oireachtas*. Currently, the *sean nós* dance style of Connemara on the west of Ireland is growing in popularity. Workshops is this solo percussive individualized dance form are held in different areas in Ireland, including Irish cities – Galway, Dublin, Limerick – and abroad. Young and old, male and female, are all participating in these workshops that are taught by well-known *sean nós* dancers, including Seosamh Ó Neachtain, Róisín Ní Mhainín, Páraic Ó Hoibicín, Mairtín MacDonnchadh, Gearóid and Páraic Ó Dubháin, Máire-Áine Ni Iarnáin, Emma O'Sullivan, Ronan O'Regan and Maldon Meehan. This interest in *sean nós* is apparent not only in the increase in numbers learning Connemara *sean nós* dance, but the increase in numbers competing at the national annual *sean nós* dance competitions at the *Oireachtas*. Also of significance is the increase in audience numbers. At the competitions in Donegal in 2004, people had to be refused entry due to the theatre being full. It is also of interest that this annual competition has been broadcast nationally by the television channel TG4 for the past decade. The programme, named *Steip*, has contributed to a further interest in, and the dissemination of, Connemara *sean nós* dance. Also it has brought a national awareness to the dance form.

since 1995 have popularized the dance form.[65] Therefore, today Irish dancing has become a global, transnational dance form. Today, more than half the registered Irish step dancing teachers within An Coimisiún live outside Ireland.[66] This, together with processes of globalization, has seen a weakening in the ideological agenda of the Gaelic League within An Coimisiún. This is made manifest in, for instance, the fact that the meetings of An Coimisiún are now conducted in English, not Irish; that the vast majority of teachers teach through English, and most could not teach through Irish due to the internationalization of Irish step dancing, and that many of the female solo dancing costumes now have abstract ornate designs in lieu of Celtic designs. In addition, some teachers and students within An Coimisiún perceive step dancing to be more akin to a sport than a cultural expressive practice.[67]

Although the Gaelic League's cultural nationalist agenda is no longer as strong within modern Ireland, in his book *Inventing Ireland* (1996), Declan Kiberd locates the invention of modern Ireland at the turn of the nineteenth and the early decades of the twentieth century. It was, according to Kiberd, the renaissance of Irish culture. The Gaelic League, among others, contributed to this renaissance and the cultural dynamic that shaped modern Ireland. In its appropriation and institutionalization of step dance and its construction of a canon of Irish *céilí* dances, the Gaelic League acknowledged the potential of dance to define, shape and transmit values and sentiments of both a communitarian and ideological nature.

Rinceoirí na Ríochta Today

The teachers of Rinceoirí na Ríochta in Kerry conform to the structures and rulings of An Coimisiún in order to belong to this international community of step dancers and to be able to participate at Coimisiún competitions, particularly 'The Worlds'. The step dancers of Rinceoirí na Ríochta have competed successfully at *feiseanna* and *oireachtais* at local, regional, national, European and international levels within the structures of An Coimisiún. However, in order for these step dancers to reach this standard, they have had to attend classes two or three times a week and practise towards winning at these competitions. In 2004, one of the students at Rinceoirí na Ríochta, John Fitzgerald, won the All Ireland Championship, the European Irish Dance Championships and was awarded second place in Oireachtas Rince na Cruinne. In 2005, another student, David Geaney, won Oireachtas Rince na Cruinne. Both John Fitzgerald and David Geaney won Oireachtas Rince na Cruinne in 2006 (see Illustration 6.1(a)), John Fitzgerald again won Oireachtas Rince na Cruinne in 2009 and 2010 (see Illustration 6.1(b)), and David Geaney again won Oireachtas Rince na Cruinne in 2012.

---

[65]   Foley (2001).
[66]   Cullinane (2003).
[67]   Hall, F. (2008).

(a)

(b)

Illustration 6.1   (a) John Fitzgerald, Rinceoirí na Ríochta, winner of Oireachtas Rince na Cruinne 2006 (The Worlds), Belfast's Waterfront Hall, Belfast, Northern Ireland. Used with permission of John Egan, FeisPix. (b) John Fitzgerald, Rinceoirí na Ríochta, winner of Oireachtas Rince na Cruinne 2010 (The Worlds), The Royal Concert Hall, Glasgow, Scotland, 2010. Used with permission of John Egan, FeisPix

When I asked John Fitzgerald about step dance competitions, he had the following to say:

My opinion of the competitions changes all of the time. It's more of a love/hate relationship with them. I tend to put a lot of pressure on myself to get things right, but most of all to win. I know people say, 'it's the taking part that counts,' but to me, unfortunately, it's not. Of course, it's such a wonderful thing to say you've competed at All Ireland and World Championship level, but when you're at the top of the podium, there's only one direction to go if you don't keep up the standard and motivation to be the best. When I won the World Championships for the third time in 2010, I told myself that I was finished with competition and that I would never place myself under that pressure again. That was very short-lived, however, as I couldn't stay away and went back competing this year [2012]. I'm never completely happy when I'm in the competition circle because of that stress I place myself under, but at the other end of the scale, I'm far more unhappy when I'm not competing, and I can never wait to get back into the training, the sweat and the making of new steps and moves. Secretly, I think I enjoy the thrill of the whole experience, and there is no possible way I

would be still competing if I didn't absolutely love the practice, the nerves, the
atmosphere and the friends I've made all over the world.[68]

The step dancers of Rinceoirí na Ríochta love to step dance. For many of them,
step dancing is their main leisure activity. Some dancers may never win a World
Championship and may not attend many competitions, but they enjoy step dancing
and the social side of the dancing class. Those step dancers of Rinceoirí na Ríochta
who have mastered the form compete at all major *oireachtais*, where they learn
life skills, the value of hard work, and the confidence to compete gracefully.
Although competition can be pressurizing, they enjoy the incentive and the buzz
of performing and competing. Also, they know that step dancing is something that
they can do well which gives them comfort and confidence.

The social dimension of this subcultural dance world is also important to these
step dancers. They travel to compete, and they get the opportunity to go to places
they may otherwise not travel to, where they stay overnight, if not for a week, and
meet other step dancers from other areas of Ireland and abroad. Some of these step
dancers have competed not only in different places in Ireland, but also in England,
Scotland, mainland Europe and the United States. Some of the dancers form strong
friendships, and going to *feiseanna* and *oireachtais* is a way of maintaining contact
with them. The *feis* and the *oireachtas* can thus be seen as a social network of step
dancers, teachers, adjudicators, musicians and step dancers' families and friends.
These dance contexts consolidate them as a subcultural community. However, like
many communities, the Irish step dancing world is also subject to both conflict and
other social forces, but it is step dancing, as a dance-music aesthetic practice, that
binds them together.

Step dancers take pride in belonging to their particular school and in
representing their school and geographical region. The dancers of Rinceoirí na
Ríochta likewise take pride in their school, their teachers and their geographical
location in the south-west of Ireland. When I asked John Fitzgerald what it meant
for him to be a dancer with Rinceoirí na Ríochta, he had the following to say:

> The first word that comes to mind is definitely 'pride'. I've danced with the
> school since the very start, and over the years the teachers have worked tirelessly
> to help develop and nurture my talent. Irish dancing has played such a major
> role in my life to date, not just in my competition life, but it has also opened so
> many different opportunities to me that would never have been possible had it
> not been for this dancing school, and I've never forgotten that. There is such a
> sense of friendship and encouragement within the school, and this is definitely
> its greatest strength. I always want to represent the school as best I can, and it is
> always a pleasure to do so.[69]

---

[68]   John Fitzgerald, questionnaire response, April 2012.
[69]   Ibid.

Jimmy Smith stresses the great camaraderie that exists between dancers from Kerry, even those from different schools in Kerry: 'They'd be delighted to see a child from another school in Kerry doing well … they've a great sense of "Up, Kerry!"'[70] This is also similar for schools from other regions. For instance, competitors from the USA take pride in somebody from their country winning a World Championship in Irish dancing. The Irish step dancing class provides a site for generating, maintaining and experiencing a strong local sense of community and belonging, and winning at a *feis* or an *oireachtas* increases this sense of belonging and community.

Although competition is the primary focus and incentive for Rinceoirí na Ríochta, step dancers of the school might also perform at social events such as family parties and weddings, school events and concerts. They also perform at cabaret and tourist events during the summer tourist season, when traditional Irish music, song and dance are performed in local hotels or in other formal venues. The latter are generally organized by Comhaltas Ceoltóirí Éireann[71] or the committee of the annual Rose of Tralee festival. For the step dancers at the school, these events provide local sites where they exhibit their dance competence and where they socialize. For the teachers, these events are less pressurizing than *oireachtais*, and they provide alternative platforms where Irish dancing and the work of the school can be exhibited and promoted:

C.F.   So how many cabarets would Rinceoirí na Ríochta step dancers do in a year?

J.S.   We've done about ten this year already.

C.F.   Would you do the same show ten times?

J.S.   I wouldn't be able to get the same kids each night. They go on holidays, so we've different kids coming in all the time. It's a very simple little piece – just put them out in a three-hander, six-hander, eight-hander, even a solo. What it does when they're children is it adds to their confidence, they gain great self-esteem out of it. When they're older, they're going to be able to face people without any trouble at all. They're not going to have any inhibitions. It gives them great self-confidence and great self-esteem.[72]

As well as being step dancers and step dance teachers, Jimmy Smith and Patricia Hanafin were also founding members of Siamsa Tíre, the National Folk Theatre of Ireland, in Tralee, for which they both taught and performed until relatively recently. Moreover, some of the current and more experienced step dancers with Rinceoirí na Ríochta, including John Fitzgerald, also perform with Siamsa Tíre. Therefore,

---

[70]   Jimmy Smith (2004), ethnographic interview with the author.

[71]   The Comhaltas Ceoltóirí Éireann cabarets generally take place in 'Dúchas' ('Heritage'), the headquarters of Comhaltas Ceoltóirí Éireann in Tralee.

[72]   Jimmy Smith (2004), ethnographic interview with the author.

although step dancers with Rinceoirí na Ríochta are competitive step dancers, some of them also learn other dance practices outside the context of the school:

C.F. Do any of your dancers do ballet, contemporary or any other dance form?

J.S. Everything now. They're involved in ballet, the school of music, disco dancing – all of that.

C.F. Would you have many dancers now back in Siamsa Tíre?

J.S. They're all in Siamsa Tíre.

C.F. How many?

J.S. A lot of them. It seems to be an automatic thing. The leaflet comes through the door saying there are auditions on for Siamsa. I hand out the pieces of paper. They go off and get into Siamsa. That would be outside now, in Listowel, in Teach Siamsa out in Finuge. They go there for three years, and then they're auditioned to come into town to the theatre.

C.F. How do you feel about that?

J.S. I don't mind at all. It's good for them – acting and singing. It takes them away from the competition side of it as well, and they're introduced to the theatrical side of it.[73]

It is clear from the above that the rule established by the Gaelic League during the early decades of the twentieth century concerning the restriction of its membership to 'Irish' dances no longer applies. Similarly to their own dance teachers, some current step dancers with Rinceoirí na Ríochta comfortably move across the different arenas of competition, theatre and social dance.[74] They use these arenas as sites to construct and negotiate their dance aesthetic according to the different contexts in which they are placed, and each site, while transforming the meaning of the dance, assists in shaping and informing individual and collective senses of identity and *habiti*.

---

[73] Ibid.

[74] It is of interest that David Geaney, one of the step dancers with Rinceoirí na Ríochta, entered and won the national Irish dance competition *The Jig Gig*, broadcast nationally by the Irish-language television station TG4 in 2011.

Chapter 7

Globalization and Siamsa Tíre, the National Folk Theatre of Ireland

From the end of the nineteenth century to the 1960s, Ireland remained politically and culturally inward-looking. This was understandable given the colonial history of the island and the efforts of various cultural nationalist movements in Ireland from the eighteenth century to establish Ireland as an independent country. Ireland became a republic in 1922 (see Chapter 5). Between 1932 and 1973, politics in Ireland was very much influenced by the government of Éamon de Valera (the *taoiseach*[1] of Ireland from 1932 to 1973). This period witnessed a strong nostalgia for the past, particularly a Catholic, rural past. This is made evident in Éamon de Valera's St Patrick's Day speech on Raidió Éireann in 1943.[2] The year marked the fiftieth anniversary of the foundation of the Gaelic League, and in recognition of this anniversary, de Valera set out his vision of an ideal Ireland:

> The ideal Ireland that we would have, the Ireland that we dreamed of, would be the home of a people who valued material wealth only as a basis for right living, of a people who, satisfied with frugal comfort, devoted their leisure to the things of the spirit – a land whose countryside would be bright with cosy homesteads, whose fields and villages would be joyous with the sounds of industry, with the romping of sturdy children, the contest of athletic youths and the laughter of happy maidens, whose firesides would be forums for the wisdom of serene old age. The home, in short, of a people living the life that God desires that men should live.

This speech was made during the Second World War, when Ireland remained neutral. However, since the 1960s, there has been a decline in the traditionalism associated with the de Valera era. Ireland has gradually begun to take its place on the global stage. In 1962, the newly established Telefís Éireann[3] paved the way for Ireland's entry into the world of mass communication. Rock and roll music became the fashion of the day, and disco dancing and cabarets were primary forms of popular entertainment. From the 1960s, Irish traditional music became popular in the international arena, and later, Irish rock groups such as U2 and The Cranberries all assisted Ireland in making its mark internationally. In 1972,

---

[1] Prime Minister.

[2] 17 March 1943.

[3] The Irish national television station.

Ireland became a member of the European Economic Community (EEC).[4] By the 1990s, a different society was emerging in Ireland: a society that was increasingly becoming secular, entrepreneurial and economically competitive.[5] This period, popularly known as the Celtic Tiger period, witnessed the global success of the Irish step dance stage shows *Riverdance* and *Lord of the Dance*. These productions assisted in placing Ireland globally, and inspired other Irish step dance stage shows to follow on the international market.[6] Ireland was emerging as a secular, modern nation-state capable of playing a part in global economics. Ireland had become a First World Western nation in an increasingly connected globalized world. This situation gave rise to questions in Ireland of culture and identity.

Siamsa Tíre, the National Folk Theatre of Ireland

> Along with the technological revolution, the transformation of capitalism and the demise of statism, we have experienced in the past twenty-five years the widespread surge of powerful expressions of collective identity that challenge globalization and cosmopolitanism on behalf of cultural singularity and people's control over their lives and environment. These expressions are multiple, highly diversified, following contours of each culture, and of historical sources of formation of each identity.[7]

In response to the process of globalization, Siamsa Tíre, the National Folk Theatre of Ireland, was established in 1974. Siamsa Tíre is a state-sponsored folk theatre whose objective is to express Irish folk culture theatrically. Siamsa Tíre seeks to locate and culturally re-present Ireland within a broader European and global arena. In this endeavour, it combines Irish traditional music, song, dance and mime within a theatrical context. Dance is an integral part of the productions of Siamsa Tíre, and the Molyneaux step dance style of North Kerry has been re-contextualized and developed as a kinaesthetic signature of this folk theatre.

Siamsa Tíre, as the national folk theatre, is placed locally in Kerry through its genesis in Kerry, its appropriation of the Molyneaux step dance style of North Kerry and its Kerry cast. It is also placed globally through its awareness of, and professional interaction with, individual artists, audiences, institutions and festivals in the international arena. Siamsa Tíre is an artistic and commercial enterprise, and as such it must compete within consumer culture. Since its inception, many choreographers, composers, dancers, musicians, singers, actors, set designers, visual artists and others have worked with the theatre to develop its artistic and folk theatrical work. This chapter focuses primarily on the dance

---

[4]   Now called the European Union (EU).

[5]   Foley (2001).

[6]   Ibid.

[7]   Castells (1997 [2004]), p. 2.

and movement aspects of the theatre. The older, regional, Molyneaux step dance practice is utilized as a resource or inspiration for the artistic movement development of the theatre. As this step dance practice is increasingly declining in its original rural context (see Chapters 3 and 4), it is acquiring new life as it is stylized, re-presented and commoditized within the context of the theatre for artistic and consumer culture.

San Am Fadó: A Performance Ethnography

It is 7.30 p.m. on 30 June 2004. I have set up my video camera in a back corner of the auditorium. The 355-seat auditorium is lit, and the raised stage is empty. All is quiet except for the comings and goings of an odd cast member or technician. I am looking forward to seeing the show, *San Am Fadó*;[8] it has been many years since I first saw an earlier production of it, then known as *Fadó Fadó*.[9] *San Am Fadó* is historically the show most associated with Siamsa Tíre, the National Folk Theatre of Ireland, and is by all accounts the most popular show with summer tourists. The show is based on rural life in Ireland in the relatively recent past, and according to the Siamsa Tíre brochure, it:

> dramatises a whole year's cycle of living and working the land. The brand new production emphasises the labour and rituals that celebrated the seasons, marked our everyday lives, and gave meaning to the cycles of the year. Through lively singing, music, dancing and mime, *San Am Fadó* moves through the open air of the bog fields and harvest festivals, to the warmth of the hearth-lit kitchen and celebrates the joys, and sorrows, of a typical family in Ireland.[10]

Since I am ready to record, I go out to the foyer. This is the third building that has been part of the history of Siamsa Tíre. Ashe Memorial Hall and the Theatre Royal in Tralee were its temporary homes but in 1991 this custom-built theatre became the permanent home to Siamsa Tíre. Together with the theatre, there is also an Arts Centre on the premises. This building allows for a wide variety of events throughout the year: contemporary theatre, dance, classical music, comedy and literary events, as well as a vibrant visual arts line-up in the dedicated gallery spaces. Siamsa Tíre also hosts activities by a large number of local amateur arts organizations.

I look at the art exhibit and make my way back to the foyer, where I meet Phil Smith, wife of Jimmy Smith, the step dance teacher with Rinceoirí na Ríochta and also a founding member of Siamsa Tíre. I am not surprised to find Phil here since it has long been my understanding that Siamsa Tíre involves not only the immediate local cast members, but also their families. This evening, Phil is working at the

---

[8]   'In Times Past'.

[9]   'Long, Long Ago'.

[10]   Siamsa Tíre brochure.

refreshments counter. Marie Whelan is in the box office; Marie is the widow of Martin Whelan, who died suddenly in 2002. Martin had been the Manager of Siamsa Tíre since its foundation in 1974, and is still fondly remembered and missed by the members of Siamsa Tíre.[11] As I look through the programme, I see that many members are related. Siamsa Tíre is a close-knit local community formed around the activities of this national folk theatre.

Phil offers me a cup of tea and informs me that the buses will be coming shortly. It is the mid-summer season, and generally, busloads of tourists include a visit to one of Siamsa Tíre's productions as part of their cultural touring package. Tourism is important to the region. It has transformed Kerry into an international cosmopolitan region where seasonal tourists (generally summertime) are drawn for a taste of Ireland, holidaying and recreation. Kerry combines the old with the new. It boasts beautiful mountainous landscapes, the Lakes of Killarney and is a relatively isolated area where a rural way of life can still be observed. The Irish language, as a first language, is heard spoken to the west of the county, while its towns have modern facilities, including schools, banks, cinemas, restaurants, pubs, hotels, clothes shops, gift shops, sports shops, recreation and entertainment facilities. These tourists are drawn to Kerry because of its landscape and culture, its geographical location on the north-western fringe of Europe, and perhaps because of a desire to visit the country of their ancestors. Tourists to the region come from all over the world, but a large proportion of them are from the USA. Tourism has therefore developed a self-consciousness in the region of Kerry, of being Irish or being of Kerry, and it has played an important cultural and economic role in the region in general, and in the emergence and development of Siamsa Tíre.

This evening, a number of these tour buses are expected. Phil is right! Within minutes, the foyer is full of lively chatter and I am struck by the prevalence of American accents. This is not surprising, considering the large Irish diaspora in the United States. I make my way back into the auditorium to take my place behind the camera. I watch as the auditorium fills up with predominantly middle-aged to elderly tourists; some families with teenagers are also in the group.

At 8.30 p.m. sharp, the lights in the house are dimmed and all eyes are focused on the stage. We listen for a few minutes to the mandatory safety announcement, and then we hear the haunting sound of the beating of the *bodhrán*. After a few bars, we hear a brisk Reel being played in unison by a group of Irish traditional musicians who are seated together in the corner of the auditorium next to, and on the same level as, the stage. This is followed by another Reel. The instruments being played include tin whistle, flute, fiddle, box, banjo, concertina and keyboard. The playing of the group is well balanced, meticulous and professional. The tin whistle then enters solo, playing the lonely and melancholy sound of the slow air 'An tSeanduine'[12] to soft, Western harmonic accompaniment on a keyboard.

---

[11]   With the sudden death of Martin Whelan in 2002, Morganne Kennedy was appointed Manager of Siamsa Tíre.

[12]   'The Old Person'.

Illustration 7.1   *San Am Fadó, c.* 1974 © Siamsa Tíre. Used with permission of
Siamsa Tíre

The stage is professionally and brightly lit, and the first scene is depicted. It is
an outdoor, summer, farmyard scene with a single-storey thatched cottage to the
right of the stage (see Illustration 7.1). A hay cart, a butter churn, a water pump
and a *súgán* chair[13] also adorn the scene. This scene is reminiscent of bygone
days in rural Ireland. A woman comes out of the thatched cottage and picks up a
bucket; she sings a melancholic Gaelic song, 'Fáinne Geal an Lae'.[14] She is joined
by other actors, who slowly walk to particular positions on stage. The melody
line is harmonized by the actors. In lieu of the song being sung in unison, as
is the norm within a monophonic song tradition, Western pentatonic harmonies
have been arranged and added to the melody line to create the very clean and
distinctive harmonic sound associated with Siamsa Tíre. These harmonies give
an air of sophistication, suggesting connections beyond 'rural' Kerry to Europe.
In the act of singing, these actors/singers are performing and reinforcing notions
about their identity and that of Siamsa Tíre; they may live locally in Kerry, but
they are globally informed and connected. This song is followed by another Gaelic
song, 'Samhradh, Samhradh'.[15] Again, the arranged pentatonic harmonies are
used. Throughout these songs, the actors either stand in particular positions on
stage or they walk slowly across the stage. During the performance of 'Samhradh,
Samhradh', children enter with garlands. A Jig commences to be played, which
is the cue for a young boy to dance a Light Jig. The young boy is the step dancer
John Fitzgerald from Rinceoirí na Ríochta. John dances around the other children

---

[13]   A *súgán* chair is a wooden-framed chair with its seat made from rushes.
[14]   'The Morning Dew'.
[15]   'Summer, Summer'.

in a circular anti-clockwise direction; he is then joined by the other children, and they all dance the side-step of the Light Jig together, facing into the centre of their circle. The adult actors, standing by and watching, eventually join them in the Light Jig. This is performed by all in unison and in a light-hearted manner. The actors perform in black, percussive dance shoes to visually and audibly beat out the rhythm of the accompanying Jig tune; some children dance bare-foot, again reminiscent of times past in an economically poorer, rural Ireland. After a while, the instrumental accompaniment of the Light Jig changes to Reel tempo, and all actors dance a series of lively percussive Treble Reel steps in unison; these are not in the local Molyneaux style, but are in a more general Irish, exhibitionistic, step dancing style. These performers are aware of the theatrical context, and they dance their planned and choreographed routines for set periods, to set music accompaniment, for the audience. This brings the first scene to a close.

Different age groups, from very young to old, are represented on stage; there is also gender equality. It is noticeable that all the actors on stage are singers and dancers. Apart from the children in this scene who dance barefoot, male and female actors wear Irish dance shoes appropriate for percussive step dances. All perform the side-step of the Light Jig; the movements are the same as those that are taught in the Coimisiún step dance class, Rinceoirí na Ríochta, and as were taught by Molyneaux as the Lead of the Light Jig. It is interesting to note the continuity of this particular step dance and the changed contexts and meanings of its performance, where each context provides a site for the performance of a different expression and story of Irish identity. Throughout the show, songs in Gaelic are interspersed with traditional dance tunes and dances: Reels, Jigs, Hornpipes, Slip Jigs, 'The Blackbird' and 'The King of the Fairies' set dances, Polkas and 'The Stack of Barley'. The dances are choreographed for specific purposes throughout the show to depict the rural way of life when Gaelic was the spoken language in Ireland. These include farming activities and rural socio-cultural experiences that were common to rural communities in Ireland prior to mechanization. The dances, movements and dramatic actions throughout the show are choreographed around these activities and experiences, and include scenes such as milking the cow, sharpening the scythe, using the flail, thatching the roof, churning butter, mending shoes, entertaining each other, celebrating Bealtaine (Mayday) and birth, and bemoaning emigration. The community depicted in the show is that of the rural peasant. This is reflected in the costumes worn on stage, which are representative of rural Ireland at the time: men wear long-sleeved shirts, waistcoats and trousers; women wear blouses and full skirts to below the knee; the young boys dress similarly to the men, while the young girls wear pinafores to below the knee.

Dance is an integral part of the show. Treble Reels, Jigs and Hornpipes are performed in both a traditional, grounded, earthy, percussive style of dancing and a more modern, elevated, travelling style. Participatory social dances are also performed, as these were traditionally danced at rural house dances; these include the Patsy Hailey couple dance, and some set dancing (similar to Quadrilles). When performing step dances, the dancers' bodies are loose. They hold their torsos upright, but softly, while their arms are allowed to swing naturally to the sides of the body. One or two of Molyneaux's step dances are also there to be observed. For example, the step from Molyneaux's advanced 'Blackbird' set dance is featured, as is the Treble Reel Lead, and one of Molyneaux's Jig steps. Motifs from the Molyneaux repertoire are also performed for theatrical purposes. One such motif emphasizes loose, curved, ankle work. This motif appears in the opening to the set section of Molyneaux's advanced 'Blackbird' set dance, and is also the opening to the Single Drum Hornpipe step.[16] Over the years, this dance motif has become a characteristic kinetic identity signature for Siamsa Tíre.

After the hour-long show, with one intermission, *San Am Fadó* comes to an end, to huge applause. The audience seems to have got what it came to see: an evening's dramatic entertainment based upon a perception of Ireland's almost idyllic rural cultural past. I slowly and reflectively pack up my camera and watch as the audience leaves. On the way out, one American lady says to me, 'You shouldn't have used your camera!' 'It's all right,' I replied, 'I had permission.' I make my way out to the foyer and meet some members of the cast after the show. They are excited and pleased with the performance. Some of them have performed in this particular show for years, and this season they have performed it every Monday, Tuesday and Wednesday night, right through from May to August. The other shows on offer during the summer season of 2004 were *Oileán*, *Oisín* and *Clann Lir*, and were performed throughout the season into September and October. With an annual five-month extended summer season, these dancers, actors and musicians are well used to performing *San Am Fadó*, as it is based on the original show *Fadó Fadó* and is the longest-running show in the theatre's repertoire.[17]

I wonder what impression of Ireland members of the audience gained from this theatrical presentation. I watch the audience as it disperses, and realize that although they may not understand Gaelic, the evening no doubt gave them a particular cultural snapshot of Ireland's rural past through the aid of visual sets, on-stage props and traditional music, song, dance and mime performed by experienced, and some professional, Irish artists. It will become part of their cultural memory of Ireland. Indeed, as Martin Whelan, the first Manager of Siamsa Tíre, stated in the Siamsa Tíre programme:

> *Siamsa Tíre* performances continue to receive standing ovations both from home and worldwide audiences, captivated perhaps by the appeal of a way of life from times past and by the intriguing Celtic resonances that are so much part of Irish heritage and traditions.[18]

---

[16] I collected and Labanotated the Single Drum Hornpipe step from a number of step dancers in North Kerry; see Foley (1988b; 2012b). Also see Catherine Foley's Step Dancing Collection at Muckross House, Killarney.

[17] *San Am Fadó* did not feature in Siamsa Tíre's summer seasons of 2010, 2011, 2012 or 2013.

[18] Martin Whelan in the Siamsa Tíre souvenir programme.

Historical Background to Siamsa Tíre

Siamsa Tíre, the National Folk Theatre of Ireland, was officially established in 1974 under the artistic directorship of a local parish priest, Fr Pat Ahern. Fr Pat Ahern had grown up on the family farm near the village of Moyvane, North Kerry, during the 1930s and 1940s; he later graduated with a degree in music (1962) from University College, Cork, under Professor Aloys Fleischmann. The mission statement of Siamsa Tíre, reads:

> to reflect Ireland's great wealth of music, dance and folklore on stage through vibrant, colourful theatrical entertainment and to continue creating new folk theatre presentations, drawing on our traditions and a rich cultural reservoir.

Founded initially on an amateur basis, Siamsa Tíre developed to become a professional folk theatre company in 1985; Fr Pat Ahern remained as Artistic Director until 1998. This chapter looks at the development of this theatre as a national folk theatre.

Housed in a specifically custom-built theatre at Town Park, Tralee, Siamsa Tíre rests on its success. Its development was originally spawned from St John's Parish Choir, under the direction of Fr Pat Ahern. The talents of some of the members of the choir inspired Fr Pat Ahern to stage a Passion Play entitled *Golgotha* in 1963. This performance was acclaimed, and subsequently, a celebratory night was held to acknowledge the performers and organizers. The night concluded with a special presentation of song, dance and music by some of those involved, including step dancers Patricia Hanafin and Liam Tarrant. Subsequent to this occasion, those interested started to experiment informally with presentations of traditional music, song, dance, traditional customs and folklore, and they gradually brought other interested people on board. A rehearsal of one of their pieces was recorded for Raidió Telefís Éireann (RTE) news, and shortly afterwards the group was invited to present four half-hour programmes for the national television programme *Ailliliú*. For this purpose, the group came up with the name Siamsóirí na Ríochta. With the profile achieved from this programme, the group was encouraged to present the four half-hour programmes together in one concert for tourists during the summer months in Kerry. Subsequently, in 1968, the summer season of Irish Folk Theatre emerged in Tralee with Siamsóirí na Ríochta. This developed into Siamsa Tíre, the National Folk Theatre of Ireland, in 1974, and has since grown in strength and in size. Thus, from its humble beginnings as a small, amateur folk theatrical group known as Siamsóirí na Ríochta, Siamsa Tíre gradually developed into the Arts Council-supported national folk theatre it is today.

Siamsa Tíre was initiated within the context of a 'Save the West' project. A proposal was written by Fr Pat Ahern in association with Patrick O'Sullivan and Partners, architects, for the establishment of a national folk theatre. The proposal, titled 'A Plan for Fostering the Growth of Traditional Irish Folk Culture' (1972), outlined how a national folk theatre could be developed. This proposal was made at the request of Éamon Casey, Bishop of Kerry, and Brendan O'Regan, Chairman of Shannon Development and Chairman of Bórd Fáilte, the national tourism board. Having seen Siamsóirí na Ríochta perform at the Abbey Theatre, Dublin, in 1970, and also having seen the Moiseyev Dance Company of Russia and the Ballet Folklorico de Mexico, these men enthused that Siamsóirí na Ríochta, the amateur folk-theatrical group in Tralee, might potentially develop in a similar way as representative of Irish folk culture. In its representation of the former USSR through folk music and dance, the Moiseyev Dance Company of Russia, founded in 1934, influenced the creation of many folk music and dance ensembles around the world.[19] Although its establishment was inspired by the Moiseyev Dance Company, Siamsa Tíre was to develop into a national folk theatre, not a dance company, nor indeed a national folk dance ensemble, as was the case with many Eastern European nation-states (for example, LADO, the Croatian State Ensemble of Folk Dances and Songs, and Mazosze of Poland).

Within the remit of a national folk theatre, Siamsa Tíre would re-present and foster the folk culture and lore of Ireland through theatre, traditional music, Irish song, dance and mime. This folk culture would be predominantly from the west of Ireland, particularly Kerry, since the rural west had long been recognized as a repository of the 'purest' and most 'authentic' folk culture. This resonated with the cultural nationalist programme of the Gaelic League earlier in the century (see Chapters 5 and 6), and indeed the European Romantic movement of the eighteenth and nineteenth centuries, when intellectuals in Europe were preoccupied with the notion that 'the peasant constituted the "pure" repository of all that is good and authentic in the national ethos.'[20] Siamsa Tíre would thus be a theatre that would utilize Irish folk culture to inspire and produce folk theatre in what the West termed 'high art'.

The proposal of 1972 argued that Tralee (and not the capital city, Dublin) was the ideal location for a national folk theatre of Ireland since the folk theatrical group Siamsóirí na Ríochta, the inspiration for the plan, was resident there. Also, the size and location of the town of Tralee was suitable for such a theatre, and it could further boast of its rich rural folk-cultural surroundings. As part of the 'Save the West' project, the establishment of the theatre in Tralee would also assist the tourist industry in the south-western region of Ireland. Siamsa Tíre, the National Folk Theatre of Ireland, thus came into being in Tralee in 1974, and it received state sponsorship.[21]

---

[19]   Shay (2008a).

[20]   Ibid., p. 167.

[21]   Siamsa Tíre received state funding from Bórd Fáilte (the National Tourist Board) and Roinn na Gaeltachta (the Department of the Gaeltachts). The latter funding was received since the theatre promoted song in the Irish language, and also because one of the Tithe Siamsa was located in Carraig, in the West Kerry Gaeltacht. Later, it received National Lottery Funding, Local Funding, and a European Development Grant for the new and current theatre, which opened in 1991. It is only recently that An Comhairle Ealaíon (the Arts Council) has funded the work of Siamsa Tíre.

Concerning the concept of Siamsa Tíre, Fr Pat Ahern stated:

> it draws its inspiration from the Irish countryside and communicates its message
> through the medium of theatre. These principles are two-fold, and they suggest
> a plan two-fold in concept: (i) The establishment of a number of rural centres as
> focal points for activities and pursuits in folk culture and (ii) The setting up of a
> folk theatre as an outlet for these centres.[22]

Conscious of the importance of folk culture and its decline at the time of writing
due to processes of modernity, demographic trends and globalization, the project
was intended to nurture Irish folk traditions within these rural centres. The rural
centres would then be used as 'filter-points', and would also sift and process
'local folk material into forms which were "marketable" in theatrical terms'.[23]
The model proposed in 1972 is the model that is followed to this day. The location
of the rural centres as suggested in the proposal also came into being; however,
the greater vision of establishing many such rural centres in key locations around
Ireland did not come to fruition. In 1974, a Teach Siamsa[24] was built as the first
rural centre in the village of Finuge, about six miles from Listowel in North Kerry,
and geographically right in the centre of the North Kerry region. Another Teach
Siamsa was built in Carraig in 1975, in the West Kerry Gaeltacht. Indeed, the Irish
language had a vital role to play in the project. According to Fr Pat Ahern, the Irish
language was where Irish people were best at 'being ourselves'.[25] For a period of
two years in the 1980s, a third rural centre was tested in Sneem, Co. Kerry, but
was discontinued. No purpose-built premises was constructed in Sneem, but a
schoolhouse was used for the purpose during this two-year test period.

The work of Siamsa Tíre was recognized in 1975 when it was awarded the
European Prize for Folk Art. Established in 1973 by the F.V.S. Foundation in
Hamburg, Germany, the prize is awarded to individuals or groups in Europe who
have 'rendered exemplary service to the preservation and further promotion of folk
art, namely in the fields of music, dancing, singing or acting'. While presenting
this award, one of the jury stated:

> It is hardly necessary to mention that even in Ireland those traditions and
> remainders of older times are badly threatened by the uniforming and equalizing
> effects of our present mass culture.[26]

According to Bishop Éamon Casey, the award had huge significance for Ireland.
First, Siamsa Tíre was recognized as a national folk theatre in Europe, and second,

---

[22] Ahern and O'Sullivan (1972), p. 15.
[23] Ibid.
[24] 'Folk Academy' or 'Folk House'.
[25] Ibid., p. 5.
[26] Dr Brednich in Siamsa Tíre souvenir booklet.

being awarded this prize implied that Siamsa Tíre was one of the most significant folk theatre developments in Europe, and as such, was worthy of support in Ireland. In response to the award, Bishop Éamon Casey stated:

> Siamsa Tíre recognizes that values are enshrined in cultural tradition and that the development of culture and tradition means not merely the preservation of these values but, in fact, their application to the living situation as it is at this moment in history. Because culture or tradition are really living things, not something that can be put away in files or put away in chests and brought out now and again, they are the response of a people to living situations through the centuries and enshrined in the mind, in *meon na ndaoine*, in the mind of the people. This is a tremendous wealth of wisdom and, of course, in the case of Ireland, Christian wisdom, because the whole culture and tradition of Ireland has been impregnated with Christianity for 1,500 years.[27]

This notion of Christian wisdom in relation to Irish culture is recognizable in the stage show *San Am Fadó*. In the kitchen scene, a Christian picture of 'The Sacred Heart' is placed above the fireplace, as it would in cottages in rural Ireland at the time the show is set. However, there are also pagan elements in the show, such as the Bealtaine scene, where dancers perform in circular patterns in relation to the Sun and the cosmos.

The European Prize for Folk Art was significant for Siamsa Tíre, which continued with more confidence in its work as a national folk theatre. Siamsa Tíre toured with the show *Fadó Fadó* to all the main theatres in Northern and Southern Ireland, as well as various cities in Europe, the USA, Canada and Australia. In 1976, Siamsa Tíre toured the USA, staging performances in New York, Chicago, Boston, New Jersey, Washington, DC, Wilmington and Philadelphia. This tour lasted approximately a month, with one week in the Palace Theatre, Broadway. Jerry Nolan and John McCarthy, two of Jeremiah Molyneaux's scholars, performed their own traditional step dances on stage during the theatrical production (see Illustration 7.2 below). In relation to this tour and Jerry Nolan, Fr Pat Ahern had the following to say:

> F. Pat.　Well, when we brought Jerry Nolan to Broadway ... I'll tell you a little story. In those days, in that particular show, it wouldn't have had any of the contemporary stuff in it, so Jerry was in context in that show ... but at the same time he outshone everything else in the show. His dance was the highlight of the evening. Why? You have to say it was the whole character of the man, as well as his step. It was the performance.
>
> C.F.　What would you say was so special about the character?
>
> F. Pat.　It was his concentration, for a start. He was very serious when he danced. He took on a very serious, concentrated look; he looked at the

---

[27]　Bishop Éamon Casey in *Radharc*, RTE documentary, 1975.

floor ahead of him, but never looked up. You felt he was working it out
as he went along … which he wasn't, of course, it was all rehearsed, but
you felt, 'What would he do next?' There was a sense of spontaneity
about it … it was almost like a conversation with you … he was talking
to you through the dance, not a performance somehow, not showing
off, communicating something to you, being himself.

The participation of the older traditional step dancers in the shows provided an
'authenticity' to the show while also assisting to validate the work of the National
Folk Theatre. In addition, it elevated the status of these step dancers within their
respective communities and brought the younger generation of actors in contact
with them, bridging the gap between these different generations.

Together with these performances, Siamsa Tíre also performed on occasion
on national television, at schools, conferences, festivals and international events,
including the International Indigenous Theatre Festival in Toronto in 1980, the
Wembley Conference Centre in London, also in 1980, and the World Expos at
Brisbane in Australia in 1988, Seville in Spain in 1992 and Hanover in Germany
in 2000. Siamsa Tíre also performed for the Pope at Castel Gandolfo in Rome
in 1981, and for the Dutch Royal Family at the Rijksmuseum in Amsterdam

Illustration 7.2   Jerry Nolan, Seán Ahern and John McCarthy outside the Palace
                     Theatre, New York, 1976. Used with permission of Siamsa Tíre

in 1986. The popular reception abroad for Siamsa Tíre, as representative of Irish culture, was welcomed by the Irish government. This international touring was also in keeping with other state-sponsored national folk ensembles. As Anthony Shay states:

> Such displays of folklore were not limited to local and national venues. Most of the governments supported international touring as well, sending their finest performing groups to sites like world fairs.[28]

As well as receiving sponsorship from the Irish state, Siamsa Tíre also relied on its own reputation and resources. Income from the theatre's five-month summer tourist season, together with box office takings from different venues both in Ireland and abroad, contributed to its financial resources.

Siamsa Tíre also had an educational and training remit, which included providing shows for schools at the theatre in Tralee and training local young people at its rural centres, the Tithe Siamsa,[29] which are still in existence today.

Tithe Siamsa

The Tithe Siamsa, or rural centres, as proposed in 1972, are training centres for the cultivation of Irish traditional music, song, dance, mime and movement; according to Fr Pat Ahern, they mine the 'local commodity'. The skills taught are those required for entry to the Performing Company at Siamsa Tíre. There are two rural centres: one in Finuge; the other in Carraig.

Young people, male and female, from approximately seven to twelve years of age train on a weekly basis from October to May at these rural centres or Tithe Siamsa. They train for three years, and are taught by the professional core members of Siamsa Tíre. Jonathan Kelliher, Artist Director of Siamsa Tíre since 2005, states:

> I first joined Siamsa Tíre, the National Folk Theatre, in 1979 at the age of 8. As a young child in North Kerry, traditional dance, music and song was part of growing up. My parents had a keen interest in music and dance and, as the training centre in Finuge was only three miles from where I lived, it was an obvious choice to go there. I also had an older brother and sister attending classes there.[30]

Entry to this training programme is by audition. Siamsa Tíre notifies the various schools in Co. Kerry when and where these auditions will be held, usually at the

---

[28]   Shay (2008a), p. 16.
[29]   Plural of Teach Siamsa.
[30]   Jonathan Kelliher, questionnaire response, 2012.

end of September to roughly coincide with the commencement of the school year. For the audition, students are required to play an instrument, to sing or to dance. The students specializing in dance usually come from the step dance schools in the region. These schools include those which are registered within An Coimisiún and those which work independently of it; all children are welcome to audition. When students demonstrate potential to perform in one or all of the above performance areas at the audition, they are accepted onto the programme and their training is free of charge. In 2004, there were approximately sixty students in each of the two rural centres. These were divided over a three-year programme, with approximately twenty students in each year.

For Siamsa Tíre and its five core professional members, Tuesday evening means Carraig. Four core members of Siamsa Tíre travel weekly from Tralee to Carraig in West Kerry to teach four different classes in traditional music, song, dance and mime; these classes last for 30 minutes, and all students participate in all four areas of expertise. The classes are organized according to level of competence and the three-year programme of the Tithe Siamsa.

Thursday evening is the class in Finuge, North Kerry, again taught by the core members of Siamsa Tíre. Here, dance, singing and mime are taught for 40 minutes per session; dancers and singers all participate in these classes according to the three-year programme structure. However, music is taught separately in two one-hour classes. Those students who are both dancers and musicians are also facilitated by being allowed to participate in both music and dance classes.

In general, particular dance material is taught at the Tithe Siamsa. In year one, dance students learn the Light Jig, the Reel, some Hornpipes and some Double Jigs; in years two and three, they learn more advanced material in a progressive manner. Steps choreographed by Jeremiah Molyneaux are also included in these classes, and it is noteworthy that a few photographs of some of the older dancers of the region adorn the walls of one of the teaching rooms, giving these students a sense of their dance history. Participatory dances, such as the Polka set (similar to a Quadrille), are taught in May, when the regular classes are finished and when students prepare for their annual summer shows, which take place in June in both Carraig and Finuge.

After three years of training at these rural centres, students have covered the basic music, song, dance and mime material for the original show *San Am Fadó*. Those students who wish to continue their training re-audition for a place in the higher Intermediate Class which takes place at the Siamsa Tíre theatre in Tralee on Monday evenings (excluding the five-month summer season). This Intermediate Class, consisting of teenagers, involves more advanced tuition in dance, drama, music and song; this is in preparation for the Performers' Class, the next level within the Siamsa Tíre training structure, where members learn the repertoire of the company at the theatre in Tralee. This Performers' Class becomes the theatre's Community Cast, who are the more advanced members of Siamsa Tíre; these classes are held on Wednesday evenings, and they also serve as a rehearsal space for new shows and productions. Consequently, the following is the training structure for a young, aspiring Siamsa Tíre performer:

- three years' training at a Teach Siamsa or rural centre;
- attendance and participation at the Intermediate Class in Siamsa Tíre;
- attendance and participation at the Performers' Class in Siamsa Tíre;
- a member of the Community Cast, and potentially
- a member of the Professional Company of Siamsa Tíre.

According to Jonathan Kelliher, he joined Teach Siamsa in Finuge in 1979 at the age of eight. He later graduated to become a member of the Community Cast, and in 1989 he joined the company as a full-time professional performer. In 2000, he became Dance Master for the company, and in 2005 he was appointed Artistic Director of Siamsa Tíre, a position he holds to the present day.

Whether or not students from the Tithe Siamsa succeed in becoming members of the Professional Company of Siamsa Tíre, they still succeed in learning and embodying part of their local cultural history and rural traditional values through classes and performances in traditional music, song and dance and mime. These events contribute not only to the transmission of the indigenous arts, but also to the social and cultural life of the rural, local communities in Finuge and Carraig and the individuals who participate in them.

Meitheal and the Construction of Community

In 2004, the Siamsa Tíre cast consisted of seven professional core members who researched, devised, rehearsed and performed new and old staged material and who acted as tutors in the classes in the training centres and in the theatre. These were Oliver Hurley, Artistic Director; Tom Hanafin, Music Director, Jonathan Kelliher, Dance Master, and actors Honor Hurley, Anne O'Donnell, Joanne Barry and Robert Heaslip. Jimmy McDonnell was Lighting Designer and Desmond Hurley was the Production Stage Manager. This professional cast was supported by a 120-member Community Cast, who had all been trained for the most part in the Tithe Siamsa, and who lived within easy reach of Siamsa Tíre. They had the specific skills required for Siamsa Tíre productions, and were on stand-by should any show require their participation. The Community Cast members performed as a hobby, not in a professional capacity, and were paid for actual performances, not for rehearsals. They worked locally, a factor that assisted the success of Siamsa Tíre. According to Oliver Hurley, Artistic Director of Siamsa Tíre in 2004, loyalty to Siamsa Tíre was strong among its members. The Community Cast, male and female, ranged in age from 10 to 70 years old, and all members, depending upon their availability, were prepared to participate when required in the theatre's five-month summer season of performances.

Members of Siamsa Tíre identify with what Siamsa Tíre represents and take pride in belonging to it. Through its well-defined hierarchical structure – Tithe Siamsa, Intermediate Class, Performers' Class, Community Cast, Professional Company, members of Siamsa Tíre's Board of Management and administrative staff – a strong sense of community is constructed around the activities of Siamsa Tíre. Siamsa Tíre is important for the employment of some professional dancers, musicians and singers, together with sound and lighting technicians, stage managers, office staff and so on. It is their livelihood, and also a primary cultural interest and social outlet. The theatre provides a site where there is a strong sense of group affiliation as well as social interactions within the group. This assists individuals in negotiating a sense of self and group identity. Siamsa Tíre thus contributes to shaping and defining the performers' relationship with their world. It also provides a means for them to experience globalization through its international audience members[31] and invited international artists who frequently work with the group.

This strong sense of community has assisted in the success of Siamsa Tíre. According to the Siamsa Tíre brochure, this type of community is reminiscent of the *meitheal*:

> Long ago the Gaelic or Irish language word *meitheal* meant inter-community co-operation. In rural Ireland neighbours rallied to help each other. Today the *Siamsa Tíre* Community Company supports the full-time professional players in this same *meitheal* spirit.[32]

As mutual aid and co-operation were important to the economic survival of rural communities in North Kerry and elsewhere in the recent past (see Chapter 5), Siamsa Tíre is also dependent upon this type of community, and hence upon its Community Cast. Members of the Community Cast share a common training provided by Siamsa Tíre, as well as a particular cultural perspective and worldview. Thus, Siamsa Tíre has constructed a community *habitus* which has assisted in shaping members' individual and collective identities within a modern, changing and global world. It is not unusual to find three generations of the one family connected to Siamsa Tíre. This notion of 'family' is important to the members of the theatre. Jonathan Kelliher, the current Artistic Director of Siamsa Tíre, has the following to say:

> To me Siamsa Tíre is a way of life. It is something that has been part of my life since I was eight years old. I am one of the lucky people in this world who have grown up with and now work in a job that offers something very special. The secret to the success of the company is that all who are involved are like family members, everyone looks out for each other.[33]

---

[31] See also Cooley (2005), p. 11.
[32] Siamsa Tíre souvenir brochure.
[33] Jonathan Kellher, questionnaire response, 2012.

According to John Fitzgerald, a member of the Community Cast:

> Siamsa Tíre is like being part of a second family. I have made some of my best friends inside those walls, and every year it is a pleasure to go back and perform in the shows. I recall one of the professional members referring to it as a 'cocoon in which they feel safe' and I remember hearing this and agreeing wholeheartedly with it. It's why I always take great pride in saying that I perform with the company .... The people involved have genuine interest in its success. It is really the only theatre of its kind. It provides something that's very unique, and it has its own unique style .... People like me grow up with the company so you have performers who really care about the work and what it stands for. The fact that it is steeped in history, and it is preserving the tradition of Irish song, music and dance in the modern world are definite contributors to the strength of the National Folk Theatre.[34]

Also important to the work of Siamsa Tíre is the collaborative efforts of core members when creating new works. According to Jonathan Kelliher:

> Everybody has a say. We do our research into whatever theme we wish to focus on in the production and then we discuss it and play around with different steps and movements until we reach some kind of consensus. There is a lot of collaboration.[35]

A sense of community and identity is important to the members of Siamsa Tíre, and these concepts are also striking themes in some of its productions, particularly *San Am Fadó* and *Oileán: Celebrating the Blasket Islands*, a more recent production.[36] Although the themes of community and identity are performed in both *San Am Fadó* and *Oileán*, each show expresses and exposes similarities and differences in their construction. These are made manifest through sets, staging, mime, dance, song and music. In *San Am Fadó*, it is the close-knit agricultural community of North Kerry's rural past which is celebrated; in *Oileán*, it is the lack of community in a modern urban setting which is contrasted with a strong, integrated sense of community in a poor south-west of Ireland seafaring community on the Blasket Island, off the west coast of Kerry. It is this sense of past community on the Blasket Island, with its stories, songs, superstitions and lore of the sea, which is theatrically and nostalgically presented to challenge Irish people's sense of identity as modern islanders.

---

[34] John Fitzgerald, questionnaire response, 2012. John Fitzgerald also dances with Rinceoirí na Ríochta and is a final year university student in physiotherapy at Trinity College, Dublin.

[35] Personal communication with Jonathan Kelliher, 13 September 2011.

[36] From talking with members of Siamsa Tíre in 2004, although *San Am Fadó* is the longest-running show, and perhaps the one perceived as most representative of the work of Siamsa Tíre, *Oileán* is one of their favourite shows to perform. To view an excerpt of *Oileán* see 'Oileán – a Celebration of Blasket Islands' at http://www.siamsatire.com/page/nft-repertory [accessed 4 July, 2013].

Illustration 7.3   *Oileán*, 2003. Used with permission of Siamsa Tíre

Oileán commences with the notion of the lack of community spirit in modern urban Irish life; the choreography has actors dressed in formal clothes, such as suits and office work attire. Actors walk or move purposefully and independently around the stage, each on his or her own individual journey with no eye contact. Dancers do not dance in unison; they dance or move purposefully and independently of each other. This choreographic strategy places emphasis and importance on the individual and the isolation of the individual in Irish urban life. The Molyneaux Single Drum motif appears here and there in the scene, but is isolated and repeated at different times by different dancers. According to the programme, this scene is suggestive of 'the chaos of today's society'.

In contrast to this, the next scene shifts to a beach on Great Blasket Island, emphasizing its 'peace and solitude' (see illustration 7.3). Also, from the outset the notion of a collective identity within this isolated, poor but close-knit island community in the Atlantic Ocean is highlighted. This identity is gendered. The girls and women collect seaweed together, the fishermen get their fishing nets ready together and they play hurling. Life on the island appears supportive and communal: people take time to talk together, to tell stories, to sing and dance together, and the whole community is perceived as supportive in times of work, joy and sorrow.

As in the other shows, Reels, Jigs, Hornpipes and Slow Airs are adapted and arranged to suit the different island activities and scenes in the show. New music pieces with new theatricalized choreographies also feature. Songs, dances, customs and traditions of Great Blasket Island life in the recent past are theatrically stylized to re-present and celebrate the strong rural communal values and ties of kinship on the island. The step part of one of Molyneaux's 'Blackbird' set dances is performed on stage, and again Molyneaux's Single Drum motif appears at different points in the show. Some contemporary dance, under the direction of the show's choreographer, Cindy Cummings, is also performed throughout the show. The show ends with the realistic occurrence of the last islanders leaving the island – an event which occurred on 17 November 1953, when the Irish government arranged for the abandonment of the island. *Oileán* celebrates and explores Blasket Island living, 'while also challenging our own notions of identity as contemporary islanders [of Ireland]'.[37]

The contrast between the urban context with its emphasis on the individual and the rural poor in the south-west of Ireland, with its emphasis on togetherness and community, again is reminiscent of eighteenth- and nineteenth-century European Romanticism. Within this framing, the urban population is perceived to have 'alien', 'foreign' traits, and to display negative behaviour, while the rural or peasant population represents the 'true' and desired ethos of the nation.[38] Thus, *Oileán* assists in theatrically portraying and reaffirming the desired values of Siamsa Tíre within the changing and challenging context of modernity.

Siamsa Tíre and the Folk-theatrical Re-presentation of the Molyneaux Step Dance Style

In the 1972 National Folk Theatre proposal, four full-time members of staff were requested: a research officer, a music teacher, a dancing teacher and an artistic director; one part-time member of staff was also requested, a local manager. Concerning the dance teacher, the proposal stated:

> The teacher will be an accomplished Irish dancer, and have a wide ranging knowledge of the art of traditional dancing. In particular, a knowledge of old-time steps and folk dances is essential. In addition, a flair for the creative side of dancing is necessary, as part of the work is intended to be that of choreographer, to experiment in recreating and building on the local native dances of the district, with a view to their theatrical presentation.[39]

The 'local native dances of the district' were perceived to be those dances associated with and performed by elderly step dancers living around the Listowel area who had been taught primarily by Jeremiah Molyneaux (see Chapters 2–4). Consequently, Fr Pat Ahern, with the help of Martin Whelan, Manager of Siamsa Tíre, video recorded two of the elderly step dancers, Jack Lyons and Paddy White. Subsequently, Fr Pat Ahern approached Muckross House Folk Museum, Killarney,

---

[37]   Siamsa Tíre theatre programme, 2003.

[38]   Shay (2008b).

[39]   Ahern and O'Sullivan (1972), p. 21.

which had initiated a project to collect traditional music, song and dance in Co. Kerry, for assistance. Since I was working as a collector of traditional music, song and dance for Muckross House at the time, I was approached to collect for posterity the remaining dances from the elderly Molyneaux step dancers in and around the Listowel area. The intention was to have these step dancers and their dances recorded for Muckross House for archival purposes (see Chapter 1). The Molyneaux dancers recorded for the Muckross House Collection in the 1980s included Phil Cahill, Seán Cahill, Michael Carroll, Jack Dineen, Marie Finucane Kissane, Willy Goggin, Jim Hartnett, Sheila Lyons Bowler, John McCarthy, Eileen Moriarty MacNamara, Jerry Nolan, John Joe O'Donnell and Michael Walsh.[40]

Although I commenced fieldwork on Molyneaux and the elderly Molyneaux step dancers in 1983, Siamsa Tíre was still at this stage an amateur folk theatre. In 1984, Michael Murphy, a young dancer, was employed to learn the Molyneaux step dances from the available video recordings, and in 1985, Siamsa Tíre became a professional folk theatre, employing for the first time five professional actors and actresses: Oliver Hurley, Michael Murphy, Ray Walsh, Tara Little and Geraldine Heaslip. These were all actors, singers and Irish step dancers. Some had already trained in competitive Irish step dance with local teachers, while others had little formal training. In my field notebook, I noted:

> The Siamsa Tíre dancers are currently learning step dances from video recordings of some of the elderly traditional step dancers in the area, in particular Jack Lyons and Paddy White.[41]

Gradually, under the artistic directorship of Fr Pat Ahern, the Molyneaux style of step dance was incorporated into the theatre's productions and became a desired kinaesthetic identity marker for Siamsa Tíre.

When speaking to Fr Pat Ahern about when he had been introduced to the Molyneaux style of dance, and its importance for Siamsa Tíre, he had the following to say:

> F. Pat.   Well, it came from my own contact with the father of all that dance, which as you know was Munnix, Molyneaux; Munnix we called him. Well, I can remember when I saw him first, as a child in the National School in Moyvane; I don't know what age I was, it must have been second or third class, in the National School, this little fellow came to offer classes in dancing. And my memory of him, my first impressions of him was of a tiny man. A very small, tiny man, and we went to his classes in the village hall, and we learned some steps .... I remember, when he'd

---

[40]   Foley (1988b) – my PhD thesis – was also deposited at Muckross House Folk Museum, Killarney, to help to contextualize the video recordings of the step dancers for the public. This work was later published. See Foley (2012b).

[41]   Catherine E. Foley, field notes, July 1983.

catch you by the arm, he would be pulling and poking your arm getting you to do it, you know, and he'd show you the way he wanted it …. I do remember him getting ratty and cross when you didn't get a thing right, and he'd say: 'It's not that! Didn't I tell you it was the other way?'

C.F. But you kind of loved that style of dance, didn't you? But what was it about that style that you liked?

F. Pat. From my great friend, Jerry Nolan, who you know as well, I got to love that dance even more, because Jerry to me was the great exponent of that style, that I knew at least, anyway. They say Paddy White was better; they say that Paddy White was even a better dancer than Molyneaux himself, but I never saw Paddy White dance because he was too old when I got to know him and his feet were too arthritic and so on, but Jerry I did know, and I was telling you about the sessions we would have on a Sunday after Mass in the kitchen of local fiddle player Barney Enright. Jerry would be in because of the fiddle, you know. He would dance, and he would love to dance for a few people in the little kitchen, and be applauded for it afterwards. Well, it was through Jerry, really, that I got to appreciate the beauty of this dance.

C.F. And then this style of dance, the Molyneaux style of dance … when you established Siamsa Tíre many years later, you kind of brought this style of dance within a theatrical context.

F. Pat. That's right. I did. Because I felt that it had something special. In my years in Dublin, I came in contact with a lot of dancers from around the country through my contact with Comhaltas,[42] because I did a lot of work for Comhaltas in those days as well – produced some shows for them in Dublin. And I had contact with a lot of dancers up and down the country, older dancers, there weren't many, but I could see nobody who could match the dance of the Kerry dance. So, I felt it was something very worth … first of all worth saving and rescuing, you know. In the early 1970s, I remember we acquired an old video camera, in the black-and-white days, and we made those tapes of the lads which you have seen, and I think that was one of the most important things that we did, in the early days of Siamsa Tíre. I really do. Because had we not done it, I am sure they would have been lost – those steps. And we rescued some wonderful steps that Lyons had, and Paddy White and … we focused on the style as a basic style of dance that we would foster in Siamsa Tíre. We have done that ever since. It is now the dance that we teach to all the pupils that come in. Some of them come in from dancing schools and they have other steps, but we don't bother with them. We teach a repertoire of steps which are taken from the old repertoire.[43]

---

[42] See Chapter 6..

[43] Fr Pat Ahern (2002), ethnographic interview with the author.

In the earlier years of Siamsa Tíre, the dances performed were not in the Molyneaux dance style; instead, dances were performed by local step dancers who had trained within the local step dance schools. It was later, with the professionalization of Siamsa Tíre, that the Molyneaux dance style took on its kinaesthetic importance within the theatre. This dance style would then also be transmitted at the Tithe Siamsa along with traditional music, song and mime. Thus, under the artistic directorship of Fr Pat Ahern, core members of Siamsa Tíre learned the Molyneaux step dances from selected dancers on the above-mentioned video recordings. These selected dancers became the representatives of the Molyneaux step dance style for Siamsa Tíre. Consequently, a process took place which included the selection of particular step dancers, their repertoires and styles of performance. These were then used as a resource for teaching and for the production of art within the context of the theatre. Once stylized, these step dances became part of the theatre's repertoire. New steps were also choreographed around basic motifs and elements associated with the Molyneaux style of dance. Within the temporally and spatially framed context of the theatre, improvisation or interpersonal variations of step dances did not feature. The Molyneaux step dances were thus artistically stylized and commodified for theatrical presentations, and took on a different and new meaning. The function and context of the performance of these dances had changed, as had the transmission process and the new required aesthetic:

> C.F.   So can I talk to you a bit about … taking the dance, the Molyneaux style of dance and representing it … within a theatrical context? Were you conscious of the way you would represent it within a theatrical context?
>
> F. Pat. I was always convinced that it had a basis for something else in it, do you know, something that could be built on. And I got in choreographers with different styles from time to time to see if they could take it on board and do something with it and make it, I suppose, more accessible to a contemporary audience, do you know? Because in a way it is for the purists, I suppose, those who would understand what it was, and knew it, would appreciate it as a pure dance. But to the ordinary sort of punters and public, it needed a little more … I suppose to show it off, whatever, but I never met anybody really who could … we failed a number of times with it. And a lot of the efforts were losing it and spoiling it …. It is hard to define what it has.[44]

According to Fr Pat Ahern, one of the successful pieces that Siamsa Tíre staged, and which was based on the Molyneaux style of dance, was *An Damhsóir*[45] (1987). This piece was theatrically choreographed by Fr Pat Ahern in collaboration with core professional members of Siamsa Tíre, and was choreographed in memory of Jack Lyons, the Molyneaux step dancer and concertina player. The theatrical

---

[44]   Ibid.
[45]   'The Dancer'.

scene in question is based on an excerpt from the Jack Lyons video recording where he performs his step dances with the aid of a chair, his hand holding on to the back of the chair for balance. In the Siamsa Tíre scene, chairs are used as theatrical props, and dancers position themselves either seated upon a chair or standing near one with a hand resting on its back. The scene commences with one step dancer performing a phrase from a percussive Jig step in the style of Molyneaux; this is unaccompanied. Another step dancer answers this by performing a different, percussive, rhythmic phrase in response to the first phrase, and bit by bit the dancers' percussive feet build up a continuous flow of motifs and phrases demonstrating the eight-bar structure of the step dance, and indeed how the step dance is structurally divided meaningfully according to the Molyneaux style of dance (see Chapter 4).[46] The scene is paced throughout. It starts slowly, and leads to a percussive climax when all the step dancers participating in the scene perform the entire step together to the accompaniment of traditional music; this is followed by other Molyneaux step dances. This performance is a theatrical choreographic arrangement, and although the step dances are stylized, adapted for theatre and performed under new conditions, the scene attempts to communicate an 'authenticity' and a 'dignity', and honours and celebrates the local dance, the local dancers and the historical contextualized past. In the words of Fr Pat Ahern:

F. Pat.   Theatre is about entertaining. But I would hope that some of the things we did had the spirit of the old way. For instance, the Jack Lyons piece … that has been by far the most successful piece that has survived in the repertoire.

C.F.   Why do you think that is?

F. Pat.   Because there is an authenticity about it. The way we set them up on chairs, that's the way we learned it. That piece came about very simply: it was a direct result of our experience with the video tapes, looking at the lads leaning against a chair, between two chairs, sitting on a chair, trying to do the best they could with the step. There was a respect in it for the dance; that was one of the things that people often said about that little piece, there was a wonderful dignity about it; a respect for what they were doing came through. Maybe that answers it. It achieved the kind of regard for the dance that the old guys had.[47]

Constructing an 'authenticity of content'[48] theatrically was important to Fr Pat Ahern as the Artistic Director of Siamsa Tíre. As a non-dialogue theatre, communication is through theatre, song in Gaelic, traditional music, dance and

---

[46] See also Foley (1988b and 2012b) for Labanotated inventories of elements, cells and motifs together with steps in Treble Reels, Jigs, and Hornpipes as practised by the traditional step dancers of North Kerry.

[47] Fr Pat Ahern (2002), ethnographic interview with the author.

[48] Shay (2008b), p. 168.

mime. The non-dialogue element of the theatre is also intended to make the theatre accessible to all nationalities. According to Fr Ahern, the themes of rural Ireland, celebrated for instance in the show *San Am Fadó*, were not just local, they were international; they expressed a way of life that people from Ireland and from abroad could readily identify with. In expressing and communicating this rural way of life, an authenticity of content was sought. Traditional music, songs, dances, folklore, customs and legends from the local and national indigenous tradition were researched and carefully selected as inspiration or a basis for the Siamsa Tíre productions; these were subsequently musically, choreographically and theatrically arranged to communicate an authenticity and a Western artistic sensibility within the context of theatre. Some movements and rhythms of movements associated with certain farming tasks also referenced an authenticity. For example, the dance rhythms in the sharpening of the scythe scene in *San Am Fadó* are in Hornpipe time due to Fr Ahern's own memories of using the scythe and observing older men on the farm using it.

   This notion of authenticity was carried further by including older performers who would also have memories of this rural lifestyle; these included on occasion some of the elderly Molyneaux step dancers. Jerry Nolan, John McCarthy and Willie Goggin all performed their steps on stage with Siamsa Tíre. Also, older dancers were remembered in theatrical productions and scenes specifically choreographed with them in mind. For example, the scene *An Damhsóir*, as mentioned above, and the productions of *Ding, Dong, Dederó*[49] and *Tearmann*. *Ding, Dong, Dederó* (see Illustration 7.4), a show produced by Fr Pat Ahern in 1990 for the opening of Siamsa Tíre's new theatre, was exclusively about the life of Jeremiah Molyneaux. In this show, Molyneaux's step dances were theatrically reconstructed around the forge and around the skills of the blacksmith, since Molyneaux had also worked as a blacksmith. Of all the Siamsa Tíre productions, this is the one with the most Molyneaux dance material. However, it is not one of the shows that is performed annually as part of Siamsa Tíre's summer season. *Tearmann*, a new production by Michael Harding in collaboration with Siamsa Tíre and under the artistic directorship of Jonathan Kelliher, is based on a dancing master, the Great Famine in Ireland, and the passing on of the step dance tradition in a workhouse. This is inspired by the fact that Múirín, the dancing master, died in Listowel Workhouse (see Chapter 3). Again, much Molyneaux material, together with contemporary dance, is included in this production.

   This authenticity of content applies also to theatrical props. For example, in *San Am Fadó*, the flail used by Fr Pat Ahern's grandfather on the family farm was found and copied for use within the theatre; house furnishings and costumes reminiscent of that period were also re-presented on stage. This authenticity of content assisted in validating the work of Siamsa Tíre as the National Folk Theatre.

---

[49]   According to Fr Pat Ahern, *Ding, Dong, Dederó* (1990) was his best production as Artistic Director of Siamsa Tíre.

Illustration 7.4   *Ding, Dong, Dederó*, 1991. Used with permission of Kevin Coleman and Siamsa Tíre

Siamsa Tíre, Art, Nostalgia and the Irish Step Dance Stage Shows

The importance of *Irish* cultural traditions and customs is significant to the Siamsa Tíre community, but it is also aware that Siamsa Tíre must constantly develop in order to survive economically and to continue with its theatrical work as the National Folk Theatre. Over the years, ballet dancers, contemporary dance choreographers, dancers from different world cultures and composers have received invitations to work in collaboration with Siamsa Tíre on particular productions. This was to complement and to enhance the Western artistic aesthetic of these productions. Thus, together with *San Am Fadó*, by 2004, there were also other shows presented during the summer season which offered a greater diversity of spectacle. These shows were produced under the artistic directorships of John Sheehan, an American theatre director (Artistic Director of Siamsa Tíre 1998–2000), and Oliver Hurley, a founding member of the professional company of Siamsa Tíre (Artistic Director of Siamsa Tíre 2000–2004).[50]

However, in spite of its successes in Ireland and abroad, Siamsa Tíre has also been subject to some criticisms. These have included the perception that the productions, particularly *San Am Fadó*, are too strongly based on rural customs and traditions and are not representative of Irish life in its more urban character.

---

[50]   These other shows included *An Gobán Saor* ('A Jack of All Trades'), *Sean agus Nua* ('Old and New'), *Clann Lir* ('The Irish Legend of the Children of Lir'), *Oileán* ('Island'), and *Óisín* ('The Irish Legend of Óisín'). In 2004, Jonathan Kelliher, who had held the position of Dance Master, became the Artistic Director of Siamsa Tíre.

As a national folk theatre, some critics feel that it should engage more with the contemporary urban audience. *San Am Fadó* was withdrawn from the summer season in 2010, but for many, until recently it was the identifying marker of the work of Siamsa Tíre. The strong connection of *San Fadó Fadó* with Siamsa Tíre was perceived by some as positive and by others as a drawback, since it was interpreted as having only tourist and nostalgic value in the way it engaged with, and re-presented, the past. Although very much influenced by Fr Pat Ahern and his own biography, it was, according to Fr Pat Ahern, both local and universal at once: 'It was a universal language; people identified with it from their own cultures ... and I don't think it's necessarily a weakness to be local.'[51]

Nostalgia and social memory of the rural past had therefore some negative and positive connotations for Siamsa Tíre. For Fr Pat Ahern the performance of memory through theatrical productions such as *San Am Fadó* was important for the theatre in a constantly changing world. It was not perceived as a drawback but as a means of strengthening social and cultural connectedness on local, national, and global levels. Working with the 'local' within the context of national and global importance was central to the vision of Siamsa Tíre. With his appointment as Artistic Director of Siamsa Tíre in 2000, Oliver Hurley attempted to counteract the nostalgic and rural image of Siamsa Tíre and build on its national profile as a contemporary folk theatre. According to Oliver Hurley, the objective was to develop the strengths of Siamsa Tíre, which included its 120-strong Community Cast, the loyalty of the members of Siamsa Tíre to the theatre, the non-dialogue format of the productions, and the vision and strong artistic foundations inherited from Fr Pat Ahern.

Siamsa Tíre and the *Riverdance* Phenomenon

Siamsa Tíre was not oblivious to the global acclaim and commercial benefits of 1990s Irish step dance shows such as *Riverdance*, *Lord of the Dance* and the other productions that followed in their wake.[52] In 2000, the commercial Irish step dance show *To Dance on the Moon* opened at the Irish National Events Centre at the Gleneagle Hotel, Killarney, Co. Kerry. This was an entrepreneurial venture by Production Manager Michael Carr, from Lisselton, Listowel, the same townland where Jeremiah Molyneaux had lived. The show was strategically located in Killarney, a prime tourist location on the famous Ring of Kerry, and also the location of Muckross House. The show alternated between Dublin and Killarney, and also toured in Germany, where it was both highly acclaimed and financially successful. But what were the implications of this style stage show on Siamsa Tíre, the National Folk Theatre in Tralee?

---

[51]   Fr Pat Ahern (2002), ethnographic interview with the author.
[52]   Foley (2001).

Both the Siamsa Tíre shows and the Irish step dance stage shows operate commercially, and Irish people together with tourists attend both styles of productions. However, they are also different, and fortunately, the market during the 2000s was able to support both enterprises. Siamsa Tíre is a state-sponsored folk theatre based in Tralee, Co. Kerry. Its cast is local, and many of them perform for years with Siamsa Tíre; however, only a handful of performers are employed as professional performers. These performers are trained in traditional step dance, traditional music, singing and mime. As a small theatre, Siamsa Tíre endeavours to negotiate between folk art, Western high art aesthetics and economics to culturally and theatrically re-present Ireland into the twenty-first century.

The step dance stage shows tour nationally and internationally, and draw from an international pool of trained step dancers, including step dancers from Kerry, and indeed from the step dance school in Tralee, Rinceoirí na Ríochta. These step dancers are employed as professional step dancers, not as actors. The step dance stage shows are commercial dance companies which present the skills of Irish step dancers within large and spectacular stage settings. Long line-ups of step dancers, male and female, stepping and gesturing in unison to fast, pulsating music have come to represent these stage shows on the global market.[53]

Both Siamsa Tíre and the commercial Irish step dance stage shows provide different types of stage productions, but each attempt to culturally represent Ireland through the traditional performing arts. Also, in their different ways, each are geared towards the commercial market, for economic survival.[54] Currently, the commercial step dance stage shows are not as strong as they once were, with a decrease in the number of large companies on the road. However, employment opportunities are still there for those step dancers who are good enough and who wish to dance professionally and to travel. Siamsa Tíre continues its work in Tralee as the National Folk Theatre of Ireland with state sponsorship and income from its tourist season. According to John Fitzgerald:

> It's titled 'The National Folk Theatre of Ireland' for a reason, in that it is the only theatre of its kind in Ireland, making it … essential in preserving past tradition and making it available to modern audiences of today.[55]

Siamsa Tíre and *rEvolution*

In 2004, Siamsa Tíre, in attempting to redefine itself, asked the question: 'What is folk?' This question was posed with reference to: (1) defining its identity and its role in Ireland as 'the National Folk Theatre'; (2) attempting to reposition itself as a folk theatre of contemporary relevance to Ireland; (3) challenging any

---

[53] Ibid.
[54] Ibid.
[55] John Fitzgerald, questionnaire response, 2012.

notion of 'tradition', and (4) exploring and interacting with dance and other multi-disciplinary areas. For several weeks, the professional members of Siamsa Tíre researched this question and worked in a collaborative manner with choreographer Cindy Cummings and visual artist Andrew Duggan. One result of this collaboration was the work *rEvolution*, which was performed at the Mansion House, Dublin in September 2005.

The aim of this multi-disciplinary piece was 'to investigate the potential to redefine and re-invent the creative vocabulary of folk theatre in a contemporary Irish context'.[56] Breaking barriers between traditional dance and contemporary dance and those between different arts disciplines was a central motivation behind the project. Using screen projection, music and dance, the work unfolded, taking a stylized interpretation of one of Molyneaux's 'Blackbird' set dances and fusing it with contemporary dance. Through this multi-disciplinary approach, the kinaesthetic with projected image and sound, *rEvolution* was a contemporary manifestation of Siamsa Tíre's exploration in re-defining itself as the National Folk Theatre of Ireland.

While watching *rEvolution* in the Mansion House, I thought of Molyneaux, Nedín Batt Walsh and Múirín, and I thought about the elderly Molyneaux step dancers who performed 'The Blackbird' set dance for me. I wondered what they would have thought of this performance. Whatever their responses, what holds true is that this 'Blackbird' set dance, choreographed by Molyneaux, continues to be an important kinaesthetic identity marker of Siamsa Tíre. And although a testimony of Molyneaux's ability as a choreographer, it illustrates that Siamsa Tíre, as the National Folk Theatre of Ireland, continues to keep the past within contemporary consciousness by exploring different but meaningful ways of communicating and performing this cultural and historical past within an ever-changing cultural environment. The study of body practices can, indeed, lead us to understand that 'images of the past and recollected knowledge of the past are conveyed and sustained by … performances'.[57]

rEvolution was well received by the arts world in Ireland, and illustrated a further development in the history of Siamsa Tíre. However, some local people perceived it as a step too far from the original vision of Siamsa Tíre. The omission of the show *San Am Fadó* from Siamsa Tíre's summer seasons in 2010 and 2011 galvanized this perception. For these local people *San Am Fadó* had represented and referenced a world of the familiar, a rural world with shared social memories and shared cultural values; *rEvolution* in spite of the fact that Molyneaux's Blackbird set dance was featured, represented and referenced a modern changing and potentially unstable world. Siamsa Tíre, however, continues with its challenging work as the national folk theatre of Ireland, balancing the old with the new, tradition with Western theatre, local with global, and commerce with art.

---

[56]   *rEvolution* programme, Siamsa Tíre, 2005.
[57]   Connerton (1989), p. 40.

Chapter 8
Conclusion: The Dynamicity of Step Dance

Step dance is culture. When step dancers perform, they embody culture. This book has proposed that step dancing as a dance-music cultural practice is not one essentialized practice; it is a complex, multifaceted, dynamic, embodied practice that exists in wider historical and socio-cultural contexts. Thus, at different points in its 250-year history, and in the midst of different cultural processes of colonialism, nationalism, postcolonialism and globalization, step dance has embodied, expressed and negotiated these processes and histories. Step dancing is a dynamic dance-music practice and a significant and potent cultural signifier. The three step dancing practices discussed in this book: the Molyneaux step-dancing practice of North Kerry, the step dancing practice associated with An Coimisiún and Rinceoirí na Ríochta, and step dancing as theatrically represented in Siamsa Tíre, illustrate this. They reference different cultural and historical contexts and embody different meaning systems, worldviews and *habiti*, or ways of *being*.

Although there are aesthetic, historical and contextual differences, all three practices are regarded as step dancing by the people of North Kerry. This is because of the persistence of the defining characteristics of step dancing: concentration on foot and leg movements moving quickly in and out of familiar and recognisable positions in time to accompanying Irish traditional dance music of Reels, Jigs and Hornpipes, the upright torso, and the arms held at the sides of the body. The specific foot and leg movements may differ stylistically and technically according to the different aesthetic systems embodied in each practice, but certain basic 'traditional' or familiar movements are constant. Different configurations of the form, including different aesthetic systems, may have been constructed and developed largely due to changing functions, contexts and conceptualizations of its practice, thus generating different meanings, but the form has continued to live on.

From its emergence at the end of the eighteenth century, the book has traced the trajectory of step dancing in Ireland, with particular reference to North Kerry. During the colonial period, it was shaped by a combination of influences from indigenous cultural practices and society, colonial culture, Catholic morality, the Great Famine, and a European dancing master aesthetic. In North Kerry, as part of the civilising process, step dancing was shaped by the itinerant dancing masters of the region, in particular Múirín, Nedín Batt Walsh and Molyneaux. Step dancing embodied, expressed and negotiated the cultural values, knowledge and history of the rural Christian communities of the region. The upright torso and the visual and percussive, rhythmical and metrical, soundings of the feet gave 'voice' to their shared colonial culture and history. Steps expressed who these people were, and where they came from. Steps rooted them in their place, North Kerry;

steps were their identity, history and culture. Steps were regarded as important tacit knowledge, and a significant part of their cultural heritage. Dancing, and particularly step dancing, was therefore valued by the people of North Kerry; it was for them an integral part of their lives. It marked and structured their social and economic calendar and contributed hugely to the quality of their lives. It also assisted in constructing a strong 'felt' sense of community and identity through the physicality of dancing and the shared experiences that these local events offered.

From the end of the nineteenth century, step dancing was appropriated and re-presented as 'Irish' dancing by the cultural nationalist movement, the Gaelic League. Within the context of colonialism, 'Irish' dancing was promoted and disseminated through competitions at *feiseanna* and *oireachtais* as an integral part of the ideological agenda of the Gaelic League and as representative and expressive of Irish Catholic culture. Schools of step dancing were established in the towns and cities of Ireland where children learned Irish step dancing as a leisure time activity. After the establishment of the Irish Free State in 1922, the Irish step dancing organization An Coimisiún was founded in 1930, under the auspices of the Gaelic League. An Coimisiún further developed and controlled Irish step dancing through a hierarchical system of step dance competitions at *feiseanna* and *oireachtais*. An Coimisiún became a hegemonic structure within the competitive world of Irish step dancing. Step dancing came to embody the ideological agenda of the cultural nationalist movement, the Gaelic League, and became iconic of the nation-state. Within this postcolonial context, step dancers unconsciously performed politics and the 'nation' and assisted in the projection of a uniform, homogenous Irish culture. In North Kerry, the dance school, Rinceoirí na Ríochta, was selected as representative of this dance practice. Step dancers identified with and conformed to rules and regulations as laid down by An Coimisiún, but they also constructed and negotiated their own individual senses of identity through their participation in other dance or leisure-time activities.

In the 1970s, Siamsa Tíre, the National Folk Theatre of Ireland, was established in Tralee, Co. Kerry, as a response to processes of modernity and globalization. It aimed:

> to reflect Ireland's great wealth of music, dance and folklore on stage through vibrant, colourful theatrical entertainment and to continue creating new folk theatre presentations, drawing on our traditions and a rich cultural reservoir.

It also aimed to promote tourism in the region by its theatrical presentation of Irish culture in its home theatre in Tralee and in other venues and theatres in Ireland and abroad. Siamsa Tíre became a professional folk theatre in 1985 with state sponsorship, and utilized indigenous cultural practices, customs and myths to inspire and produce folk theatre in what the West terms 'high art'. The traditional, Molyneaux, step dance practice of the region was stylized, integrated and re-presented for this theatrical context. Gradually, it became a significant kinaesthetic identifying marker for Siamsa Tíre, with different dancers and choreographers stylizing and working with the form. This theatricalized practice thus embodied a folk-theatrical commodity situated within the context of Western art theatre, tourism, consumer culture and globalization. Siamsa Tíre, as the National Folk Theatre, thus mediated aesthetics and economics while also negotiating issues of identity: local, national and global.

Synchronically, these three step dance practices illustrate the diversity of step dance practices present in the region of North Kerry at a specific moment in time. All three embodied practices were present during my fieldwork period in the 1980s and 2004,[1] and although the Molyneaux practice is not as vibrant today as a living tradition, there are still a few of the Molyneaux step dancers alive who will perform on occasion at weddings, pubs or local cultural events. Rinceoirí na Ríochta continues its work as a registered step dancing school with An Coimisiún, and Siamsa Tíre continues to include the Molyneaux step dance style within both its educational work at the Tithe Siamsa and its artistic and folk-theatrical work in the theatre.

These three practices carry their own meaning and value systems, and they each assist in constructing, shaping and being shaped by place, history and the culture out of which each has emerged. Each practice has its own 'authenticity', and illustrates different ways that people experience their world through step dancing. However, these practices are not fixed. They are transforming and transformative practices that shape and are shaped by dancers, dance teachers, dance directors, musicians, institutions, and changing socio-cultural and economic circumstances.

These dance communities have their symbolic markers, both expressive and material, and these effectively define their boundaries. As Anthony Cohen states, 'community' seems to imply simultaneously both similarity and difference. The word thus expresses a *relational* idea: the opposition of one community to others or to other social entities.[2] However, as illustrated in this book, although these communities of step dance practitioners in North Kerry may belong to different meaning and value movement systems, and have adapted a particular *habitus*, it no longer precludes them from participating in the other step dancing or leisure-time activities available to them. This is, of course, dependent upon an individual's motivation, ability, cultural values, time, money and socio-environmental factors. Thus, whether participating in one or more overlapping multiple allegiances, individuals endeavour to shape a sense of self and collective identities and to enhance their own sense of well-being.

It would be a mistake, however, to think that all step dancers representative of any one of the embodied step dance practices in North Kerry at the beginning of the twenty-first century embraced all the other practices. Some step dancers were totally involved in their own step dance worlds; others acknowledged differences,

---

[1]   Although I conducted two periods of intensive fieldwork during the 1980s and 2004, I have been constantly in touch with what is going on in dance in North Kerry between these periods and since 2004. As I have lived and worked in Limerick since 1996, I have visited and met dancers from North Kerry regularly, and I have been kept up to date with changes that have occurred there, not only in dance, but also in the lives of the dancers.

[2]   Cohen (1985), p. 12.

and negotiated their dance aesthetic in whatever step dance context they found themselves; and others still made conscious decisions to remain apart. Questions of authenticity and authority often arose in conversations with step dancers in the area. Some perceived the Molyneaux style of dance to be the 'real' Kerry tradition; others believed that no institution had the right to speak for them; others still believed that dance practices change and develop, and one has to change with the times or be left behind. Therefore, the presence of different expressions and embodiments of step dance in the region of North Kerry at the time of my field research was a manifestation of the co-existence of different meaning and value systems, different worldviews and different ways of *being* in the world. It represented a process that aligns many cultures where old ways, new ways and emergent cultures co-exist. This situation highlights a particular human and cultural predicament when some people situate themselves in the old 'familiar' world, with its particular cultural values and belief systems, while others embrace cultural change and a new and different value system. This can be interpreted as tradition versus innovation, or tradition versus modernity – a debate that has relevance for many cultures in the modern world.[3] The three step dance practices in this book highlighted moments of cultural adaptation, change and resistance in Ireland, with particular reference to North Kerry.

Postscript: Step Dancing as a Transnational Dance Practice

Step dancing within the internationally acclaimed, commercial step dance stage shows such as *Riverdance* and *Lord of the Dance* influenced the perceptions of step dancing in Kerry, Ireland and abroad.[4] Step dancing was no longer perceived as a rural 'low art' dance practice, it was now part of popular culture[5] playing to huge audiences in the largest and most renowned theatres in the world. The step dancers in these shows were professional dancers, and some step dancers with Rinceoirí na Ríochta, the Coimisiún school in Tralee, joined these commercial shows. They were now not only paid to step dance, but had the opportunity to travel around the world as professional step dancers; this provided them with status and value as dancers.

These shows exposed many different cultures to Irish step dancing. Step dancing was seen as skilful, exciting and challenging, and a demand for step dancing classes and teachers grew, not just in Ireland and the Irish diaspora, but also further afield. Some of these teachers included the professional show step dancers. Step dancing had thus become transnational, with individuals of all

---

[3]   See Vallely et al. (eds) (1999).

[4]   Foley (2001; 2007a).

[5]   Another Irish dance group, Prodijig, won the televised 'Got to Dance Series 3' award in 2012. It is available for viewing on 'Got to Dance Series 3 Prodijig Final Performace' at http://www.youtube.com/watch?v=oy3gCVaYk8E [accessed 4 July, 2013].

ages and from different cultural backgrounds wishing to learn the form and to participate in the vibrant and social world of step dancing.

In 1999, a Master of Arts degree in Irish Traditional Dance Performance was established at the Irish World Academy of Music and Dance, University of Limerick, Ireland. This was the first university programme of its type in the world.[6] I designed and have directed the programme to date, and have firsthand knowledge and experience of its development since its inception. The programme has attracted dancers from Ireland, the diaspora and from other diverse dance and cultural backgrounds. Some dancers were experienced dancers from shows such as *Riverdance*, *Lord of the Dance* and so on; others were experienced competitive dancers; and others, having seen *Riverdance*, took step dancing up for the first time and immersed themselves in the form, taking classes wherever and whenever they could. A requirement for entry to the MA programme was a successful audition. The demographic of these MA step dancers assisted in reinforcing a perception of step dancing as a transnational and inclusive dance form. This would concur with a statement made by the sociologist Reginald Byron, with reference to Irish-Americans in Albany some years ago:

> There are no longer any recognizable practices that belong exclusively to people of Irish decent … the remaining icons of Irishness … now belong to everyone, and anyone is free to play with these public symbols of Irishness, whether they have several Irish ancestors, just one or two, or even none at all ….[7]

Currently, Irish step dancing is no longer confined on the grounds of ethnicity or geography (including Ireland and the diaspora). Step dancing has become a transnational dance form, and sits on the global kinetic palette of diverse movement systems to be selected, or not, by individuals who embrace whatever movement systems they choose to avail of, based on matters of self-interest, self-expression, identity or the meaning it may hold for them. Today, step dancing is practised, enjoyed and studied by thousands of step dancers, not only in Kerry, Ireland and its diaspora, but also in Japan, Russia, Norway, Eastern Europe, Africa and further afield. It is performed within social, competitive, theatrical and third-level academic contexts, and is practised by young and old, amateur and professional step dancers. There are those who do it, those who actively watch it, those who research it, and those who combine all of these.

The MA Irish Traditional Dance Performance programme offers advanced training in Irish step dancing, but also fosters respect for past masters and their repertoires and styles; this includes Jeremiah Molyneaux. A further objective is to assist individual students to 'find their own individual voice' through the medium of step dancing; this allows students to also explore the dance form creatively within a contemporary theatrical context utilizing physical theatre and

---

[6] See Foley (2007b; 2012a; 2012d).
[7] Reginald Byron in Fintan O'Toole, *The Irish Times*, 17 March 2007.

contemporary dance principles.[8] Irish contemporary theatrical dance is also being explored by other dance artists, such as Jean Butler, Colin Dunne[9] and Breandán de Gallaí.[10] These three dance artists were lead dancers with the Irish step dance stage show, *Riverdance,* and have developed their careers further through dance exploration and third level education.

The MA Ethnochoreology programme was established at the Irish World Academy of Music and Dance in 1996. This was the first programme of its kind in a European university. I had the privilege of designing it, and continue to direct the programme. While students focus on researching a dance or human movement practice of their choice, some students research step dancing, and these students are generally step dancers. Step dance thus continues to provide a distinctive and meaningful dance-music experience for practitioners, observers and researchers. As the anthropologist, Cynthia Novack, states:

> dance is a part of life and culture – as metaphor for social interaction and values, as a focal point for different kinds of organizations and institutions, and, not least of all, as the direct apprehension of moving with and for a community of people. In the moment of dancing, people experience powerful occasions of meaning in their lives.[11]

Step dance as an embodied dance-music practice is dynamic and adaptable; throughout its historicity it has contributed significantly to expressing, negotiating and representing culture and identity, and it continues to do so. Step dancing is meaningful to those who do it, watch it, re-present it and research it. Step dancing is made meaningful and relevant to people's lives through the different experiences that it offers and the opportunities these provide to express their *being* in the world.

---

[8]   See Foley (2007b; 2012a; 2012d) and 'Dance Masters' in *Rising Steps* (Stirling Film and Television Productions, 2000).

[9]   Colin Dunne's solo multi-media full-length production, *Out of Time* (2008). See also Foley (2010).

[10]   Breandán de Gallaí's stage shows *Noctú* (2011) and *Rite of Spring* (2012); part of a PhD in Arts Practice Research at the Irish World Academy of Music and Dance.

[11]   Novack (1990), p. 235.

Appendix

Step

A step is an eight-bar choreographic structure in step dancing. A step is danced first commencing on the right leg; this is called the right leg of the step. Once completed, it is then repeated commencing on the left leg; this is called the left leg of the step. Steps are choreographed to Reel, Jig or Hornpipe music. The three primary step dance types are similarly named the Reel, Jig and Hornpipe.[1]

Reel

A dance performed either solo or in a group. The Reel is danced to tune types of the same name in $\frac{4}{4}$ time or $\frac{2}{2}$ time. They are believed to have been played in Ireland for the first time in the late 1700s. Reels are danced solo by both male and female dancers, in either competitive step dance contexts, exhibitions, commercial stage shows or as a vernacular dance form. They are danced with either hard shoes for a percussive, rhythmic sound, or soft shoes to display a lightness and gracefulness. Male and female dancers perform hard-shoe Reels; these are commonly named *Treble Reels*. Reels are also danced percussively in a close-to-the-floor style in places such as Connemara; this style is named *sean nós*, or 'old-style'. Reel steps are generally structured within eight bars of Reel music, and each step is choreographed and performed commencing with the right foot, followed immediately by a repeat of the whole step commencing with the left foot (total 16 bars). In a group performance, step dancers may perform *céilí* dances (see An Coimisiún's *Ár Rinncidhe Fóirne*) or figure dances (newly choreographed dances).

Jig

A dance performed either solo or in a group. There are many variants of the Jig. The *Double Jig* is generally a solo percussive hard-shoe step dance performed by both males and females in competitive and exhibition contexts, stage show and vernacular contexts to Jig tunes in $\frac{6}{8}$ time. These tunes are structured in two eight-bar sections, each section repeated twice (AABB). Generally, a Jig step is structured within eight bars of music, and each step is choreographed and performed commencing with the right foot, followed immediately by a repeat of the whole step commencing with the left foot (total 16 bars). A Double Jig performance will consist of a sequence of these step dances. The Double Jig is

---

[1]   Foley in Vallely (2011).

also associated with solo set dances – traditional and modern. Solo set dances are musically irregular in structure, and specific dances are choreographed to fit these structures (see below).

The *Light Jig* is a solo light-shoe step dance performed by both males and females in competitive, exhibition and social contexts to Jig tunes in $\frac{6}{8}$ time. The tempo of the Light Jig is lively, and similarly to the Double Jig, a Light Jig step is structured within eight bars of the accompanying music and is repeated to the opposite side (total 16 bars).

The *Single Jig* is a specific solo light-shoe step dance performed by predominantly females to Single Jig tunes in $\frac{6}{8}$ time or $\frac{12}{8}$ time. Musically, this is also known as a 'slide', and is danced in some set dances (Quadrilles). The Single Jig differs from the Double Jig in that its characteristic rhythmic pattern is a crochet followed by a quaver, in lieu of the three-quaver pattern of the Double Jig. Likewise, a Single Jig step is structured within eight bars of the accompanying music, and is repeated to the opposite side.

The *Slip Jig* (or *Hop Jig*) is different from the other Jig dances. It is a light-shoe step dance performed today predominantly by female step dancers in competitions, exhibitions or stage show choreographies to Slip Jig tunes in $\frac{9}{8}$ time. Similarly to the other Jig types, the Slip Jig step is structured within eight bars of the accompanying music, and each step is choreographed and performed commencing with the right foot, followed immediately by a repeat of the whole step commencing with the left foot (total 16 bars). Unlike the other Jig types, musically the Slip Jig is in single form; its two-part eight-bar music structure is not repeated. It is often referred to as 'the queen of step dances', to indicate the required gracefulness of the dance. Historically, the Slip Jig was also a couples dance, performed by both male and female dancers.[2]

Hornpipe

A dance performed either solo or in a group, historically the Hornpipe was introduced to Ireland at the end of the eighteenth century via England, where it was performed by professional dancers between acts in plays; the Hornpipe also has maritime associations. In Ireland, the Hornpipe was developed by dancing masters as an exhibitionistic solo percussive step dance genre. The Hornpipe is danced to tune types of the same name in $\frac{4}{4}$ time with a characteristic dotted rhythm and with accents occurring on beats one and three. It is danced in competitive step dance contexts, exhibitions, social contexts and commercial stage-shows. As a solo percussive step dance, it is performed today by both male and female dancers; historically, it was predominantly associated with male dancers. Exceptions include step dancers in North Kerry, where both male and female step dancers performed Hornpipes (see Foley 1988b), and Cork City, where in the 1920s women commenced performing Hornpipe percussive solo dances. In its solo format, the

---

[2]   Sheehan (1902 [1986]); O'Keeffe and O'Brien (1902 [1944]).

Hornpipe is generally performed to lively Hornpipe music, but a reduced tempo is required for competitive step dancers who wish to illustrate their virtuosity of footwork. Hornpipe step dances are generally structured within eight bars of music, and each step is choreographed and performed commencing with the right foot, followed immediately by a repeat of the whole step commencing with the left foot (total 16 bars). A Hornpipe performance will consist of a sequence of these step dances. There are also Hornpipe solo set dances, both traditional and contemporary. Solo set dances are musically irregular in structure, and specific dances are choreographed to fit these structures. Traditional Hornpipe solo set dances include 'The Blackbird', 'An Súisín Bán' ('The White Blanket') and 'The Garden of Daisies'; contemporary solo Hornpipe set dances include 'Kilkenny Races' and 'Bonaparte's Retreat'. Hornpipes and are also danced in groups, particularly in some set dances (Quadrilles), at exhibitions and in stage show choreographies.

Solo Set Dances
Solo set dances are performed to specific pieces of Irish traditional dance music of irregular structure. Dance steps are therefore choreographed specifically to these pieces of music. Within the competitive structures of An Coimisiún, there are traditional solo set dances and modern solo set dances. These are performed with hard or heavy dance shoes, and are in either Jig or Hornpipe time. The traditional solo set dances are believed to be old, and are performed at a relatively lively tempo. The modern solo set dances (non-traditional) are contemporary choreographies, and are created by individual teachers for their students; these change all the time, and are danced to music of a much slower speed to allow step dancers to fit in as many beats as possible. Set dances are the showpieces for step dancers.

Traditional Solo Set Dances (An Coimisiún List)
'The Blackbird': Hornpipe ($\frac{4}{4}$; step: 7½ bars; set: 15 bars)
'The Hurling Boys': Jig ($\frac{6}{8}$; step: 8 bars; set: 16 bars)
'The Job of Journeywork': Hornpipe ($\frac{4}{4}$; step: 8 bars; set: 14 bars)
'Jockey to the Fair': Jig ($\frac{6}{8}$; step: 8 bars; set: 14 bars)
'King of the Fairies': Hornpipe ($\frac{4}{4}$; step: 8 bars; set: 16 bars)
'Saint Patrick's Day': Jig ($\frac{6}{8}$; step: 8 bars; set: 14 bars)
'The Three Sea Captains': Jig ($\frac{6}{8}$; step: 8 bars; set: 20 bars)
'The White Blanket': Hornpipe ($\frac{4}{4}$; step: 6 bars; set: 12 bars)
'The Blackbird', 'Saint Patrick's Day', 'Garden of Daisies' and 'The Job of Journeywork' were institutionalized by An Coimisiún as the traditional set dances in the 1970s (see Chapter 6 and Foley, 1988b; 2012b); more recently, these four set dances have been extended to include 'King of the Fairies', 'Jockey to the Fair', 'The Three Sea Captains' and 'The White Blanket' for competitive purposes.

Modern Solo Set Dances (An Coimisiún List)

'Ace and Deuce of Pipering': Hornpipe ($\frac{4}{4}$; step: 12 bars; set: 12 bars)
'Blackthorn Stick': Jig ($\frac{6}{8}$; step: 15 bars; set: 15 bars)
'Blue-Eyed Rascal': Hornpipe ($\frac{4}{4}$; step: 8 bars; set: 12 bars)
'Bonaparte's Retreat': Hornpipe ($\frac{4}{4}$; step: 8 bars; set: 20 bars)
'Deep Green Pool': Jig ($\frac{6}{8}$; step: 8 bars; set: 20 bars)
'Downfall of Paris': Hornpipe ($\frac{4}{4}$; step: 12 bars; set: 12 bars)
'The Drunken Gauger': Jig ($\frac{6}{8}$; step: 15 bars; set: 15 bars)
'Four Masters': Hornpipe ($\frac{4}{4}$; step: 8 bars; set: 12 bars)
'The Fiddler Around the Fairy Tree': Jig ($\frac{6}{8}$; step: 8 bars; set: 12 bars)
'Humours of Bandon': Jig ($\frac{6}{8}$; step: 8 bars; set: 16 bars)
'Hunt': Hornpipe ($\frac{4}{4}$; step: 8 bars; set: 12 bars)
'Hurry the Jug': Jig ($\frac{6}{8}$; step: 8 bars; set: 16 bars)
'Is the Big Man Within?': Jig ($\frac{6}{8}$; step: 8 bars; set: 8 bars)
'Kilkenny Races': Hornpipe ($\frac{4}{4}$; step: 12 bars; set: 24 bars)
'Lodge Road': Hornpipe ($\frac{2}{4}$; step: 12 bars; set: 24 bars)
'Madam Bonaparte': Hornpipe ($\frac{4}{4}$; step: 8 bars; set: 12 bars)
'Miss Brown's Fancy': Jig ($\frac{6}{8}$; step: 8 bars; set: 16 bars)
'Orange Rouge': Jig ($\frac{6}{8}$; step: 8 bars; set: 16 bars)
'Piper Thro' the Meadow Straying': Hornpipe ($\frac{4}{4}$; step: 8 bars; set: 12 bars)
'Planxty Davis': Hornpipe ($\frac{2}{4}$; step: 16 bars; set: 16 bars)
'Planxty Drury': Jig ($\frac{6}{8}$; step: 12 bars; set: 16 bars)
'Rambling Rake': Hornpipe ($\frac{4}{4}$; step: 8 bars; set: 16 bars)
'Rodney's Glory': Hornpipe ($\frac{2}{4}$; step: 8 bars; set: 12 bars)
'Roving Pedlar': Hornpipe ($\frac{4}{4}$; step: 8 bars; set: 14 bars)
'Rub the Bag': Jig ($\frac{6}{8}$; step: 8 bars; set: 14 bars)
'Sprig of Shillelagh': Jig ($\frac{6}{8}$; step: 8 bars; set: 10 bars)
'Story Teller': Jig ($\frac{6}{8}$; step: 8 bars; set: 16 bars)
'Wandering Musician': Jig ($\frac{6}{8}$; step: 8 bars; set: 16 bars)
'Youghal Harbour': Hornpipe ($\frac{4}{4}$; step: 6 bars; set: 14 bars)

For the music to these set dances, see, for example, *The Final Round*, double CD by Kevin Joyce (CLJ Productions, 2000,).

Céilí Dances

Céilí dances are group dances which were promoted by the Gaelic League from the end of the nineteenth century and were commonly performed socially at *céilí* dance events (Foley 2011). They derived from round and long dances, and were choreographed and transmitted by itinerant dancing masters, particularly in Co. Kerry (see Chapter 5). *Céilí* dances and/or set dances (Quadrilles) are danced today at *céilithe*. The most popular of the *céilí* dances include 'Ballaí Luimní' ('The Walls of Limerick'), 'Ionsaí na hInse' ('The Seige of Ennis'), 'Baint an Fhéir' ('The Haymaker's Jig') and 'Cadhp an Chúil Áird' ('The High-cauled Cap'). *Céilí* dances are taught at specific *céilí* dance classes and in step dance classes. They are danced at exhibitions and at *céilí* dance competitions under the jurisdiction of different organizations. For example, from the 1970s, *céilí* dance competitions were included in *Scór*, a festival organized under the auspices of the Gaelic Athletic Association. Also, to mark the centenary of the first Irish *céilí*, Cairde Rince Céilí na hÉireann ('Friends of Irish *Céilí* Dancing') was established in 1997 to celebrate the centenary and to promote non-competitive *céilí* dancing in Ireland. Examples of *céilí* dances can be found in J.J. Sheehan's *A Guide to Irish Dancing* (1902), O'Keeffe and O'Brien's *A Handbook of Irish Dances* (1902), Burchenal's *Rince na hÉireann: National Dances of Ireland* (1925), O'Rafferty's *The Irish Folk Dance Book* (Book One, 1934; Book Two, 1950), P. and G. O'Rafferty's *Dances of Ireland* (1953), Burchenal's and An Coimisiún's *Ár Rincidhe Fóirne, Volume 1* (1939), *Ár Rincidhe Fóirne, Volume 2* (1943) and *Ár Rincidhe Fóirne, Volume 3* (1969).

Figure Dances

Figure dances are group dances which are newly choreographed to Irish traditional music and portray through movement an Irish theme or item. These dances are choreographed with eight to 16 step dancers, and are performed at exhibitions and at competitive events.

Sean Nós Dancing ('Old-style' Dancing)

A solo, improvisatory, percussive dance-music form predominantly associated with Connemara on the west coast of Ireland, s*ean nós* has undergone a revival in recent years, with master classes being taught in the form in different parts of the world. Although associated with men in the past, it is now performed by both old and young, male and female dancers. *Steip*, a televised programme of the *sean nós* dance competitions at the national *Oireachtas* (separate from An Coimsiún's *oireachtais*) is broadcast every year by the Irish-language television station TG4.

An Coimisiún le Rincí Gaelacha ('The Irish Dancing Commission')

An Coimisiún is the largest international Irish competitive step dancing organization. It was established in 1930 by the cultural nationalist movement the Gaelic League to preserve and promote the dance form. Formal dance classes and competitions, culminating in Oireachtas Rince na Cruinne ('The Worlds'), assist in promoting the form.

Comhdháil na Muinteoirí le Rincí Gaelacha ('The Organization of Irish Dancing Teachers')

An Comhdháil is another Irish step dance organization, established in 1969 when some teachers split from An Coimisiún to form a separate organization independent of the Gaelic League. Like An Coimisiún, formal dance classes and a hierarchical system of competitions promote the dance form.

Cumann Rince Náisiúnta ('The Organization of National Dance')

Commonly referred to as CRN, Cumann Rince Náisiúnta is another step dancing organization which separated from An Comhdháil. It was established by dance teacher Ita Cadwell. Like An Coimisiún and An Comhdháil, CRN also preserves and promotes Irish dancing through formal dance classes and competitions.

Comhaltas Ceoltóirí Éireann ('The Organization for Irish Musicians')

Comhaltas Ceoltóirí Éireann is commonly referred to as 'Comhaltas'. It was established in 1951 to preserve and promote Irish traditional music, song and dance. Formal classes in instrumental music, singing and dancing (particularly set dancing) are characteristic of the organization. Competitions are held at county, regional and national levels, the main one being Fleadh Cheoil na hÉireann (see Henry 1989).

Festival Dance Teachers' Association (FDTA)

Commonly referred to as 'Festival Dancing', the association was established in 1971 after An Comhdháil split from An Coimisiún. It is generally a Northern Ireland step dancing association, whose dancing competitions are organized under the auspices of the British Federation of Festivals for Music, Dance and Speech and the Festival Dance Teachers' Association. Patricia Mulholland, musician, dancer, choreographer and teacher, is very much associated with Festival Dancing. She was the founder of the Irish Ballet in 1951 (see Scullion 2003; MacCafferty 2007).

World Irish Dance Association (WIDA)

Following the global acclaim of the Irish step dance stage shows in the 1990s, WIDA was established to facilitate the growing demand in mainland Europe for classes and competitions in Irish dance. WIDA organizes its own classes and competitions independently from other step dance organizations.

Céilí

A *céilí* (pl. *céilithe* or *céilís*) is an Irish social dance event, first established on 31 October 1893 by the cultural nationalist movement the Gaelic League (Conradh na Gaeilge) in Bloomsbury Hall, London (see Foley 2011).

Feis

Feis (pl. *feiseanna*) means 'festival', and within the context of Irish step dancing, it means a small local step dancing festival with a number of competitions, such as a class/school *feis*.

Oireachtas

Oireachtas (pl. *oireachtais*) is translated as 'deliberative assembly'. Within the world of Irish dancing, it means a major competitive step dancing event, such as a regional, national (The All Irelands) or international competition (The Worlds).

Ríocht

The word *ríocht* ('kingdom') is associated with Co. Kerry; when one speaks of 'the Kingdom' in Ireland, one is referring to the county of Kerry. Hence, we have names such as Rinceóirí na Ríochta ('Dancers of the Kingdom') and Siamsóirí na Ríochta ('Players of the Kingdom') in Kerry.

Bibliography

Printed Primary Sources

An Coimisiún le Rincí Gaelacha (1981), *Ár Rinncidhe Fóirne: Thirty Popular Figure Dances*, Book One (1939), Book Two (1943), and Book Three (1969). Dublin: An Coimisiún le Rincí Gaelacha.

—— (1977), *Rialacha Comórtaisí Cláraithe*: Rules of Registered Competitions. Dublin: An Coimisiún le Rincí Gaelacha.

Comhaltas Ceoltóirí Éireann (1985), *Iubhaile Cúig mBliana Fichead*. Tralee, Co. Kerry: Comhaltas Ceoltóirí Éireann, Co. Kerry Branch.

National Folklore Collection, Manuscripts 659, 1169, and 1719: Schools' Manuscripts, no. V 404. Dublin: University College, Dublin.

Public Dance Halls Bill (1934), National Archives, Department of Justice, ref. no. 8/21, Dáil Éireann, Dublin.

Ros (1978) (Journal of Kerry Folk Life), vol. 8, no. 3.

This is Listowel (1970), official guide. Tralee, Co. Kerry: Kerryman.

Secondary Sources

Ahern, Pat and Patrick O'Sullivan and Partners, Architects (1972), 'A Plan for Fostering the Growth of Traditional Irish Folk Culture'. Unpublished.

Anderson, Benedict (1983), *Imagined Communities: Reflections on the Origin and Spread of Nationalism*. London: Verso.

Arbeau, Thoinot (1589), *Orchesography*, Langres, transl. into English by Mary Stewart Evans (1948), New York: Kamin Dance Publishers; reprinted 1967 with corrections, a new Introduction, and notes by Julia Sutton, and representative steps and dances in Labanotation by Mireille Backer, New York: Dover Publications.

Barz, Gregory. E. and Cooley, Timothy J. (eds) (1997; second edition 2008), *Shadows in the Field: New Perspectives for Fieldwork in Ethnomusicology*. Oxford and New York: Oxford University Press.

Beckett, J.C. (1966), *A Short History of Ireland*. London: Hutchinson University Library.

Berlin, Isaiah (1991), 'The Bent Twig', in Henry Hardy (ed.), *The Crooked Timber of Humanity*. London: Fontana Press.

Blacking, John (1973a), 'Fieldwork in African Music', *Review of Ethnology*, vol. 3, no. 23.

—— (1973b), *How Musical is Man?* Seattle, WA: University of Washington Press.

Blasis, Carlo (1820), *Traité élémentaire, théorique et pratique de l'art de la danse*, transl. Mary Stewart Evans (1968), *An Elementary Treatise upon the Theory and Practice of the Art of Dancing*. New York: Dover Publications.

Boas, Franz (1944), 'Dance and Music in the Life of the Northwest Coast Indians of North America.' In Franziska Boas (ed.) *The Function of Dance in Human Society*, New York: The Boas School, pp. 5–20.

Boas, Franziska (1944; ed.) The *Function of Dance in Human Society*, New York: The Boas School.

Bourdieu, Pierre (1977), *Outline of a Theory of Practice*. Cambridge: Cambridge University Press.

—— (1984), *Distinction: A Social Critique of the Judgement of Taste*. London: Routledge.

Brainard, Ingrid (1998a), 'Dancing Masters', in Selma Jeanne Cohen (ed.), *International Encyclopedia of Dance*, vol. 2. Oxford and New York: Oxford University Press, pp. 336–41.

—— (1998b), 'Renaissance Dance Technique', in Selma Jeanne Cohen (ed.), *International Encyclopedia of Dance*, vol. 5. Oxford: Oxford University Press, pp. 336–40.

Breathnach, Breandán (1977), *Folk Music and Dances of Ireland*. Cork: Mercier Press.

—— (1983), *Dancing in Ireland*. Miltown-Malbay, Co. Clare: Dal gCais Publications.

Brennan, Helen (1999), *The Story of Irish Dance*. Dingle: Brandon Press.

Brody, Hugh (1982), *Inishkillane: Change and Decline in the West of Ireland*. London: Jill Norman and Hobhouse.

Browning, Barbara (1995), *Samba: Resistance in Motion*. Bloomington, IN: Indiana University Press.

Buckland, Theresa Jill (ed.) (1999), *Dance in the Field: Theory, Methods and Issues in Dance Ethnography*. London: Macmillan Press.

—— (2006), 'Dance, History and Ethnography: Frameworks, Sources, and Identities of Past and Present', in Theresa Jill Buckland (ed.), *Dancing from Past to Present: Nation, Culture, Identities*. Madison, WI: University of Wisconsin Press, pp. 3–24.

Burchenal, Elizabeth (ed.) (1925), *Rince na hÉireann: National Dances of Ireland*. New York: A.S. Barnes.

Carleton, William (1840), 'The Country Dancing Master', *Irish Penny Journal*, vol. I, no. 9 (29 August), pp. 69–72.

—— (1845), *Tales and Stories of the Irish Peasantry*. Dublin: James Duffy.

Castells, Manuel (1997 [2004]), *The Information Age: Economy, Society and Culture. Volume 11, The Power of Identity*. Oxford: Blackwell Publishing; reprint, 2004.

Clifford, James (1988), *The Predicament of Culture: Twentieth-century Ethnography, Literature, and Art*. London: Harvard University Press.

Cohen, Anthony P. (1985), *The Symbolic Construction of Community*. Oxford: Routledge.

Connerton, Paul (1989), *How Societies Remember*. Cambridge: Cambridge University Press.

Cooley, Timothy J. (2005) *Making Music in the Polish Tatras: Tourists, Ethnographers, and Mountain Musicians*. Bloomington, IN and Indianapolis, IN: Indiana University Press.

Cornazano, Antonio (1455 [1981]), *The Book on the Art of Dancing*, transl. Madeleine Inglehearn and Peggy Forsyth. London: Dance Books.

Cowan, Jane K. (1990), *Dance and the Body Politic in Northern Greece*. Princeton, NJ: Princeton University Press.

Cregan, David (2009), *Deviant Acts: Essays on Queer Performance*. Dublin: Carysfort Press.

Crehan, Junior (1977), 'Junior Crehan Remembers', *Dal gCais*, pp. 72–7.

Csordas, Thomas (1990), 'Embodiment as a Paradigm for Anthropology', *Ethos*, vol. 18, pp. 5–47.

Cullinane, John (1996), *Irish Dancing Costumes: Their Origins and Evolution*. Cork: self-published.

—— (2003), *An Coimisiún le Rincí Gaelacha* [Irish Dancing Commission]*: Its Origins and Evolution*. Cork: self-published.

Daniel, Yvonne (1995), *Dance and Social Change in Contemporary Cuba*. Bloomington, IN: Indiana University Press.

Derrida, Jacques (1981), *Positions*. London: Athlone Press.

Dumont, Jean-Paul (1978), 'Introduction' and 'Entering the Field', in *The Headman and I: Ambiguity and Ambivalence in the Fieldworking Experience*. Long Grove, IL: Waveland Press.

Elias, Norbert (1994), *The Civilizing Process*. Cambridge, MA: Blackwell Publishers.

Emmerson, George (1972), *A Social History of Scottish Dance: Ane Celestial Recreatioun*. Montreal and London: McGill-Queen's University Press.

Evans-Pritchard, E.E. (1928), 'The Dance' in *Africa: Journal of the International African Institute*, Vol. 1, No. 4. (Oct.). pp. 446 – 462. Published by: Edinburgh University Press.

Feld, Steven and Basso, Keith H. (eds) (1996), *Senses of Place*. Santa Fe, NM: School of American Research Press.

Flett, Joan P. and Flett, Thomas M. (1985), *Traditional Dancing in Scotland*. London: Routledge and Kegan Paul.

—— (1996), *Traditional Step Dancing in Scotland*. Edinburgh: Scottish Cultural Press.

Foley, Catherine E. (1988a), 'Irish Traditional Step Dance in Cork', in Theresa Buckland (ed.), *Traditional Dance*, vols 5 and 6. Crewe: Crewe and Alsager College of Higher Education, pp. 159–74.

—— (1988b), 'Irish Traditional Step Dancing in North Kerry: A Contextual and Structural Analysis', unpublished PhD thesis (text and video). London: Laban Centre for Movement and Dance at Goldsmith's College; published as Foley (2012b).

—— (2001), 'Perceptions of Irish Step Dance: National, Global and Local', *Dance Research Journal*, vol. 33, no. 1 (Summer), pp. 34–45.

—— (2005a), 'Representing Irish Step Dance Heritage: Bridging Theory and Practice', keynote address, in Ingibjörg Björnsdóttir (ed.), *Dance Heritage: Crossing Academia and Physicality – Proceedings of the 7th Nordic Forum for Dance Research 2004*. Reykjavik: Nordic Forum for Dance Research, pp. 48–55.

—— (2005b), 'What is My Nation? What is My Dance? Ethnochoreology in Ireland', unpublished paper presented at the 38th World Conference of the ICTM, Sheffield, UK.

—— (ed.) (2007a), *At the Crossroads: Dance and Irish Culture*, conference proceedings of Dance Research Forum Ireland's 1st International Conference. Limerick: Dance Research Forum Ireland.

—— (2007b), 'Maintaining, Redefining and Challenging Dance Boundaries: Irish Traditional Dance within Third Level Education', in Catherine E. Foley (ed.), *At the Crossroads: Dance and Irish Culture*, conference proceedings of Dance Research Forum Ireland's 1st International Conference. Limerick: Dance Research Forum Ireland, pp. 64–70.

—— (2007c), 'The Creative Process within Irish Traditional Step Dance', in Adrienne L. Kaeppler and Elsie Ivancich Dunin (eds), *Dance Structures: Perspectives on the Analysis of Human Movement*. Budapest: Akadémiai Kiadó, pp. 277–302.

—— (2008), 'Percussive Relations: An Exploration of Percussive Dance at Tráth na gCos 2002', in Mick Moloney et al (eds), *Close to the Floor: Irish Dance from the Boreen to Broadway*. Madison, WI: Macater Press, pp. 47–56.

—— (2010). 'Negotiating Boundaries in Irish Step-dance Performance Practice: Colin Dunne and Piano One', *Inbhear*, vol. 1, issue 1. © Inbhear, Journal of Irish Music and Dance, 2010. www.inbhear.ie

—— (2011), 'The Irish *Céilí*: A Site for Constructing, Experiencing, and Negotiating a Sense of Community and Identity', *Dance Research*, vol. 29, no. 1, pp. 43–60.

—— (2012a) 'Contemporizing Irish Step Dance within a University Context', in Elsie Ivancich Dunin, Daniela Stavelová and Dorota Gremlicová (eds) *Proceedings of the 26th Symposium of the ICTM Study Group on Ethnochoreology*. Academy of Performing Arts, Prague, and the Institute of Ethnology of the Academy of Sciences of the Czech Republic. Prague: Czech Republic, pp, 220–28.

—— (2012b), *Irish Traditional Step Dancing in North Kerry: A Contextual and Structural Analysis*, text and video. Listowel: North Kerry Literary Trust.

—— (2012c) 'The Notion and Process of Collecting, Recording, and Representing Irish Traditional Music, Song and Dance: The Muckross House Collection', in Thérèse Smith (ed.), *Ancestral Imprints: Histories of Irish Traditional Music and Dance*. Cork: Cork University Press, pp. 107–17.

—— (2012d), 'The roots and routes of Irish step dancing: issues of identity and participation in a global world', in Ian Russell and Chris Goertzen (eds),

Routes & Roots: Fiddle and Dance Studies from around the North Atlantic 4. Aberdeen: The Elphinstone Institute, University of Aberdeen, pp. 145–56.

—— (2012e), 'Ethnochoreology as a Mediating perspective in Irish Dance Studies'. *New Hibernia Review/ Iris Éireannach Nua*, vol. 16, no. 2, pp. 143–54.

Foucault, Michel (1977), *Discipline and Punish*. Harmondsworth: Penguin.

Franko, Mark (1993), *Dance as Text: Ideologies of the Baroque Body*. Cambridge: Cambridge University Press.

Friel, Mary (2004), *Dancing as a Social Pastime in the South-east of Ireland, 1800–97*, Maynooth Studies in Local History, no. 54. Dublin: Four Courts Press.

Frith, Simon (1996), 'Music and Identity', in *Questions of Cultural Identity*. London: Sage Publications, pp. 108–27.

Gadamer, Hans-Georg (1960 [1986]), *Truth and Method*. New York: Crossroad Publishing; reprint, 1986.

Gareiss, Nicholas (2012), 'Queering the Feis: An Examination of the Expression of Alternative Sexual Identity in Competitive Irish Step Dance in Ireland', unpublished MA Ethnochoreology thesis. Limerick: The Irish World Academy of Music and Dance, University of Limerick.

Gaughan, J. Anthony (1973), *Listowel and its Vicinity*. Cork: Mercier Press.

—— (2004), *Listowel and its Vicinity: Since 1973*. Dublin: Currach Press.

Geertz, Clifford (1973), *The Interpretation of Cultures*. New York: Basic Books.

Giurchescu, Anca and Torp, Lisbet (1991), 'Theory and Methods in Dance Research: A European Approach to the Holistic Study of Dance', *Yearbook for Traditional Music*, vol. XXIII, pp. 1–10.

Green, E.R.R. (1984), 'The Great Famine (1845–50)', in T.W. Moody and F.X. Martin, (eds), *The Course of Irish History*. Cork: Mercier Press, pp. 263–74.

Guest, Ivor (1960 [1977]), *The Dancer's Heritage: A Short History of Ballet*. London: The Dancing Times; 5th edn, 1977.

Hahn, Tomie, (2007) *Sensational Knowledge: Embodying Culture through Japanese Dance*. Hawai'i: University of Hawai'i Press.

Hall, Frank (1997), 'Your Mr. Joyce is a Fine Man, but Have You Seen Riverdance?', *New Hibernia Review – Iris Éireannach Nua*, vol. 1, no. 3, pp. 134–42.

—— (2008), *Irish Dance: Discipline as Art, Sport, and Duty*. Madison, WI: Macater Press.

Hall, Mr and Mrs S.C. (1984), *Halls Ireland*, vol. 1. London: Sphere Books, first published 1840.

Hall, Stuart (1990), 'Cultural Identity and Diaspora', in J. Rutherford (ed.), *Identity: Community, Culture, Difference*. London: Lawrence & Wishart, pp. 222–37.

—— (1991), 'The Local and the Global: Globalization and Ethnicity', in Anthony King (ed.), *Culture, Globalization and the World-system: Contemporary Conditions for the Representation of Identity*. London: Macmillan Press, pp. 19–39.

—— (1996), 'Introduction: Who Needs "Identity"?', in Stuart Hall and Paul du Gay (eds), *Questions of Cultural Identity*. London: Sage Publications, pp. 1–17.

Hanna, Judith Lynne (1980), *To Dance is Human: A Theory of Nonverbal Communication*, London: University of Texas Press.

Heidegger, Martin (1962), *Being and Time*, transl. John Macquarrie and Edward Robinson. San Francisco, CA: Harper & Row Publishers.

Henry, Edward O. (1989), 'Institutions for the Promotion of Indigenous Music: The Case of Ireland's Comhaltas Ceoltóirí Éireann', *Ethnomusicology*, vol. 33, no. 1 (Winter), pp. 67–95.

Herzfeld, Michael (1983), 'Looking Both Ways: The Ethnographer in the Text', *Semiotica*, vol. 46, nos 2–4, pp. 151–66.

Hilton, Wendy (1981), *Dance of Court and Theatre: the French Noble Style 1690–1725*. London: Dance Books.

Hobsbawm, Eric J. (1977), *The Age of Revolution 1789–1848*. London: Sphere Books.

—— and Ranger, Terence (eds) (1985), *The Invention of Tradition*. Cambridge: Cambridge University Press.

Hughes-Freeland, Felicia (2008). *Embodied Communities: Dance Traditions and Change in Java*. Oxford: Berghahn Books.

Inglis, Tom (1987), *Moral Monopoly: The Catholic Church in Modern Irish Society*. Dublin: Gill and MacMillan.

—— (2002), 'Pleasure Pursuits', in Mary P. Corcoran and Michael Peillon (eds), *Ireland Unbound: A Turn of the Century Chronicle*. Dublin: Institute of Public Administration, pp. 25–35.

Kaeppler, Adrienne L. (1972), 'Method and Theory in Analyzing Dance Structure with an Analysis of Tongan Dance', *Ethnomusicology*, vol. 16, no. 2, pp. 173–217.

—— (1978) 'Dance in Anthropological Perspective', *Annual Review of Anthropology*, vol. 7, pp. 31–49.

—— (1986), 'Cultural Analysis, Linguistic Analogies and the Study of Dance in Anthropological Perspective', in Charlotte Frisbie (ed.), *Detroit Monographs in Musicology*, vol. 9, pp. 25–33.

—— (1991), 'American Approaches to the Study of Dance', *Yearbook for Traditional Music*, vol. XXIII, pp. 11–22.

—— (2000), 'Dance Ethnology and the Anthropology of Dance', *Dance Research Journal*, vol. 32, no. 1, pp. 116–25.

—— and Dunin, Elsie Ivancich (eds), *Dance Structures: Perspectives on the Analysis of Human Movement*. Budapest: Akadémiai Kiadó.

Kealiinohomoku, Joann W. (1972a), 'Dance Culture as a Microcosm of Holistic Culture', *CORD Research Annual*, vol. VI, pp. 99–106.

—— (1972b), 'Folk Dance', in R.M. Dorson (ed.), *Folklore and Folklife: An Introduction*. Chicago, IL: University of Chicago Press, pp. 381–404.

Keane, John B. (1964), *Self-portrait*. Cork: Mercier Press.

Kearney, Richard (ed.) (1985), *The Irish Mind: Exploring Intellectual Traditions*. Dublin: Wolfhound Press.

Kennedy, Patrick (1875), *The Banks of the Boro: A Chronicle of County Wexford*. London: Simpkin Marshall; reprinted 1989, Enniscorthy, Co. Wexford: Duffry Press.

Kennelly, Brendan (2011), *The Essential Brendan Kennelly: Selected Poems with Live CD*. Newcastle upon Tyne: Bloodaxe Books.

Kiberd, Declan (1996), *Inventing Ireland: The Literature of the Modern Nation*. London: Vintage Books.

—— (2006), 'Foreword', in Deirdre Mulrooney (ed.), *Irish Moves: An Illustrated History of Dance and Physical Theatre in Ireland*. Dublin: The Liffey Press, pp. xi–xiv.

Koning, Jos (1980), 'The Fieldworker as Performer: Fieldwork Objectives and Social Roles in County Clare, Ireland', *Ethnomusicology*, vol. 24, no. 3, pp. 417–29.

Kurath, Gertrude (1960), 'A Panorama of Dance Ethnology', *Current Anthropology*, vol. 1, no. 3, pp. 233–54.

Lenihan, Maurice (1867), 'Reminiscences of a Journalist no. 104', *The Limerick Reporter and Tipperary Vindicator*, 8 November.

Lyons, F.S.L. (1973), *Ireland Since the Famine*. London: Fontana Press.

Mac Aodha, B. (1972), 'Was This a Social Revolution?', in Seán Ó Tuama (ed.), *The Gaelic League Idea*. Cork: Mercier Press, pp. 20–30.

McArdle, Gráinne (2003), 'Dance on the Early Dublin Stage', unpublished paper presented at the Irish Dance Research Forum as part of the Society of Dance History Scholars 26th Annual International Conference, University of Limerick, Ireland, 28 June 2003.

—— (2005), 'Signora Violante and Her Troupe of Dancers 1729–32', in Michael Brown (ed.), *Eighteenth-century Ireland: Iris an dá chultúr*, vol. 20. Dublin, pp. 55–78.

MacCafferty, Joyce Ann (2007), *The Deep Green Pool: The Life, Work and Legacy of Patricia Mulholland*. Derry: Guildhall Press.

McCartney, Donal (1984), 'From Parnell to Pearse (1891–1921)', in T.W. Moody and F.X. Martin (eds), *The Course of Irish History*. Cork: Mercier Press, pp. 294–312.

McDowell, R.B. (1984), 'The Protestant Nation (1775–1800)', in T.W. Moody and F.X. Martin (eds), *The Course of Irish History*. Cork: Mercier Press, pp. 232–47.

McGann, Art (1936), 'Irish Dancing: Some Aspects of its Development and Status, Part 1', *An Raitheachán*, no. 1 (June), pp. 65–6.

McKenzie, John M. (1995), *Orientalism: History, Theory and the Arts*. Manchester: Manchester University Press.

Mackenzie, Robert Shelton (1855), *Bits of Blarney*. New York: Redfield.

MacMahon, Bryan (1992), *The Master*. Dublin: Poolbeg.

Malinowski, Bronislaw (1922), *Argonauts of the Western Pacific*. New York: E.P. Dutton.

Marcus, George E. and Fischer, Michael M.J. (1986), *Anthropology as Cultural Critique: An Experimental Moment in the Human Sciences*. Chicago, IL: University of Chicago Press.

Martin, Györgi and Pesovar, Ernö (1961), 'A Structural Analysis of the Hungarian Folk Dance', *Acta Ethnographica Academiae Scientiarum Hungaricae*, vol. x, pp. 1–40.

Mathews, P.J. (2003), *Revival: The Abbey Theatre, Sinn Fein, The Gaelic League and the Co-operative Movement*. Cork: Cork University Press in association with Field Day.

Mauss, Marcel (1973) 'Techniques of the Body', transl. Ben Brewster, *Economy and Society*, vol. 2, pp. 70–87.

Maxwell, Constantia (ed.) (1983), *Arthur Young: A Tour in Ireland*. Belfast: Blackstaff Press.

Mead, Margaret (1928), *Coming of Age in Samoa*. New York: Morrow.

Mendoza, Zoila S. (2000), *Shaping Society through Dance: Mestizo Ritual Performance in the Peruvian Andes*. Chicago, IL: University of Chicago Press.

Merriam, Alan P. (1974), 'The Anthropology of Dance', in Tamara Comstock (ed.), *New Dimensions in Dance Research: Anthropology and Dance*. New York: Committee on Research in Dance (CORD), pp. 9–27.

Mitchell, J. Clyde (1956), *The Kalela Dance*, Paper No.27, Manchester: Manchester University Press.

Moody, T.W. (1984), 'Fenianism, Home Rule, and the Land War (1850–91)', in T.W. Moody and F.X. Martin (eds), *The Course of Irish History*. Cork: Mercier Press, pp. 275–93.

Ness, Sally Ann (1992), *Body, Movement, and Culture: Kinesthetic and Visual Symbolism in a Philippine Community*. Philadelphia, PA: University of Pennsylvania Press.

Nettl, Bruno (1964), *Theory and Method in Ethnomusicology*. London: The Free Press of Glencoe, Collier-Macmillan.

Ní Bhriain, Orfhlaith (2008), *The Terminology of Irish Dance*. Madison, WI: Macater Press.

—— (2010), 'The Creative Process in Competitive Irish Step Dance', unpublished PhD thesis. Limerick: The Irish World Academy of Music and Dance, University of Limerick.

Ní Shúilleabháin, Eibhlís (1936), *Letters from the Great Blaskets*. Cork: Mercier Press.

Noland, Carrie and Ness, Sally Ann (eds) (2008), *Migrations of Gesture*. Minneapolis, MN: University of Minnesota Press.

Novack, Cynthia (1990), *Sharing the Dance: Contact Improvisation and American Culture*. Madison, WI: University of Wisconsin Press.

Ó Cinnéide, Barra (2002), *Riverdance: The Phenomenon*. Dublin: Blackhall Publications.

Ó Criomhthain, Tomás (1929; 1980), *An tOileánach*. Dublin: Helicon Teoranta.

Ó Cúlacháin, Ciarán (1980), *Tobar na Gaeilge: Litríocht agus Teanga*. Dublin: Helicon Teoranta.

Ó Fearaíl, Pádraig (1975), *The Story of Conradh na Gaeilge*. Dublin: Clódhanna Teo.

Ó Tuama, Seán (ed.) (1972), *The Gaelic League Idea*. Cork: Mercier Press.

Ó Tuathaigh, Gearóid (2005), 'Language, Ideology and National Identity', in Joe Cleary and Claire Connolly (eds.), *The Cambridge Companion to Modern Irish Culture*. Cambridge: Cambridge University Press, pp. 42–58.

O'Connor, Barbara (1998), 'Riverdance', in Michael Peillon and Eamonn Slater (eds), *Encounters with Modern Ireland: A Sociological Chronicle 1995–1996*. Dublin: Institute of Public Administration, pp. 51–62.

O'Crohan, Tomás (1955) *The Islandman*, transl. Robin Flower from the Irish *An tOileánach*, 1951. Oxford: Oxford University Press.

O'Donnell, Patrick D. (1975), *The Irish Faction Fighters of the 19th Century*. Dublin: Anvil Books.

O'Keeffe, J.G. and O'Brien, Art (1902 [1944]), *A Handbook of Irish Dances*. Dublin: M.H. Gill & Son; 6th edn, 1944.

O'Neill, Francis (1973a), *Irish Folk Music*. East Ardsley, Yorkshire: EP Publishing.

—— (1973b), *Irish Minstrels and Musicians*. East Ardsley, Yorkshire: EP Publishing.

O'Rafferty, Peadar (1934), *The Irish Folk Dance Book: Book One*. London: Paterson's Publications.

—— (1950), *The Irish Folk Dance Book: Book Two*. London: Paterson's Publications.

—— and O'Rafferty, Gerard (1953), *Dances of Ireland*. London: Max Parrish.

Ortner, Sherry (1984), 'Theory in Anthropology Since the Sixties', *Comparative Studies in Society and History*, vol. 126, no. 1, pp. 126–66.

O'Sullivan, Donal (1958 [1991]), *Carolan: The Life Times and Music of an Irish Harper*, vol. 2. London: Routledge and Kegan Paul, 1958; reprint, Louth: Celtic Music, 1991.

Parle, John (2001), *The Mummers of Ireland*. Drinagh, Co. Wexford: JJP Publications.

Quirey, Belinda (1987), *May I Have the Pleasure: The Story of Popular Dancing*. London: Dance Books.

Radcliffe-Brown, A. R., (1922) *The Andaman Islanders*. Cambridge: Cambridge University Press.

Ralph, Richard (1985), *The Life and Works of John Weaver: An Account of his life, writings and theatrical productions* (with an annotated reprint of his complete publications). London: Dance Books.

Reed, Susan (1998), 'The Politics and Poetics of Dance', *Annual Review of Anthropology*, vol. 27, pp. 503–32.

Reynolds, William C. (1974), 'Foundations for the Analysis of the Structure and Form of Folk Dance: A Syllabus', *Yearbook of the International Folk Music Council*, vol. 6, pp. 115–35.

Rice, Timothy (1994), *May it Fill Your Soul: Experiencing Bulgarian Music*. Chicago, IL: University of Chicago Press.

—— (1997), 'Toward a Mediation of Field Methods and Field Experience in Ethnomusicology', in Gregory F. Barz and Timothy J. Cooley (eds), *Shadows in the Field: New Perspectives for Fieldwork in Ethnomusicology*. Oxford: Oxford University Press, pp. 101–20.

Ricoeur, Paul (1981), *Hermeneutics and the Human Sciences*, ed. and transl. John B. Thompson. Cambridge: Cambridge University Press.

Robb, Martha (1998), *Irish Dancing Costume*, The Irish Treasures Series. Dublin: Country House.

Roche, Francis (1982), *The Roche Collection of Traditional Irish Music*, vols 2 and 3. Cork: Ossian Publications.

Royce, Anya Peterson (1977), *The Anthropology of Dance*. Bloomington, IN: Indiana University Press.

—— (2002), *The Anthropology of Dance*, 2nd edn. Alton, Hampshire: Dance Books

—— (2007), *Anthropology of the Performing Arts: Artistry, Virtuosity, and Interpretation in Cross-cultural Perspective*, New York: Altamira Press.

Said, Edward W. (1978 [1991]), *Orientalism: Western Conceptions of the Orient*. Harmondsworth: Penguin Books; reprint, Harmondsworth: Penguin Books, 1991.

Savigliano, Marta E. (1995), *Tango: The Political Economy of Passion*. Bloomington, IN: Indiana University Press.

Scullion, Úna (2003), 'Musical Bodies: The Art of Expression in the Festival Tradition of Irish Step Dance', unpublished MA Ethnochoreology thesis. Limerick: The Irish World Academy of Music and Dance, University of Limerick.

Shay, Anthony (ed.) (2008a), *Balkan Dance: Essays on Characteristics, Performance and Teaching*. London: McFarland.

—— (2008b), 'Choreographing the Other: The Serbian State Folk Dance Ensemble, Gypsies, Muslims, and Albanians', in Antony Shay (ed.), *Balkan Dance: Essays on Characteristics, Performance and Teaching*. London: McFarland, pp. 161–75.

Sheehan, J.J. (1902 [1986]), *A Guide to Irish Dancing*. London: John Denvir; reprinted 1986 by Peggy McTeggart and Maureen Hall, Midleton, Co. Cork: Litho Press.

Sheets-Johnstone, Mazine (1979), *The Phenomenology of Dance*. London: Dance Books.

Sklar, Deidre (2008), 'Remembering Kinaesthesia: An Inquiry into Embodied Cultural Knowledge', in Carrie Noland and Sally Ann Ness (eds), *Migrations of Gesture*. Minneapolis, MN: University of Minnesota Press, pp. 85–112.

Smith, Antony D. (1992), *National Identity*. London: Penguin Books.

Snyder, Allegra Fuller (1972), 'The Dance Symbol', *CORD Research Annual, Volume 1. New Dimensions in Dance Research: Anthropology of Dance – The American Indian*, pp. 213–24.

Solis, Ted (ed.) (2004), *Performing Ethnomusicology: Teaching and Representation in World Music Ensembles*. Berkeley, CA: University of California Press.

Spencer, Paul (ed.) (1985), *Society and the Dance: the Social Anthropology of Process and Performance*. Cambridge: Cambridge University Press.

Sparti, Barbara (1993), *Guglielmo Ebreo of Pesaro: De Pratica Seu Arte Tripudii* ('On the Practice or Art of Dancing'). Oxford: Clarendon Press.

Stokes, Martin (ed.) (1994), *Ethnicity, Identity and Music: The Musical Construction of Place*. Oxford: Berg Publishers.

Sutton, Julia (1998a), 'Caroso, Fabritio', in Selma Jeanne Cohen (ed.), *International Encyclopedia of Dance*, vol. 2. Oxford: Oxford University Press, pp. 73–7.

—— (1998b), 'Negri, Cesare', in Selma Jeanne Cohen (ed.), *International Encyclopedia of Dance*, vol. 4. Oxford: Oxford University Press, pp. 579–83.

Vallely, Fintan (ed.) (2011), *The Companion to Irish Traditional Music*, 2nd edn. Cork: Cork University Press.

—— et al. (eds) (1999), *Crosbhealach an Cheoil: The Crossroads Conference 1996 – Tradition and Change in Irish Traditional Music*. Dublin: Whinstone Music.

Washabaugh, William (1996), *Flamenco: Passion, Politics and Popular Culture*. Oxford: Berg Publishers.

Wilde, William R. (1979), *Irish Popular Superstitions*. Dublin: Irish Academic Press.

Williams, Drid (1991), *Ten Lectures on Theories of the Dance*. Metuchen, NJ: Scarecrow Press.

Wulff, Helena (2007), *Dancing at the Crossroads: Memory and Mobility in Ireland*. Oxford and New York: Berghahn Books.

Archival Sources

Irish Traditional Music Archive, Dublin

Muckross House Archive, Killarney, Co. Kerry. The Muckross House Collection of Irish Traditional Music, Song, and Dance (1980–1985). Collector: Catherine E. Foley.

National Archives of Ireland, Dublin. Public Dance Halls Bill (1934). Department of Justice, File Number 8/21.

The National Folklore Collection, University College Dublin. Manuscript Number 1169: 45. Muiris Seoighe, Killorglin, Co. Kerry. Collector: Seosamh Ó Dálaigh (1950).

The National Folklore Collection, University College Dublin. Manuscript Number 1169: 314. Doncha Ó Flartharta, Collector: Seosamh Ó Dálaigh (1950).

Siamsa Tíre, The National Folk Theatre of Ireland, Archive, Tralee.

Newspaper Sources

Chute's Western Herald, 16 February 1828. Co. Kerry Archives. Tralee, Co. Kerry.

Chute's Western Herald, 5 March 1828. Co. Kerry Archives. Tralee, Co. Kerry.

Chute's Western Herald, 24 May 1828. Co. Kerry Archives. Tralee, Co. Kerry.

The Freeman's Journal, 13 October 1817. Glucksman Library. University of Limerick.

The Freeman's Journal, 22 December 1818. Glucksman Library. University of Limerick.

The Freeman's Journal, 1 December 1855. Glucksman Library. University of Limerick

Audio and Video Recordings

An Coimisiún le Rincí Gaelacha, *World Irish Dance Championships, 25th Anniversary, Dublin, Ireland* (1984), Trend Studio Production, written and directed by Olive Hurley.

Comhaltas Ceoltóirí Éireann, *Comhaltas Concert Tour of Australia: Echoes of Erin* (1997), Dublin, Comhaltas Ceoltóirí Éireann and RTE Production.

Feet of Flames (1998), VVL Production in Association with Polygram Visual Programming for Unicorn Entertainment.

Lord of the Dance (1996), VVL Production for Unicorn Entertainment.

Riverdance – Eurovision Song Contest, Point Theatre, Dublin (1994), RTE Production.

Riverdance – the Journey (1996), Tyrone Production for Abhann Productions.

Riverdance – The Show (1995), Tyrone/RTE Production.

The Final Round (2000), double CD by Kevin Joyce, CLJ Productions.

Televised Programmes and Films

Jig (2010 Film). Director Sue Bourne.

Oireachtas na hÉireann, *Steip: Comórtas Rince ar an Sean Nós*, TG4 (2004–11).

Radharc, Documentary: Bímís ag Rince – Siamsa Tíre, RTE (1975), Dublin.

Rising Steps, Stirling Film and Television Productions (2000), Belfast.

Ethnographic Interview Recordings

Eileen Moriarty MacNamara (1983; 1985): Catherine E. Foley.

Fr Pat Ahern (2003): Catherine E. Foley.

Honor Flynn (1985; 2004): Catherine E. Foley.

Irene Gould (1985): Catherine E. Foley.

Jack Dineen (1985): Catherine E. Foley.

Jack Lyons: Fr Pat Ahern, personal archive.

Jimmy Smith (1985; 2004): Catherine E. Foley.

John Fitzgerald (2004): Catherine E. Foley.

John Flavin (1983): Catherine E. Foley.

John McCarthy (1985): Catherine E. Foley.

John-Joe O'Donnell (1985): Catherine E. Foley.

Jonathan Kelleher (2000; 2004): Catherine E. Foley.
Liam Ó Duinín (1983): Catherine E. Foley.
Michael O'Carroll (1985): Catherine E. Foley.
Michael Walsh (1985): Catherine E. Foley.
Miriam O'Sullivan (1985; 2004): Catherine E. Foley.
Mossie Walsh (2004): Catherine E. Foley.
Oliver Hurley (2004): Catherine E. Foley.
Paddy White: Fr Pat Ahern, personal archive.
Patricia Hanafin (1985): Catherine E. Foley.
Paudy Hanrahan (1985): Catherine E. Foley.
Phil Cahill (1983): Catherine E. Foley.
Seosamh Ó Bruadair (1985): Catherine E. Foley.
Sheila Lyons Bowler (1985): Catherine E. Foley.
Tim Hanrahan (2004): Catherine E. Foley.
Tríona Breen (2004): Catherine E. Foley.
Willie Goggin (1985): Catherine E. Foley.

Index

References to illustrations are in **bold**.

traditions, invented 131–2
    céilí as 136
Treble Reels 82, 86, 96, 110, 111, 169, 233

Walsh, Edward 77
Walsh, Michael 99, 118
Walsh, Nedín Batt 74, **75**, 78, 227
    family 76
    teaching circuit 76, **77**
waltzes 29, 53
Weaver, John 45–6, 71
    lectures on dance 46
    Orchesography or the Art of Dancing
        47, 51
weddings, Molyneaux step dancers 113–14
Whelan, Kevin 140

Whelan, Martin 202, 205, 217
White, Paddy 70, 83, 98, 106, 166, 217,
    219
Whiteboys, North Kerry 60–61
Wild Geese 45
Wilde, William, on the Great Famine 73–4
World Irish Dance Association 238
The Wren ritual
    Molyneaux at 116
    Molyneaux step dancers at 115–16
    origins 114

Young, Arthur 86
    A Tour of Ireland 62
    on dance 63